For Others to Follow

For Others to Follow

An Ethos of Leadership Grounded in Spirituality

Paul K. Bates

WIPF & STOCK · Eugene, Oregon

FOR OTHERS TO FOLLOW
An Ethos of Leadership Grounded in Spirituality

Copyright © 2021 Paul K. Bates. All rights reserved. Except for brief quotations in critical publications or reviews, no part of this book may be reproduced in any manner without prior written permission from the publisher. Write: Permissions, Wipf and Stock Publishers, 199 W. 8th Ave., Suite 3, Eugene, OR 97401.

Wipf & Stock
An Imprint of Wipf and Stock Publishers
199 W. 8th Ave., Suite 3
Eugene, OR 97401

www.wipfandstock.com

PAPERBACK ISBN: 978-1-7252-9969-6
HARDCOVER ISBN: 978-1-7252-9970-2
EBOOK ISBN: 978-1-7252-9971-9

06/07/21

For Sally

Contents

Acknowledgements | ix
A Glossary of Terms | xiii
Spirit-Led Leadership: A Definition | xv

Introduction | 1
1. Approaching the Challenge | 8
2. Research Foundation | 34
3. The Roots of the Contemporary Workplace | 56
4. Spiritual Leadership in a Secular World | 120
5. Leadership as a Divine Calling | 174

Reflections | 205
Bibliography | 209

Acknowledgements

My sincere thanks to Tim Arnill, human resources executive, for his reflections on this work.

My sincere thanks to Harriet Ekperigin, senior healthcare lead and telemedicine specialist, for her reflections on this work.

My sincere thanks to Dr. Janet Harvey, educator, for her review and suggestions in the completion of this work.

My sincere thanks also to Rev. Dr. Michael Knowles for his review and suggestions in the completion of this work.

My very special thanks to Dr. Janet P. Moreland, educator, for her constant encouragement and suggestions.

My sincere thanks to Fr. Brian J. Morris for his review and suggestions in the completion of this work.

My sincere thanks to Andrea Swinton, board director and executive in the healthcare sector, for her reflections on this work.

My sincere thanks also to Rev. Sue-Ann Ward for her review and suggestions in the completion of this work.

My sincere thanks also to Dr. Phil Zylla for his guidance in the completion of this work.

This book, founded in my doctoral research, is written from a Christian perspective. Many of my own lessons are from colleagues of other faiths and, indeed, colleagues who profess no faith affiliation but are deeply spiritual. While I cannot, clearly, offer the depth of commentary that those of other faiths and spiritual orientations will have on this topic of leadership, I hope that many of the perspectives presented will find some degree of resonance. An ethos of leadership that is conducive to human flourishing is a goal that we all share. Leadership, from the perspective of this book, is a ministry of presence.

A Glossary of Terms

It may aid you in reading this work to have a succinct glossary of terms as used, with brief definitions. These follow below:

Annihilato Mundi: Complete destruction of the world; to reduce the world to nothing, complete destruction of the world. As contrasted with Transformatio Mundi, the transformation of the world; a metamorphosis.

Cognitive Dissonance: Having inconsistent thoughts or beliefs.

Discernment; perceiving clearly, in the context of this work this is achieved through divine inspiration.

Dissonance: to be discordant, or inharmonious.

Epistemology: In the context of this book, belief or understanding.

Eschatology: The branch of theology dealing with end times.

Flourishing: To succeed, thrive, prosper, blossom. To achieve our full potential as persons.

Grounded theory: In the context of this work, a proposition derived from an analysis of, and reflection on, responses to a research questionnaire.

Liminal: A threshold, a place where one perception crosses over into another.

Paraclete: An advocate, comforter, intercessor. Often used to describe the Holy Spirit.

Phenomenology: The study of phenomena: events or circumstances.

Postmodern: Replacing modernism approximately in the 1960s; in the context of this work, the term postmodern is used primarily to reflect an epistemology (see above) regarding the nature of truth and the acquisition of knowledge.

Practical Theology: In the context of this book, an understanding of how theology can be applied to certain practices.

Ontology: Dealing with the nature of being.

Sacramental: In the context of the book, having a sacred characteristic.

Sacred: In the context of this book, set aside by God.

Secular: worldly.

Teleology: The study of final causes. This brings us to Telos: the inherent, ultimate purpose of a thing or person.

Spirit-Led Leadership
A Definition

The Spirit-led leader, as presented in this work, is a complex person who brings a broad range of integrated attributes to the role. Foundational are what we might term as management skills, leadership skills, and those attributes which I offer as gifts of the Spirit.

Drawing from Peter Drucker, management acumen includes acquired skill in "decision-making, people decisions, communications, budgeting measurement and controls, and information literacy."[1] To be proficient in these areas, one must be strong in analytical ability, measurement, finance, economics, information technology, communications, marketing and organizational systems. Further, leaders, according to Warren Bennis, possess four essential qualities. They must have the ability to engage others by creating shared meaning. They must have a distinctive voice. They must have integrity. They must possess adaptive capacity.[2] To all these attributes, I would add the characteristics of the Spirit-led leader, which under the broad quality of servanthood include being a deeply passionate attentive listener, nurturer, and counsellor. The Spirit-led leader is prayerfully concerned with personhood, community, and legacy. Spirit-led leadership, then, is an activity, it is a profession, and indeed it is a vocation.

---

1. Drucker, *Management*, xxiv.
2. See Bennis, *On Becoming a Leader*, xxv-xxvi.

Introduction

A Leadership Vignette

NOT SO LONG AGO, a young man began a career as a Traffic Warden: an auxiliary officer with the British police. It was the first morning of the first day of training specific to his new assignment. Indeed, it was his very first—proud—day in uniform. He arrived early for his first class. The first to arrive, he chose a desk in the classroom—two rows back at the left-most end of the row. He positioned his officer's peaked cap at the front right-hand side of his desk, centred his note paper and pen, and waited. Other recruits began to arrive. Eventually, precisely at the top of the hour, the assigned senior instruction officer arrived. Before the assembled students, the instructor walked directly, in a very straight line, to the young man, to whom he barked, "I'm getting old, and I'm getting cranky! Put your cap on the hook outside, then come back and sit down!"

The message received by the class, intended or not, was that they were going to be subjected to a week of perfunctory instruction. It would be a routine that the instructor had likely carried out many times. Inferable, also, was that the instructor had no interest in learning anything from the students. Barbara Kellerman writes, "Leaders become incompetent for various reasons. Some lack experience, education, or expertise. Others lack drive, energy, or the ability to focus. Still others are not clever enough, flexible enough—or whatever enough."[1] It may not be fair simply to write off our police instructor as incompetent. He may have been going through illness, emotional stress, or some other distraction that particular week. He may have been assigned to a task that he did not want to do. Perhaps it was an assignment that he was ill-suited to do. Perhaps he started his career with the same verve as the young man whom he

---

1. Kellerman, *Bad Leadership*, 51.

had disciplined; somewhere along the way losing sight of his purpose as a dedicated and caring instructor. Good, well-intentioned, people sometimes lose their compass. Indeed, it can happen to us all.

For most people, work presents us with mixed emotions. Rishad Tobaccowala asserts that "people with a niche, voice, and story work more productively."[2] Yet, in terms of flourishing and in finding true purpose—a purpose hungered for—work can be a struggle. From my research, while people take pride in their chosen endeavours, they also experience work-related dissonance, to a lesser or greater extent. This study will explore the quality of leadership actions that might enhance, or inhibit, the opportunity for true flourishing, examined through the lens of faith. Support for this inquiry is a *grounded theory* derived from my own qualitative research;[3] analyzed through a review of critical literature, as well as personal reflection.

It is important at the outset to make an anthropological assertion here. Tanya Luhrmarin offers that "when you are secular you think of the difference between you and believers as being the belief . . . But to a person of faith, the tension between the world as it is and the world of God as the point."[4] John Baillie makes the statement, "God, it is said, is the first reality to exist but the last to be known."[5] It took me a very long time, with many conversations, to become a person of faith. As a Christian, I arrive at Jesus, who said, "I came that they might have life, and have it abundantly."[6] Abundance implies plentiful-ness: more than sufficiency. Our expectation of work—our daily contribution to our chosen field of endeavour—should hold the hope that as we contribute to the abundance of the enterprises that we are part of, we too will experience life abundantly—that we will experience a sense of flourishing. Daniel Finn emphasizes the place of work in Catholic social thought. He writes, "John Paul II, who himself had been a labourer in Poland . . . interprets God's command to Adam and Eve . . . as an invitation, a call to enter into God's creative action through work."[7] Work is elemental to human existence.

---

2. Tobaccowala, *Restoring the Soul of Business*, 102.

3. I do not cover the entirety of my research methodology in this book, simply a brief outline of the process. Focus is placed on the conclusions drawn.

4. Luhrmarin, "Understanding the Work of Faith," 148.

5. Baillie, *Our Knowledge of God*, 166.

6. John 10:10b.

7. Finn, "Human Work in Catholic Social Thought," 874–75.

Introduction

It is valuable to reflect on indigenous thought regarding Medicine Wheel teaching of the four aspects of the self in relation. Celia Haig Brown and John Hodson explain:

> Each human being has a spiritual, physical, emotional and intellectual reality. For the individual to be in balance, each aspect must be in balance; any impact on one reality has an impact on the whole.[8]

This is flourishing, and it should be the cultural aspiration for every enterprise, alongside all other success metrics pursued. Indeed, to bring about flourishing at the enterprise level is to set in motion a chain of events that contributes to flourishing at the societal level. Damon So offers this:

> When thinking about economic forces operating in the world, one must be very careful in assessing their positive contributions as well as their possible drawbacks which emerge when they are exercised without proper restraint and an ethical framework.[9]

Here is the call for Spirit-led leadership. Practical theology offers an interpretation of situations, resulting in a constructive analysis which offers insights, in the case of this book, for leadership. As alluded to earlier, my research resulted in a grounded theory emerging from a multi-layered analysis of rich, first-hand narratives given by respondents to a research questionnaire. This grounded theory will guide the balance of my enquiry.

Taken together, the recommendations presented underpin an *ethos*—a *character*—of leadership that will invite others to follow and to emulate; while the leader herself grows and blooms. Specifically, this work presents Spirit-led leadership as archetypical of the approaches recommended. With the assumption that the actions of leadership have a direct effect on human flourishing at work, Mary Shideler offers:

> To be a person is to act, to work. In working we become our true selves and know ourselves and each other truly. Therefore, work which is essentially trivial or shoddy, or consists of making things that are not worth making at all, diminishes the persons who engage in it at every level of production, exchange and use. In contrast, those who love their work, and love to do it well, grow into the full measure of personhood.[10]

---

8. Brown and Hodson, "Indigenous Thought in Canadian Education," 170.
9. So, *The Forgotten Jesus and the trinity you never knew*, 2.
10. Shideler, "Introduction," 14–15.

Our philosophies change in terms of the way we see work intersecting with other aspects of life. We transition from modern to postmodern epistemologies around faith, spirituality, religion and ethics. Jean-Francois Lyotard rejected the concept of metanarratives. From this we might deduce that reason is constantly evolving. Ronald Hendel suggests that, "Reason is a 'self-correcting enterprise,' which means we are capable of learning, and even of learning to reason better."[11] Elements of this perspective will emerge later in this book. Our organizational structures change and our societies change. I would postulate, however, that *with God all things are possible.* Karl Barth writes:

> When revelation takes place, it never does so by means of our insight and skill, but in the freedom of God to be free for us and to free us from ourselves, that is to say, to let His light shine in our darkness, which does not comprehend His light. In this miracle, which we can only acknowledge as having occurred, which can receive from the hand of God as it takes place by His hand. His Kingdom comes for us, and this world passes for us. It is in this coming and passing that there takes place for us the movement which Holy Scripture calls revelation.[12]

Revelation is a deeply personal event. For some it is immediate, for others it occurs over time. For those who are called to leadership, this work argues that revelation involves a divine instruction and preparation to be stewards and to be shepherds. From Genesis to Revelation God calls us to work. Jesus teaches us to come alongside those we engage with as coworkers. We are called to be people who bring our faith to God's workplace as God's revelation unfolds, broken as we are. Charles Winquist asserts, "Practical theology is a theology specially grounded in theory and practice and it is needed to bring self-consciousness to ministry."[13] There is, indeed, work to be done. Bartholomew and O'Dowd write, "The secular humanist project has not succeeded as hoped, yet our culture bids us to press on, trusting that we just need to tinker with our knowledge and technology until we are finally happy with ourselves."[14] This book presents the compelling view that work is a human response to a divine

---

11. Hendel, "Mind the Gap: Modern and Postmodern in Biblical Studies," 426.
12. Barth, *Church Dogmatics*, 67.
13. Winquist, "Revisioning Ministry," 27.
14. Bartholomew and O'Dowd, *Old Testament*, 185.

call. Thus, leadership becomes practical theology—theology in practice, in that leadership may be grounded in theological values.

With the foundational argument that organizational culture and ethos are driven, for better or worse, by leadership, this book offers a study in practice-led research, leading to research-led practice. The practice in view here is leadership. Practice-led research is concerned with the nature of a practice, leading to new knowledge that has operational significance for that practice. Specifically, I propose that Spirit-led leadership is a critical, honed, practice if people are to achieve a workplace environment that is conducive to human flourishing. When we acknowledge the spiritual dimension of our labour, we are likely to have a deeper sense of meaningfulness and purpose. Leadership strategies that foster spiritual awareness may facilitate community and human flourishing in the workplace and beyond. Kimberley Bell asserts that "Individuals today are wanting more out of their work because work has become an integral part of individual's lives."[15] Men and women are defined to a large extent by their profession. Their work shapes, to a considerable degree, their sense of worth and identity as well as their economic circumstances. For most, work is where we express ourselves—our aspirations, and our growth as unique and marvelous individuals.

Drawing from my earlier definition, a characteristic of Leadership may be described as *showing the way*, both in the sense of organizing work processes, and in terms of safeguarding the ethos of the workplace. John Stott emphatically states, "*Leadership* is a word shared by Christians and non-Christians alike, but this does not mean that their concept is the same."[16] Indeed, note my earlier definition of Spirit-led leadership. Stott offered these words to a community that, in its time (2002), was comprised largely of individuals who generally had a relatively robust relationship with their faith and their faith traditions. However, an increasing number were beginning to turn away from faith, choosing to fashion their ideals and habits in secular, or temporal, terms. Much has changed as the modern era has given way to the postmodern era. Andrew Gustafson adroitly points out that "deconstruction is not destruction, but rather it is a destructuring or dismantling in order to more carefully examine."[17] Joel Thiessen confirms, "Religious nones are the

---

15. Bell, *Spirituality in the Workplace*, 12.
16. Stott, *Basic Christian Leadership*, 11 [emphasis original].
17. Gustafson, "Making Sense of Postmodern Business Ethics," 648.

fastest growing 'religious' group in Canada, the United States, and many other Western Countries."[18] While an increasing number may eschew the term 'religious,'[19] my research suggests that a significant number describe themselves as 'spiritual.' Bell confirms that, "Spirituality . . . may be more of an inward reflection that allows individuals to experience inner feelings, personal experiences, a desire to care for others and having a relationship with them."[20] As will be seen, this is evident.

This book constructs a 'warp and woof': a structure for a theological practice of leadership that emerges from the weaving together of a qualitative study and a critical literature review, integrated with my impressions drawn from five decades of personal lived experiences which include roles in the capital markets, regulatory agencies, government service and the academy. It was midway through my career that I experienced a faith re-awakening, leading eventually to ordination as a Deacon in the Anglican Church.[21]

Practising a life of faith, for many, means finding deep spiritual meaning in the great number of hours to which we devote our working lives—seeing the product of our work, and our contribution to the lives of others—as a commitment to God's Kingdom. This book reflects a deep commitment to the aspiration that every human being might flourish—in this context defined as to grow vigorously, succeed, thrive, and prosper. I will argue that true human flourishing can only be achieved when, as Elizabeth Liebert writes, it is through discernment that we, "come to know ourselves in the light of God, thereby coming to know God."[22] Given its centrality to our existence and fulfillment as persons, work should lead to this deeper knowledge of God. In my view, we should be satisfied with nothing less.

A key assumption made in approaching this study includes the perspective that, with the exception of a very small minority, people wish to make a meaningful contribution to society through their workplace efforts. However, this study is also grounded in the view that few people fully achieve a deep and complete sense of purpose, even though we devote the greater part of our lives to our work.

18. Thiessen, *Meaning of Sunday*, 94.

19. We may view the term 'religious' as to be 'tied' to a particular faith—from the Latin root, to tie or bind.

20. Bell, *Spirituality in the Workplace*, 5.

21. Aligned with the Episcopal Church in the U.S.

22. Liebert, *The Way of Discernment*, 5.

Introduction

Thus, my study concentrates on arriving at the confluence of a deep sense of purpose and meaningfulness at work, in the sense that work satisfies a person's economic needs (fair pay and job security), and that it satisfies a person's sense of spiritual vocation in a workplace that has become largely secularized, i.e., transformed from close identification with religious values to an environment with essentially no such basis. I will explore the ways in which persons of faith and spirituality express a deeper sense of vocation and purpose versus those who do not identify as persons with such values. By direct inference, I argue that, broadly, the practice of leadership is failing to create and maintain an environment in which a state of flourishing is achieved. If we aim for less, we will accomplish less. I seek to offer a leadership practice that might ameliorate this shortcoming. The five chapters of this book are laid out as follows:

Chapter 1 introduces the challenges of the post-modern workplace, together with a resulting impact on workers as they seek to flourish. This chapter outlines an approach to understanding the circumstances that we find ourselves in, as seen through the lens of faith. Chapter 2 brings deeper insights from responses to a research questionnaire interpreted through the lens of marketplace forces, organizational structure, leadership practices, and the role of faith or spirituality in our working lives. Chapter 3 offers a deeper reflection and analysis of workplace structure and dynamics. Here I offer dimensions of the demand for an ethos of leadership. Chapter 4 calls for, and offers, rationale for spirituality in leadership, which I offer as foundational for the emergence of flourishing in the workplace. Chapter 5 presents a discussion of leadership as a deep, divine, calling. This chapter explores faith as the catalyst for developing a more complete understanding of leadership.

1

Approaching the Challenge

It was just before the Passover Feast. Jesus knew that the time had come for him to leave this world and go to the Father. Having loved his own who were in the world, he now showed them the full extent of his love . . . Jesus knew that the Father had put all things under his power, and that he had come from God and was returning to God; so, he got up from the meal, took off his outer clothing, and wrapped a towel around his waist. After that, he poured water into a basin and began to wash his disciples' feet, drying them with the towel that was wrapped around him.

(JOHN 13:1 NIV)

ALTHOUGH SECULAR CULTURE DEFINES remunerated labour effectively in economic terms, I suggest that work is actually best understood as spiritual in nature. Work activities (at their best) serve to express personal vocation (an internal and personal good). Work is (at its best) meaningful and purposeful in that it contributes to human flourishing (an external and communal good). Vocation and human flourishing hold, in turn, both anthropological, i.e., cultural/social, and spiritual characteristics, invoking and expressing the divine-human relationship. Nowhere, perhaps, is the divine-human endeavour more critical than in the exercise of leadership. If the essential act of leadership is the *reshaping* of the way we do things, then Jesus' act of washing the feet of his disciples, as portrayed in John 13, is at the core of divinely-inspired leadership.

If leadership is a practice, what is the practical purpose of Leadership? Yishuang Meng elucidates, writing:

> Modern theories of leadership such as strategic leadership theory emerged as early as the 1980s when outdated theories of behavioral contingency were questioned, resulting in the beginning of a shift in focus, leading to the emergence of modern theories hypothesizing the importance of vision, motivation and value-based control of clan and culture.[1]

Marguerite Rigoglioso adds, "By engaging more of workers' total selves, organizations hope to develop staff who are more satisfied, productive and innovative."[2] While this shift in focus may be underway, my research suggests that the human search for meaning and coherence continues to be frustrated by what appears to be a large number of work environments. Ann Morisy declares, "People have a hunger for meaning."[3] As suggested through my research, many employees risk being reduced to factors of production as organizations prioritize profit and output over human flourishing.[4] There is a further risk to human flourishing wrought by increased urbanization, post-modernism, marginalization of faith communities, and social change in general. For example, cultural transmutation being brought about by rapid advancement of multiculturalism. As will be explored later, multiculturalism[5] ultimately brings broad societal benefits—I argue that it is the rate of change that can bring potential challenges, such as the perceived loss of tradition among some, resulting in feelings of dislocation, or distortion. The working lives that are the central concern of my work may well be described by Swinton and Mowat when they state, "Most of us tend to live within situations in ways which are unreflective and uncomplicated."[6] In other words, we tend to accept an 'it is what it is' approach to work. We may not seek greater

---

1. Meng, "Spiritual Leadership at the Workplace," 408.
2. Rigoglioso, "Spirit at Work," para. 1.
3. Morisy, *Beyond the Good Samaritan*, 45.
4. Tim Arnill writes: "Nothing speaks to this more than the widespread use of the phrase Human Capital" which reduces the role of human beings in an organization to the same level as any other aspect of capital."
5. Assimilating new and sometimes dramatically changing environments which affect our cognition, even our ways of conducting ourselves and the ways we communicate. Consider the rapidly forced adoption of virtual communications during the COVD 19 pandemic.
6. Swinton and Mowat, *Practical Theology and Qualitative Research*, 16.

meaning. We become resigned to our situation, perhaps in order to keep it uncomplicated. We keep our heads down. We accept minimal affirmation of our work. We bend to the mores of the environment—sometimes at the suppression of our true values. We accept and tolerate weak, even bad leadership. We brush aside value-less 'performance' feedback from a supervisor who has surprisingly little real awareness of our work, and we settle into a state where we seldom ask, 'is this all there is?' Shrugging our shoulders, we plod along.

This book contributes to a growing field of enquiry. Meng continues, "Spiritual leadership and workplace spirituality are in their infancy, and consequently, theoretical knowledge related to this subject in Western religious theology and practiced leadership ethics is limited."[7] A number of business schools have undertaken to incorporate, in their curricula, the deeper spiritual dimension of human flourishing at work, moving beyond a focus which is primarily on the development of strategies that enhance productivity and profitability; eschewing the spiritual dimension of work. There is much more to be done. The church, also, is broadening its discourse on the search for deep spiritual contentment at work. Again, however, much learning is required.

Theological *gravitas* is drawn from the vocational perspective that work is important in the full sense of *transformatio mundi* over *annihilatio mundi*, in that our work may be a contribution to the new kingdom. Thus, work may be viewed within a framework of the *doctrine of last things*, implying a divine-human cooperation empowered and enabled by the Spirit. We must recognize and embrace, then, the practice, and deep human value of spirituality in the workplace. Miroslav Volf underscores this, when he states, "The picture changes radically with the assumption that the world will not end in apocalyptic destruction, but in eschatological transformation."[8]

Drawing from the research conducted for this work, viewed through the lens of research and personal experience, the fundamental threads to the argument are as follows:

- There is a deep thirst for meaningfulness in work, evidenced frequently by an expression of caring for others, as well as personal achievement.

- Dissonance, mild to severe, is pervasive.

7. Meng, "Spiritual Leadership at the Workplace," 408.
8. Volf, *Work in the Spirit*, 91.

- Human beings are generally settling for less in terms of achieving a state of flourishing in their work.
- Leadership that is self-centred must be replaced by leadership that is other-centered.
- Practices of leadership must reflect and respond to societal views of success and the impact of organizational structures.

A respondent to my research questionnaire stated:

> [I feel] that I have been put in a position of being taken advantage of, reducing my drive and loyalty. But I am blessed to continually receive what I need. Many events have placed a sense of doubt in my job security. E.g., others not being supported, not being assigned to a position that I felt qualified to do; being assigned a role that suited the company, but which impeded my development.[9]

Here is a heartfelt and loud cry to be noticed, recognized and nurtured.

When someone in a senior role puts together a schedule for tasks to be completed and, accordingly, assigns and communicates those tasks, these are acts of management (organization). When the concerns of the persons assigned to the tasks are ignored or disrespected, that is a leadership issue. Peter Drucker provides that a manager "sets objectives, organizes, motivates and communicates, measures, and develops people."[10] Henry Mintzberg pinpoints, "The overriding purpose of managing is to ensure that the unit serves its basic purpose."[11] Such comments imply that management activities are generally procedural and transactional in nature. Essentially then, something is done in return for extrinsic reward. Warren Bennis turns to intrinsic factors. He writes:

> All leaders have four essential competencies. First, they are able to engage others by creating shared meaning . . . Second all authentic leaders have a distinctive voice; something we now call emotional intelligence . . . The third quality that all true leaders have is integrity. The fourth and key competence is adaptive capacity.[12]

---

9. Verbatim respondent 22.
10. Drucker, *Management*, 8.
11. Mintzberg, *Managing*, 49.
12. Bennis, *On Becoming a Leader*, xxv–xxvi.

Biblical stories of leadership are frequently of such a nature. Using the story of Nehemiah, commissioned to carry out the rebuilding and repopulation of Jerusalem, Matthew Carter explains:

> Leadership is providential. God raised up Nehemiah to accomplish an important mission. God is the active agent leading and directing. Leadership is spiritual hard work. Nehemiah exemplifies the interplay between prayer, planning, and hard work . . . Leaders persevere. Nehemiah faced adversity and conflict.[13]

The story of Nehemiah encompasses both the organizational *and* the ethical elements of leadership. Aubrey Malphurs adds a dimension to the distinction between and leadership and management. He insists, "The basic difference between leadership and management is that the former strives to accomplish change, while the latter seeks to control complexity."[14] This coincides with my broad definition of Spirit-led leadership as stated earlier. In the context of this book, management is viewed as essentially about the organization of work. Leadership is viewed as being about the ethos of the organization, and its impact on the work environment.[15] This work is about leadership founded in fidelity. It is about the creation of a pervasive ethos, or character of leadership, that nurtures human flourishing in the workplace, while concurrently attending to the organization of work for optimum productivity and output. We could do well to revisit Matthew's account of the Beatitudes as offered by Jesus' Sermon on the Mount (cf. Matt 5). Martin Lloyd-Jones describes the Beatitudes as "a description of character."[16] Jonathan T. Pennington goes further, stating

---

13. Carter, "4 Leadership Lessons from Nehemiah," para. 4.

14. Malphurs, *Developing a Vision*, 191. In my very first office job, a government agency, my supervisor was obsessed with ensuring that if seven hours had been set aside for a task load, I had better not get it done in less than seven hours.

15. Harriet Ekperigin writes, "In my first job after completing my MBA I worked as a manager of an outpatient mental health hospital managing a team of about 30 people. I had a flexible management style where staff were able to balance their time accordingly. A few months after leaving that job, a few of my former staff asked to go to lunch, upon arriving there were more of them than I had thought. They asked me to sit down for an intervention. They pleaded that I returned to my former position because the new manager had a less flexible style. Her office was right by the elevator and she would keep a log of staff goings and comings and inform them each time they were late, took extra minutes for lunch or left to go home early regardless of whether they had worked through their lunch. I was saddened to hear of this. I did not return to the position but encouraged the staff to be vocal. The manager did not last long.

16. Lloyd-Jones, *Studies in the Sermon on the Mount*, 25.

that *"the sermon is offering Jesus's answer to the great question of human flourishing."*[17] A culture of flourishing should be central. I argue that there is a spiritually-centric approach to the construction and operation of an enterprise. David Miller and Wambura Ngunjiri offer detail, writing:

> Workplace spirituality is a framework of organizational values evidenced in the culture that promotes employees' transcendence through work processes, facilitating their sense of being connected to others in a way that provides feelings of completeness and joy.[18]

A respondent to my research questionnaire stated, "I experience very deep joy and meaningfulness in my work."[19] This sense of completeness exemplifies a state that most seek for. Victor Frankl writes, "Man's [sic] search for meaning is the primary motivation in his [sic] life and not a 'secondary rationalization' of instinctual drives."[20]

Spirituality, as a factor in the achievement of purpose at work, is complex. Scott Quatro explains that the topic of workplace spirituality, "is perhaps one of the most compelling and least understood forces driving organizational practice today."[21] I would offer that it is at the heart of practical theology.

Denise Ackerman and Riet Bons-Storm define practical theology as "the theological discipline which is essentially involved with living, communicating and practising the life of faith."[22] I argue that this life of faith *must* pervade the workplace experience through the actions of the leader. Work simply occupies too great a component of our existence not to.

For greater emphasis, the goal of this book is to develop a 'research-informed practice,' leading primarily to a deeper understanding of, and more effective approach to, the practices of organizational leadership. Swinton and Mowat underscore this goal when they discuss the goal of practical theology as "facilitating faithful participation in God's practices in, to and for the world."[23] There may be no single practice more critical

---

17. Pennington, *The Sermon on the Mount and Human Flourishing*, [emphasis original]36.
18. Miller and Ngunjiri, "Leadership View," 130.
19. Verbatim respondent 6.
20. Frankl, *Man's Search for Meaning*, 99.
21. Quatro, "New Age," 228.
22. Ackerman and Bons-Storm, *Liberating Faith Practices*, 1.
23. Swinton and Mowat, *Practical Theology and Qualitative Research*, 6.

to achieving this end than the practice of spiritually awakened enterprise leadership. Dent et al. write, "Leaders who bring their spirituality to work transform organizations from merely mission-driven activities into places where individual and collective spirituality are encouraged and spiritual development is integrated into the day-to-day work life."[24] Creating such an environment requires deeply thoughtful and prayerful application. Those that try may be subject to indifference, even ridicule. People may be, at best, tentative when it comes to fully expressing their work in terms of their faith. Yet, Jeff Woods asserts that "it is in human nature that we find God's revelation."[25] Thus Spirit-led leadership will shape the nature of the workplace. I also hold to the belief that God is revealed in our response to him through our work, and that we are not fully satisfied with our work—we do not experience true flourishing—until we discover this revelation. In fact, our professional restlessness may never end until we do. That said, it may be, however, that consciously or unconsciously, some abandon this search, resulting in a failure to recognize the opportunity for divine encounter in our work—for a full sense of flourishing.[26]

In a previous article, "Paracletic Ministry: A Study in Pastoral Encounters with Male Mid-career Spiritual Searchers," I offered the following:

> This article presents a conceptual distinction between silence, stillness and solitude, surrender and divine encounter; all within what is offered as a *paracletic* ministry journey. In addition to Henri Nouwen the work accesses a fairly broad range of practical and pastoral theologians, together with literature regarding spirituality, to support the author's assertions regarding a *paracletic* approach for coming alongside, and encouraging those who are struggling with and searching for faith.[27]

The circumstance presented here is the life situation of an energetic and career-driven, but otherwise spiritually adrift, mid-career male figure for whom paracletic ministry is viewed as critical. For this individual, a spiritually sound view of life and achievement has been lost, or was never found at all. Sadly, he is uninspired. C.S. Lewis addresses this, writing:

---

24. Dent et al., "Spirituality and Leadership," 627.
25. Woods, *Designing Religious Research*, 53.
26. Harriet Ekperigin writes, "I would even go as far as saying that some are unaware of this revelation, thus being unaware of the need for this search."
27. Bates, "Paracletic Ministry," 66 [emphasis original].

> There are two ways in which the human machine goes wrong. One is when human individuals drift apart from one another, or else collide with one another and do one another damage, by cheating or bullying. The other is when things go wrong inside the individual—when the different parts of him [sic] (different faculties and desires and so on) either drift apart or interfere with one another.[28]

Lewis describes a situation where the core elements of a sense of flourishing are absent. Such circumstances and phenomena are among those that this work seeks to encounter and understand, founded in a research methodology which layers and then enfolds an examination of the responses to my research questionnaire together with a multi-domain literature review. Sharon Ravitch and Matthew Riggan state:

> The process of developing your research questions is primarily one of *excavation*. You disembark onto a vast swath of intellectual terrain, formed by an amalgam of what you care about and are interested in, the field(s) you have been exposed to and are working within, and what is already known about the problems or questions that pique your interest.[29]

The terrain that is the focus of my study is the postmodern workplace, and the effects of leadership on this workplace. I set out to understand the depth to which people feel spiritually anchored, or adrift, at work. Further, I sought to explore the extent to which constructs and behaviours of leadership influence and shape the circumstances which influence a person's achievement of deep flourishing at work. This is at the heart of my chosen field of practical theology, and presents the question asked by Swinton and Mowat, i.e. "What appears to be going on; what is actually going on?"[30] I attempt to respond to these questions.

The essential goal of my research was to arrive at a series of recommendations for leadership practices by which the dissonance between purpose and work might be ameliorated.

My approach is qualitative in nature—i.e., exploratory research employed to gain an understanding of the underlying perspectives, opinions, and motivations of people at work, particularly the spiritual dimensions of work, anchored by the written words of individuals. This includes taking

---

28. Lewis, *Mere Christianity*, 71.
29. Ravitch and Riggan, *Reason and Rigour*, 29 [emphasis original].
30. Swinton and Mowat, *Practical Theology and Qualitative Research*, v.

a phenomenological approach, i.e., the interpretation of structures of consciousness as experienced from the first-person point of view as narrated by the respondents to my research survey. With the emerging grounded theory, this enabled the conceptualisation of the latent social patterns that emerged from the collective perspectives of the respondents.

Research questionnaire responses were completed by thirty-two men and women between the ages of mid-twenties and mid-seventies. These respondents live in Canada, the United Kingdom, and the United States. They work in for-profit, not-for-profit, public service, and faith-based environments. They include people who are, or were, in supervisory roles, in non-supervisory roles, as well as those who are entrepreneurs. The respondents narrate their feelings about work, and their sense of fulfillment, meaning, and purpose in their work. They narrate their *situations* and their *lived experiences* in those situations. Don Browning points out, "The interpretation of situations seldom is thought to include the personal histories that bring people into praxis. This is a significant loss to practical theology and theological education in the church, the seminary, and the university."[31] By contrast, and as stated earlier, this work is grounded in the narratives of the lived experiences of the respondents to the research questionnaire presented herein. Reflection is critical to sorting through complex data, ultimately resulting in the grounded theory which underpins the recommendations for praxis as put forward. In my own case this reflection is deepened, and hopefully enriched, by my work experience. I also carried out an extensive literature review. Reflection involves what Hazel Smith and Roger Dean introduce as the "Iterative Cyclic Web."[32] Of particular interest, the authors point out, "is the concept of iteration, which is fundamental to both creative and research processes. To iterate a process is to repeat it several times (though probably with some variation) before proceeding, setting up a cycle: start—end—start."[33] The coding, interpretation, analysis and reflection efforts in this work followed this iterative approach.

The data gathered in the research underpinning this work led to an interpretation—an exposition—of life stories from individuals of broad social and cultural backgrounds, growing up and working through

---

31. Browning, *Fundamental Practical Theology*, 59.
32. Smith and Dean, *Practice-Led Research*, 19.
33. Smith and Dean, *Practice-Led Research*, 19.

different eras, in different countries, and in vastly different professional environments.

A Perspective: Modern to Post Modern

Egon Golomb offers a valuable element of the deep altering of work-life experience—the massive social impact wrought by urbanisation. He writes, "The social evolution of modern urbanism appears to have outstripped pastoral institutions."[34] We see this phenomenon almost everywhere. By way of underscoring this thought, former villages have been transformed from tight-knit communities where people, live, work, worship, purchase the essentials of life, and socialize, into what are now largely 'bedroom' communities from which people commute to work in a wide arc, frequently resulting in commuting times of up to several hours each way.[35]

The term *secularization*—in the context of this work, may be interpreted as social disassociation or separation from religious or spiritual affiliations. This is amplified by Michael Northcott. He writes:

> Industrialization and urbanization were accompanied by a new sociological phenomenon, known as secularization, in which churches lost members and influence to other social forces, influences and actors. One cause of this decline in influence was the break-up of the old organic social context of the village and the small town in which the church was set as a central institution. In the new cities face-to-face relationships of production and trade were increasingly characterized by cash and contract, and rationality, rather than face-to-face exchanges and moral codes... The demise of the organic community was also characterized by social differentiation whereby whole sectors of social life gradually moved beyond the influence of the church and its functionaries.[36]

Thus, people choose, generally through economic necessity, to live in suburban environments.[37] This results in long commutes as stated above,

---

34. Golomb, "Model Theoretical Considerations," 359–60.

35. A 2011 Statistics Canada report suggests that 17.2% of Canadian commuters took 45 minutes or more to get to work (Statistics Canada Catalogue no. 99-12-X2011003). It is possible that the Covid 19 pandemic may result in changes to this trend. We shall see.

36. Northcott, "Pastoral Theology," 156.

37. This is particularly true for newcomers to the area.

and a disruption of community. Add to this the diminishing perspective of a church or other religious place of worship as an anchoring element of a sense of belonging. Thus, in the postmodern context we are witnessing upheaval, breakdown, and reconstruction of society and the workplace. Communities and workplaces are coming to grips with significant ethnic and cultural reshaping as we consider what is just. Workplaces are coming to terms with, and adjusting to, the recognition and acceptance of women as equal in stature. We are acknowledging LBGTQ communities as equal. We are coping with the recognition and acceptance of broadened political perspectives, together with social media bringing positive and, in some cases, negative effects on the way we view the world. Warren Bennis adds to this list of change-drivers:

> Single-parent families, working mothers, one-person households, and non-traditional families are now having a significant impact on workforce make-up. Housing costs are exploding. Society is increasingly litigious. We are witnessing persistent poverty, drug abuse, and homelessness.[38]

In some cases, also, there is deep political polarization, as we are witnessing.

My research suggests that the postmodern workplace can be an environment of discord. As will be seen in the analysis, respondents frequently report dissonance, sometimes acute dissonance, in their workplaces. This can only carry over into one's sense of self-worth, one's choices with where to live, one's effort to incorporate family life into sometimes crushing work and financial challenges; particularly credit-card debt.[39] Dissonance erodes one's sense of belonging. Butler-Bass adds, "Instead of being grounded, people feel unmoored."[40] Thus the observations made by Golomb some five decades ago are being proven today. He declares:

> The urban religious crisis in the industrial age was accompanied from the beginning by the breaking up of the social structures; so that the structure of pastoral care inevitably became unsuitable. Population increases resulting from industrial development,

---

38. Bennis, *On Becoming a Leader*, 172.

39. A 2019 article in Bloomberg News offers that household debt in Canada has reached levels that could be qualified as excessive. Canadians owe C$2.16 trillion—which, as a share of gross domestic product, is the highest debt load in the Group of Seven economies. https://www.bloomberg.com/news/articles/2019–13-26/canadians-are-feeling-the-debt-burn.

40. Butler Bass, *Christianity after Religion*, 172.

social mobility up-rootings and feelings of being strangers all brought problems which broke the old parish conception.[41]

At the time of Golomb's writing, most people enjoyed employer-sponsored defined-benefit pension plans, together with broad and extensive on-the-job training. The work-day was defined by regular in-person attendance at the workplace. A Sabbath-type rhythm of work, worship and recreation was largely common. Today, the vast majority of people have to make their own retirement investment decisions (and are largely ill-equipped to do so[42]), on-the job training has been replaced by 'just-in-time' expertise, and multiple income sources are a necessity—leading to an extended, often stressful, work week. Modern communications technology, rather than increasing our leisure time, has resulting in 'twenty-four-seven' work-related demands.[43] Beyond this, whereas as little as five decades ago the notion of 'one career-one employer' was largely anticipated—indeed hoped for by many—as a possibility, today many employees are on short-term contracts. For most, a career that encompasses working in numerous organizations across several industry sectors is the accepted norm—a norm that requires almost constant new learning and upskilling. In times of workforce upheaval and restructure, for some the traumatic effect of being 'let go' by their employer can be extreme. Career transition counsellors report a tragic number of situations where a person being terminated has been prone to violence, and to depression, or worse.

My arguments assume that the current era has brought many momentous changes and challenges to the workplace. These include dramatic and distinctly new communication methods and technologies, significantly increased complexity in market structures, a substantially increased complexity in supply chain management (i.e., the relationship between product manufacturers and distribution structures) together with workforce arrangements. This upheaval is brought sharply into view through the lens provided by Mary-Jo Hatch and Anne Cunliffe when they articulate the contrasting view of the organization in the post-modern era vs. the modern era. Hatch and Cunliffe suggest that in the

41. Golomb, "Model Theoretical Considerations," 359.

42. My work as Board Chair of the Ontario Securities Commission funded entity, 'Get Smarter About Money,' conducted research which suggests that Ontario residents have a financial acumen, on average, at the educational level of Grade 4.

43. If one works in a globally-reaching organization, there is literally no end to the work-day as we once understood it.

modern era, organizations may be viewed as, "Objectively real entities operating in a real world. When well-designed and managed they are systems of decision and action driven by norms of rationality, efficiency and effectiveness toward stated objectives."[44] However, Hatch and Cunliffe assert that in the postmodern era, organizations are, "Sites for enacting power relations, giving rise to oppression, irrationality, and falsehoods but also humour and playful irony; as they are texts or dramas, we can rewrite organizations so as to emancipate ourselves from human folly and degradation."[45] Drawing closer to deeper spiritual values may underpin such emancipation.

Employers may have four generations under the same roof, each relating to fundamentally different work traditions, each having different expectations. This generational dilemma is just one dimension of the challenges impacting workplace dynamics. Add to this the impact of multiculturalism which, depending on the setting can have a significant effect on the perspectives and bases for response to situations. Adjustment to multiplicity of languages may be the simplest example of the changes introduced by multiculturalism as we grow and adapt. Eve Haque explains:

> There is an assumption that a shift from non-official-language to official proficiency is inevitable and desirable . . . Critical here is the conflation of language and culture so that concerns about non-official languages become concerns about racialized immigration and that English and French come to stand in for the founding cultural groups.[46]

The foregoing suggests the need for critical theological reflection on the human experience: a central element of practical theology. We may have reached a time in society where we have, in terms of our working lives, arrived at what is a virtual separation of the sacred and the secular. We must consider that this separation has resulted for some, in a setting aside completely, of personal purpose and meaning in one's chosen endeavours. In 1966, Simon Phipps asserted, "The biblical outline of the world shows it as man's [sic] means of freedom, God's means of communication, and man's [sic] means of response . . . and it all happens in the one

---

44. Hatch, *Organization Theory*, 15.

45. Hatch, *Organization Theory*, 15.

46. Haque, "Multiculturalism," 206–7.

secular world."⁴⁷ I have sought to understand the degree to which people today attempt to navigate this secularization. The Church may be at fault. I note that Phipps goes on to criticize an evangelism that implies a duality in our lives, i.e., our religious world and our secular world. In concurring with Phipps, I do not accept a simplistic duality of the sacred and the secular. Pippa Norris and Ronald Inglehart appear to support this rejection. They write:

> The seminal social thinkers of the nineteenth century—Auguste Comte, Herbert Spencer, Emile Durkheim, Max Weber, Karl Marx and Sigmund Freud—all believed that religion would gradually fade in importance and cease to be significant with the advent of industrial society . . . During the last decade [2000's], however, this thesis of the slow and steady death of religion has come under growing criticism; indeed, secularization theory is currently experiencing the most sustained challenge in its long history.⁴⁸

No wonder.

Phipps' assertion implies the hope that, through his agents (in the context of this book, Spirit-led leaders) God might stitch back together an economic effort that fully encompasses divine-human purpose. For those called to the task of agency in this endeavour, there is much to learn if we are to reconcile what appears to be a widening divide, a divide made greater when the lexicon of economic activity is contemplated within a broader framework of theological reflection which, it seems, we must undertake. Although Norris's and Inglehart's comments may, with hindsight, be only partly correct, my thesis assumes that practices of leadership, when viewed as Spirit-led, are pivotal to human flourishing. Through a theological lens, the broad practice of leadership argued for here is the synthesis of all the factors that influence the potential for a deep sense of flourishing in which economic endeavour—at all levels—is perceived as a divine-human expression of God's kingdom. Indeed, this may be perceived as preparatory for our eschatological *telos*. Thus, the practices which this work will hopefully influence, include organizational governance, the chain of leadership within an organization and, indeed, the chaplain, should there be one, together with those who would provide the capital for such endeavours.

---

47. Phipps, *God on Monday*, 35.
48. Norris and Inglehart, *Sacred and Secular*, 3.

Multiple Research Dimensions

This work welds together several fields of study. Each is viewed through the lens of the others. The foundational premise of this work asserts that workplace dynamics and resulting challenges, when viewed through the lens of the worker's need for a sense of deep spiritual fulfillment and satisfaction, are poorly understood, possibly even ignored.

My aim is to set a fresh and enhanced template for the development of essential practices of leadership that will promote flourishing in the workplace. When we consider that, for most, more than fifty percent of our waking hours are spent in professional and economic pursuit, *there is arguably no greater domain to achieve faithful living and authentic practice than the workplace*. Swinton and Mowat offer that, "Practical Theology has a *telos* and a goal that transcends the boundaries of human experience and expectation."[49] For emphasis, my work seeks to construct leadership as the means to encourage workers to rediscover deeper meaning and purpose.

In the context of this endeavour, the term *leadership practice* may be interpreted as what Erlene Grise-Owens and Jay Miller describe as a "synthesizing framework."[50] I seek to broaden this framework to encompass and combine leadership and operational management with flourishing, as imagined through the prism of practical theology. Shelley Trebesch offers a definition of what it means to flourish. She writes that it is, "to live within an optimal range of human functioning, one that connotes goodness, generativity, growth, and resilience."[51] I will argue that sustained peak achievement of workplace output is impossible without an environment where human flourishing is complete.

As indicated above, a challenge to this endeavor is wrought by the confluence of three fundamental challenges to a very significant underpinning of human spiritual flourishing. These are:

1. Erosion of meaningfulness at work, both in the sense that work satisfies a person's economic needs (e.g., equitable pay, job-security etc.), and that it satisfies a person's sense of vocation. This yearning for meaningfulness is challenged by a workplace that has become

---

49. Swinton and Mowat, *Practical Theology and Qualitative Research*, 9.
50. Grise-Owens and Miller, "Responding to Global Shifts," 47.
51. Trebesch, *Made to Flourish*, 11.

largely bereft of any purpose other than an economic, administrative, or legislative as perceived by the enterprise and its funder.
2. A Church that, largely, does not respond comprehensively to the spiritual needs of workers, leaving congregants uncertain of how to link their remunerated labour with the call of their faith, and,
3. Human beings that have had little to no interaction with—even introduction to—the Gospel.

Further, there is for many a risk of a spiralling state of distress, or at the very least, ennui, made worse by a lack of understanding of the reason for that state. The result is that people increasingly accept work as simply the route to a paycheque and hoped-for social status, defined largely in economic terms. Consciously or not, people are putting greater distance between themselves and those that might counsel them. As those that might offer such ministry increasingly become unaware of the issue of diminishing purpose and its spiritual *gravitas*, each generation of workers is at risk of drifting further and further away from God's intended purpose for our work.

Simply arriving at this circumstance presents a multi-dimensional challenge requiring special and dedicated effort. Scholars have attempted to deal with elements of the challenge which this work will address. For example, Wesley Carr distinguishes between organizations and institutions. He provides, "The organization demands managers and people who will get things done . . . The institution looks for leadership, which has to recognize and work with what is mostly inaccessible—the unconscious aspects of the body's life."[52] One asks however, 'Does the organization respond to values, or impose them?' Carr continues, "If the organizational image dominates, then values will be felt to be imposed. They become apparent practicalities: cutting costs, downsizing, restructuring and so on. The management approach focuses in terms of motivation by rewards and incentives."[53] While presenting a laudable approach, I argue that Carr's observations fall short in terms of fully exploring the complexity of the situation and lack the granular nuances of both organizational design and leadership practice.

As mentioned, an increasing number of schools of business and management are exploring spirituality and business. For example, there

---

52. Carr, "Spirituality of Institutions," 115–16.
53. Carr, "Spirituality of Institutions," 116.

is an emerging discussion of 'people-first organizations,' and work-life balance in the sense that this discussion contributes to a positive work environment. We need to see much more of this.[54]

Many organizations are aware, and are sensitive to, employee wellness. For example, the 2017 Annual Report of the Public Guardian and Trustee for Ontario states, "As part of a larger Wellness Strategy supporting positive mental health within the organization the OPGT provided compassionate fatigue and vicarious trauma training."[55] Swinton and Mowat note that, "[S]pirituality and religion (understood as related but not synonymous concepts), are fast becoming recognized as a significant aspect of the healthcare agenda."[56] It would appear these aspects have not yet, however, become pervasive in the lexicon of leadership.

Career concepts and expectations are changing. As suggested, it is apparent that for most, a long-term career-path with the same enterprise is no longer an obtainable expectation. Job loss and the sometimes-wrenching changes that accrue are significant factors of our era. In a work by Al Emid and myself, we wrote:

> Losing a job can be a devastating blow. It undermines a person's emotional well-being at the same time that it knocks down the pillars of financial stability. After all, a job not only puts bread on the table but also, for a lot of people, instills a sense of purpose into everyday life. And because we spend so many hours each day at a job, we expect to love what we do.[57]

For many who go through a forced termination, the experience can be shocking to the point of being overwhelming. This, sadly, is far from uncommon. It can be at least unnerving, causing individuals to become anxious and uncertain.[58]

William Pollard asserts, "People want to work for a cause, not just for a living. When there is alignment between the cause of the firm and

---

54. Harriet Ekperigin writes, "My MBA course in 2006 included an option for ethics and management. I focused my essay on the importance of corporate social responsibility and the ethical need for this. It was an emerging trend at that time and it did and still continues to influence the work I do today. I always felt that this should have been a mandatory rather than an optional course." I agree.

55. Public Guardian and Trustee for Ontario (OPGT) 2017 Annual Report, 3.

56. Swinton and Mowat, *Practical Theology and Qualitative Research*, 159.

57. Bates and Emid, *What I Have Learned*, 95.

58. This can be particularly vexing for new-comers to the country without established networks.

the cause of its people, move over—because there *will* be extraordinary performance."⁵⁹

Work as Struggle: A Search for Purpose

Many observers describe work as a struggle at best, bruising at worst. In the introduction to his book *Working*, Studs Terkel offers:

> This book being about work, is, by its very nature, about violence—to the spirit as well as to the body. It is about ulcers as well as accidents, about shouting matches as well as fistfights, about nervous breakdowns as well as kicking the dog around. It is above all (or beneath all), about daily humiliations ... It is about a search, too, for daily meaning as well as daily bread, for recognition as well as cash, for astonishment rather than torpor.⁶⁰

It is clear that work can be, and usually is, laborious. But this is not the end of the story—certainly, it does not have to be. While work can be exhausting, Katherine Dell writes, "Work brings structure to a day and it brings us into contact with others: there is nothing more rewarding than a job well done."⁶¹ You will hear this in several research respondent narratives presented later in this book.

It is likely that we can all think of discussions of the workplace that are expressed in pejorative ways: a place to 'kiss up, kick down,' a place of bullying, aggression, conflict, deviance, discrimination, harassment, incivility, mobbing, revenge, sabotage, swearing, violence, and worse.⁶²

---

59. Pollard, *The Soul of the Firm*, 45.
60. Terkel, *Working*, xiii.
61. Dell, *Seeking a Life*, 34.

62. A USA Today article in June 2019 reports that a postal worker on disability retirement for psychological issues returned to her workplace years later and killed six people. A Connecticut beer delivery worker irate over being forced to resign opened fire as he was being escorted out of the building, killing eight co-workers.
Just a week ago, a long-time municipal engineer submitted his resignation in the morning and within hours went on a rampage inside the building, killing 11 co-workers and a contractor. The Virginia Beach killing is one of 11 mass workplace killings dating back to 2006 in the U.S., according to a database of mass killings maintained through a partnership between The Associated Press, USA TODAY and Northeastern University. In all, nearly 90 people have died in these mass shootings, which are defined as 4 or more people killed, not including the perpetrator.
And while such workplace shootings remain rare among the tens of thousands of gun deaths each year, they resonate among Americans who worry they might become

Indeed, we can probably all recall such circumstances. By contrast, Robert Bruno offers:

> The working-class Christians, Jews and Muslims that I spoke with described a living faith that was realized in God's name but was all about finding God in relation with others. While making no claims to a grand theology, I found the daily relational nature of spirituality to be a central tenet of working-class faith ... God seems to be everywhere to the painter, the nurse, bus-driver, massage therapist, butcher, processing clerk, cemetery worker, and teacher.[63]

While Bruno's work with a group of Chicago's working poor is inspiring, it is the assumption of my enquiry that contemporary culture is sufficiently secularized that remuneration and the goals of workplace productivity conspire to redefine both work and workers largely in materialistic, non-spiritual terms. Both are conceived of in utilitarian (and thus intrinsically de-humanizing) terms.

To put it simply, labour—the fundamental human input to production—appears to be considered by many enterprises as simply a factor of production. For example, we read frequent accounts of longstanding employees being denied expected benefits in the event of corporate restructuring.[64] Further, it appears that few work environments can be guaranteed to be free of some form of demeaning behaviour. Mental illness leaves of absence are increasingly common. Jean Twenge confirms, "[S]tudies conclude that anxiety and depression are markedly higher than they were in earlier eras."[65] Indeed, in 2016, the Canadian Federal Government announced a sweeping 'Federal Public Service Mental Health Strategy.' Taken together, the circumstances of the modern workplace described in the foregoing paragraphs may well be precursor to deeper psychological issues, violence, ill-health, even suicide. Beate Muschalla et al. write:

> The workplace is an important part of people's lives and thus exerts a strong influence on general well-being and health ...

---

an aggrieved co-worker's next victim.

63. Bruno, *Justified by Work*, 214.

64. At the time of writing, business press, Money.com covers the story that Sears Canada seeks court protection from its creditors, while letting go seventeen percent of its seventeen thousand employees, and confirms, "that it does not intend to pay severance to those laid off."

65. Twenge, "Mental Health Issues" (blog) October 15 2015.

> The nature of workplace influences is two-sided. The workplace can exert positive influences by providing social support, identity and self-esteem, but it also involves demands, pressures, and even threats that can provoke anxiety.[66]

No doubt, every reader of this book will identify to some degree with Muschalla's observation.

There are occasions when an organization's majority owners seek massive change in the structure and leadership of the enterprise. This can occur when significant, or controlling, shareholders perceive that there is greater value in the business than is reflected in the common share price of the company. This was the case at CP Rail in late 2011, when Hunter Harrison was hired as the company's Chief Executive Officer. Harrison was a railway executive known as a 'turnaround specialist.' What followed at CP Rail was extreme disruption. A 2016 news article chronicled the impact on CP Rail during the period that Hunter Harrison held the role of Chief Executive Officer. Journalist Kristine Owram writes:

> Hunter Harrison is legendary in the industry for his operating method, known as precision railroading, which is designed to create a leaner company by introducing longer and faster trains, better service and lower costs. Including both unionized and non-unionized employees, CP cut its total workforce by 40 per cent, to 11,700 from 19,500, during his four-and-a-half-year reign.[67]

One might argue that the journalist does not provide information regarding views on the quality of management and reliability of operations *prior* to Harrison's arrival. Certainly, the financial analysts who covered the company during his tenure were largely favourable in their assessments of Harrison's directives' effect on profitability. Indeed, Mr. Harrison went on to receive a reported U.S. $84 million as his annual salary from his subsequent employer, US based rail company CSX Corp. Assessing the effectiveness of management solely through the lens of financial performance, especially relatively short-term financial performance, is not enough, however. The CP Rail story, if taken on a *prima facie* basis, epitomizes a workplace situation which, if looked through the paradigm of work as an expression of divine-human endeavor, may be argued as being at risk of becoming corrupt; essentially destroying the opportunity for work to be a source of flourishing. Without question, organizations reach

---

66. Muschalla et al., "The Significance of Job-Anxiety," 415.
67. Owram, "The Other Side," 2.

inflection points where significant disruption is required to correct a perceived weakness. The critical question is the degree to which the pace and nature of change incorporate the imperative of human flourishing as part of the change planning exercise.

Hospitality and Community

The prevailing view of work, as an expression of spirituality, represents an area of social upheaval that, I argue, must be addressed. It is a premise of this book that exposure to the message of the Gospel[68] is a rapidly decreasing, if not non-existent, element of the moral compass of many in western society. In other words, an increasing number have not been exposed, and therefore enlightened or given spiritual sight through an encounter with the Gospel, discovering that *God is love*, and that we are to respond by loving others, while continuing to be effective leaders of an enterprise. It is possible that the Church itself may, unintentionally, be a significant contributor to the state of cognitive dissonance with respect to a theological understanding of work. Peter Marty introduces a significant change in church culture. Following Pentecost, writes Marty, "In Acts 4 we learn that believers began to experience palpable unity with one another . . . Every individual in the community had the necessities of life met."[69] This was complete integration of community, the organization of work, and mutual caring. Marty observes:

> Today, we are direct descendants of a pattern of promoting private and personal spirituality that has long overwhelmed the much more difficult work of forming and sustaining Christian community. Some theologians argue that modernity has brought on a rampant individualism never seen before in church history, but it would be more helpful to say that contemporary consumerism and a market ideology have merely exacerbated the longstanding impulse among believers for a privatized faith.[70]

This notion of individualism is in direct contrast to the mutual dependence and concept of community in ancient times. The need for hospitality has endured through millennia as a key element of community. If we consider the word 'forgiveness' in terms of reducing stress, and allowance

---

68. Or any faith-based doctrinal perspective.
69. Marty, "Shaping Communities," 308.
70. Marty, "Shaping Communities," 309.

for, or overlooking, differences, then we can perceive the linkage between attributes of forgiveness and hospitality. Interestingly, the very foundation of modern commerce could be the ancient precept of hospitality. Henri Nouwen writes:

> [I]f there is any concept worth restoring to its original depth and evocative potential, it is the concept of hospitality . . . Old and New Testament stories not only show how serious our obligation is to welcome the stranger in our home, but they also tell us that guests are carrying precious gifts with them, which they are eager to reveal to a receptive host.[71]

Here Nouwen is echoing one of Jesus' most fundamental instructions. Jesus' admonishment is clear, "I was a stranger and you welcomed me (Matt 25:25)." Arguably, without hospitality, commerce between different communities would have never become a reality. Jesus, too, is drawing back together love of God and love of neighbour (cf. Matt 22:36–40). Gainful work, too, is critical to neighbourhood. Without a strong and healthy economic foundation, neighbourhoods falter and decline.[72] Arguably, a thriving economy may be perceived as eschatological. Miroslav Volf asserts an eschatological value of work:

> It is possible that the statement in Revelation about the saints resting 'from their labours (*kopon*), for their deeds (*erga*) follow them' (Rev 14:13; cf. Eph. 6:8) could be interpreted to imply that earthly work will leave traces on resurrected personalities . . . Human work is ultimately significant not only because it contributes to the future environment of human beings, but also because it leaves an indelible imprint on their personalities.[73]

The word 'deed' is taken in another of its meanings—that of action or performance. Jesus has demonstrated to us that forgiveness is the act that shapes everything we do (cf. John 8:7). In the workplace, when deep dissatisfaction or behaviour is perceived as abusive, one frequently simply leaves the environment, thus there is no opportunity for reconciliation. Further, when litigation is involved, while settlement may be achieved (usually through pecuniary means), the opportunity to arrive at apology, let alone reconciliation, almost never occurs. Beyond this, very little, if any opportunity is created for an exploration of spiritual and emotional

---

71. Nouwen, *Reaching Out*, 66.
72. Consider the circumstances of many 'rust belt' communities.
73. Volf, *Work in the Spirit*, 97–98.

damage that occurs. It may be interesting to explore the First Nations' concept and employment of healing—or peacemaking—circles, as a method for reconciliation and restorative justice, in which adversarial litigation is set aside. In other words, forgiveness is central to restoration. Forgiveness is at the very heart of faith. When viewed as practised, or operative theology, work and leadership—imbued with a culture of forgiveness—will have cooperation as the working model over interpersonal competition.

Jaco Hamman states further, "[F]orgiveness has a forensic component, a therapeutic component, and a *redemptive component*."[74] Frequently, although not always, abusive behaviour in the workplace, if it reaches a legal process, will involve a forensic component—but only a societal forensic component. There is seldom recognition for a need to explore a biblical perspective on sin—of straying from the right path, or God's justice and forgiveness. Thus, while civil litigation may be completed, therapeutic and redemptive processes and activities may not occur at all—leaving lasting scars that may manifest in physical as well as emotional illness. These are outcomes that people carry with them for the rest of their lives.[75]

As my research moved through the many iterative cycles of data collection, coding, analysis and theological reflection described earlier, interpretation sought to identify both profound and subtle linkages between professed faith and a deeper sense of purposefulness at work. Paul Ballard writes, "In theological reflection as a structured method, there is a conscious and deliberate exploration of belief and practice in a given situation. This could range from a moment in ministry, to working with a congregation, to a personal life decision."[76] While Ballard does not discuss workplace experiences as explicitly integral, or even foundational to personal life decisions, this comment contains instruction. As Ballard states, "Theological reflection, as a deliberate process, aims to enable us to discern the wisdom of God in the scriptures for faithful living in the present."[77] We must find the right moment to explore biblical tenets and

---

74. Hamman, "Revisiting Forgiveness," 444 [emphasis original].

75. Harriet Ekperigin writes, "I would go as far as saying that this can sometimes negatively affect the way that those that have experienced such interact with others where the bullied becomes the bully and the cycle is perpetuated."

76. Ballard, "The Use of Scripture," 168.

77. Ballard, "The Use of Scripture," 169.

perspectives as we contemplate work. Ballard describes the dynamic that must be anticipated. He writes:

> The rapid social, economic, and political changes that are overtaking [and frequently polarizing] the world mean that we are increasingly living in a mobile, pluralistic society that can so easily lose cultural roots and cultural cohesion. In the West, certainly, it is no longer possible to assume a widespread familiarity with the Christian faith and the Bible, in particular—its stories, its language, and its perspective—which have for so long been at its heart. What does it mean to live in a Bible-poor, post-Christian culture? What does this mean for Christian practice, witness, and ministry?[78]

We may not be called to proselytize, but we are called to act.

The research endeavour at the heart of this work seeks to achieve what John Patton offers when he writes, "[P]astoral theology is not just concerned with human experience, but human experience in relationship to God and other persons."[79] While the lexicon of the workplace may not permit a literal discussion of work as contribution to the coming eschatological transformation, we can certainly act in such a way that allows the Spirit to enter the conversation, bringing deeper reflection on the purpose of work. Stanley Grenz writes:

> We have characterized the fundamental theological assertion concerning the relationship between God and the world by use of the term's 'creator' and 'creation.' The triune God is the creator of the world; and the universe is the creation of God. But the divine act of creation, while including the primordial calling of the world into existence, ultimately is an eschatological event ... This conclusion naturally leads us to inquire regarding God's purposes for the world he is making and God's active directing of history toward the accomplishment of these purposes ... We may summarize God's intention for the world by employing the term, 'community.'[80]

When the workplace is seen through the lens of community, that workplace may be imbued by an ethos of mutual collaboration rather than competition.

---

78. Ballard, "The Use of Scripture," 170.
79. Patton, "Practical Theology Asks," 54.
80. Grenz, *Theology for the Community of God*, 112.

Seasons of Life

The seasons of a person's life appear to have a bearing on one's coping mechanisms. Older research respondents demonstrated an ability to derive inner strength in the face of less-than-optimal workplace experiences. This calls to mind the thought that career changes over time gradually help older workers to find work environments that are more in line with their values, resulting in an amelioration of dissonance. This suggests that experiences, education, communities of civic engagement, such as volunteer activities, will shape the way we respond to situations.[81] Bill Mowry writes:

> Instead of a universal reality which is scientifically provable, there is a growing belief that people construct their sense of reality . . . This means that research and interpretation must consider the cultural and historical factors which make up the ministry or individual context. The emphasis now is on *interpretation* and not on predicting through universal laws.[82]

This will be helpful in interpreting what Teresa Amabile and Steven Kramer describe as, "workday events that ignite emotions and fuel motivation."[83]

I have not encountered a broad-reaching, multi-domain, effort to draw together the multivariate influences on the changing workplace, together with the resulting effect on the worker. These include economic priorities and influences, operations efficiencies, urbanization and resulting changes in commuting patterns, changes in job-training, changes in provision for financially secure retirement; ethnic, religious, and gender diversity, plus corporate structural changes. An example is the flattening of corporate hierarchy which has reduced, or eliminated middle management. This elimination distances senior management from the worker, thus removing opportunities for real coaching and mentorship. Consider also that all these phenomena have occurred in one generation.

---

81. In my own experience, it is these public and not-for-profit activities that have shaped leadership careers through the breadth of exposure to numerous environments with vastly different cultures, goals and methods.

82. Mowry, "A Reflective Approach," 56 [emphasis original].

83. Amabile and Kramer, "The Power of Small Wins" 2.

Conclusion

For most, our work is a deep expression of who we are. Among the first questions that we ask someone whom we meet for the first time is, "What do you do?" This question, perhaps without our realization, instantly invokes all the aspirations, fears, goals, and unresolved conflicts that we all hold in our workplace endeavours. Virtually all of us seek to find deeper purpose in our work, although we express this in different ways. We seek a purpose that is far beyond economic security, even beyond achieving a sense of a job well done. We want to flourish—to blossom, to thrive, to be liberated; to be at the peak of our development—and, for the most part, we want our neighbours and co-workers to flourish also. The proposition which undergirds this book is that for many, if not most, this aspiration is unfulfilled. We are settling for less, much less in some cases.

Spirit-led leadership is presented here as critically important, indeed urgent, in the postmodern era. Gustafson offers, "Insofar as postmodern thought engenders a sense of caution and concern about the limits of one's ability to know 'the truth,' it may actually bring about a sense of awe and humility, akin to worship."[84] To this I add the view that leadership is providential. My work recasts leadership as practised theology. If work is a means to flourishing, then the ethos of the workplace is the energy source from which flourishing may be achieved. Spirit-led Leadership is the means by which that energy is released. God called Abraham to lead (cf. Gen 12:22). God called Moses to lead (cf. Exod 3), and God called Ananias to an act of leadership (cf. Acts 9:17). God called and equipped many others to lead. In each situation the act of equipping this resulted in a release of energy that formed a new ethos—by which situations and people were transformed, and by which flourishing followed.

---

84. Gustafson, "Making Sense of Postmodern Ethics," 649.

2

Research Foundation

For by the grace given me I say to every one of you: Do not think of yourself more highly than you ought, but rather think of yourself with sober judgment, in accordance with the measure of faith God has given you. Just as each of us has one body with many members, and these members do not all have the same function, so in Christ we who are many form one body, and each member belongs to all the others. We have different gifts, according to the grace given us.

(ROM 12:3 NIV)

IF THE GIFT OF leadership is to be understood as a praxis which is rooted in practical theology, then it is critical to understand how people view their work, particularly through the lens of faith and spiritual flourishing. In order to explore such views, a six-part questionnaire was devised for my research, using closed-end and open-end questions,[1] to elicit contemplative observations regarding the respondents' sense of meaningfulness and purpose at work, together with spirituality and faith as elements of their orientation in terms of finding that meaningfulness. This chapter

---

1. Closed-end questions seek a 'yes or no' answer, whereas open-end questions elicit a longer, detailed, response.

is revelatory in terms of attitudes toward work, as articulated by the respondents, reflected upon through the prism of a half-century of work.

Workplace experiences present significant narratives, creating deep interest from a research point of view in that workplace experiences pervade and impact all facets of one's life. By design, the research questions elicit lived experiences which, inductively, may be assumed to be wrought largely by the impact of leadership on workplace ethos. It is critical to note that the narratives recorded by the respondents offer crucial insights into the implied effects that leadership styles, approaches and decisions have on the degree to which a state of flourishing is achieved. Also provided by the respondents are examples of coping mechanisms, and ways in which people achieve some level of meaningfulness, together with those factors which trigger changes in career paths.

Research Questionnaire

An invitation was distributed via several contact networks in Canada, the United Kingdom, and the United States. The goal was to receive between twenty-five and thirty-five completed responses from men and women across a broad range of occupations, and of varying ages. Thirty-two completed responses were received.

The participant questionnaire included the following:[2]

Please respond to as many of the questions below as you are comfortable answering and as they apply to your own experience: I am looking for as much as you are willing to share. Please use additional space if you require. It will take approximately 10–20 minutes to complete this questionnaire.

1. *Please identify whether you: (a) Work in a supervisory role, (b) non-supervisory role or, (c) are a retiree?*

2. *Please offer your thoughts regarding the degree to which you enjoy a sense of deep meaningfulness at work, both in the sense that work satisfies your economic needs (e.g., equitable pay, job-security etc.), and that it satisfies your sense of vocation—even calling. Has this changed over time? Do you feel that your views are shared by your peers and co-workers? Please take as much space as you need to answer this question in detail, using specific examples and experiences where you wish.*

---

2. As you read this, you may wish to take a sheet of paper and write down your own answers to these questions.

3. Would you describe yourself as a person of faith? Please answer yes or no.

4. If you are a person of faith, how does your spiritual or faith-orientation have a bearing on your views as expressed in question 2 above? Please offer your thoughts on the ways in which your faith impacts or affects your views of work.

5. Are you comfortable in speaking about your faith and the ways in which your faith affects your approach to work? Please answer yes or no, and explain further if you wish.

6. If you have experienced a conversation with an advisor, e.g., a minister in your faith tradition, please offer your thoughts on the ways in which these conversations have assisted you in putting your work in a more satisfying perspective.

A spreadsheet was populated with each verbatim response to the six questions asked in the questionnaire. In this primary gathering process, all responses were rendered anonymous, with responses tabulated under 'respondent 1,' 'respondent 2,' and so on. Further, the responses were edited to remove information that might provide a reader with knowledge of the respondent's identity through discussion of work location or other specific information that might identify the respondent.

Analysis

With this spreadsheet completed, several analytical methods were employed. These included substantive and axial coding stages, concept mapping, phenomenological examination, and the identification of several tenets of emergent theories, leading ultimately to the formation of a grounded theory. In this chapter, and in the balance of this work, where considered germane, verbatim quotations from research participants will be included, in some cases used in multiple instances to underscore different perspectives and arguments. The questions were designed to cause the respondents to contemplate their circumstances quite deeply. The respondents did not disappoint.

Workplace environments of the respondents include capital markets, accounting, agriculture, communications, construction, teaching, nursing, long-term and palliative care, together with administrative roles in public service, church/faith-based, and not-for-profit enterprises.

Although age information was not requested, responses suggest that the sample includes individuals that range in age from mid-twenties to mid-seventies.

Several identify a strong sense of God's calling in their work. A respondent stated, "I believe that I am doing good works, utilizing God-given talents."[3] Many, however, describe injustice in their environment. A respondent stated, "Many events have placed a sense of doubt in my job security. E.g., others not being supported or not being assigned to a position that I felt qualified to do; being assigned a role that suited the company, but which impeded my development."[4] There are trust implications here. Carlton Snow suggests:

> Trust is an elusive abstraction. Like the air we breathe, trust is taken for granted, drawing little attention to itself until the atmosphere goes bad. At the same time, trust, elusive though it is, is a concept that has practical importance: the issue of trust is central to the development and continuation of a productive work experience.[5]

Generally, it would seem certain among all the respondents that trust is assumed to be offered automatically and immediately by them, in their workplace, to both their manager and their peers. This appears particularly to be emphasized among those who articulate a spiritual calling to their work. Trust appears central to faith and spirituality. When trust is eroded, it is frequently the workplace environment that has caused it, deliberately or inadvertently.

The seasons of life have an impact on the response to views regarding a sense of purpose. A respondent stated, "[In my] second career [I am doing] what I am meant and called to do."[6] This may be partly the result of learning more about our gifts and capabilities vs. our aspirations. This suggests that aging results in one's becoming more completely aware of one's calling. It may also be about becoming more comfortable in our own skins as we age. Capps writes, "To reconnect with [our] earlier time, then, is more than an expression of nostalgia for bygone years—though it is partly that. It is the attempt to understand ourselves so that we become

---

3. Verbatim respondent 13.
4. Verbatim respondent 22.
5. Snow, "Rebuilding Trust," 35.
6. Verbatim respondent 15.

better at living in the here and now."⁷ Respondents whose narratives made it clear that they had been working for several decades, frequently offered a response to their circumstances that reflected deeper resolve in the manner in which they internalized and coped with their situations.

In a number of their narratives, respondents discuss personal values and goals, choices and compromises. There is frequently suggested a stronger or weaker sense of calling, but this calling is often set aside or left unanswered for the sake of economic necessity, or the converse, i.e., enjoyment of the work circumstance means a loss of economic return. A respondent stated, "I will be working out of financial necessity until I am at least 70. My work is a calling."⁸ Richard Higginson underscores this when he writes, "Organizational life offers many dilemmas that have no easy answers. Ethical complexity is all around, and so leading with integrity is often a matter of walking through a moral minefield."⁹ Clearly the same is true of followers. We make compromises in order to earn a living wage.

The workplace, and the marketplace more broadly, appear to create dissonance for some in terms of their personal values and the resulting desire for perfection in their chosen endeavour. Br. Lucas Hall describes a "dissonance between what is and what should be."¹⁰ This straightforwardly describes the intuitive sense that we have when a situation is not right—that it should be better. Expressed, on occasion, is a deep desire to figure out how their faith should guide one's actions. A respondent stated, "I pray for the wisdom to make the most of every day."¹¹ For some, modelling their values, or faith, is not generally made easy by the workplace. Several commented on being taken advantage of, yet they still felt blessed. Others felt sadness at seeing how colleagues were being treated. A respondent stated, "I believe that easing the suffering of others is an easing of my own suffering."¹² 'Suffering' is a strong term, implying that one is witnessing a dire situation.

Numerous respondent comments underscore the sense of dissonance, or disharmony. Dissonance is perceived and described in varying

---

7. Capps, *The Decades of Life*, 120.
8. Verbatim respondent 13.
9. Higginson, "Integrity and the Art of Compromise," 28.
10. Hall, "Remember the Words He has Taught You," [n.d.].
11. Verbatim respondent 9.
12. Verbatim respondent 17.

degrees, manifest by feelings of lost empowerment. Despite feelings of dissonance—that a circumstance is beyond one's capability to change—respondents still held an underlying sense of commitment to their work. Isabel Lopez writes, "[In chaotic times] I am convinced that we must find our own center, and that once we have found it all the chaos becomes irrelevant."[13] We find our way. Situations may not become irrelevant, but we may learn to compartmentalize them.

Finding one's spiritual centre is expressed, albeit sometimes tentatively, by respondents. A respondent stated, "I'm still trying to figure it all out."[14] Another respondent stated, "I gained a sense of vocational enjoyment and I am committed."[15] *This is an issue for leadership*. It is leadership, solely, that is empowered to create an environment that is conducive to resolving such dissonance. Regrettably, however, a number of respondents' comments suggest evidence of a pervasive lack of leadership relative to their expectations. Comments point to the goals of the organization taking primacy over needs of the employee. Kellerman emphasizes, "[L]eadership can be considered the exercise of influence, or a power relation, or an instrument of goal achievement . . . The point is that each of these definitions is value-free."[16] Fully competent leaders insert values into their calculus; however, it appears that sometimes it is incompetence that results in a lack of good leadership. Sometimes it is also a lack of commitment. It is clear that, on occasion, employees are being overtly coerced toward a particular goal, without regard to implications in terms of meaningfulness and purpose. The end justifies the means.

While several speak of their faith, few respondents see the church as a place of spiritual guidance in terms of work challenges and choices. Some respondent narratives describe faith in the message of scripture, yet these same respondent narratives articulate real despair in the nature of the workplace situation alluded to. John Beckett writes:

> God wants a greater role not only with individuals, not just in church, but also in our families, our schools, in government, *and* in commerce and industry. He has a purpose for us and our work and a dynamic role to play. For God to have greater

---

13. Lopez, "Finding Wisdom," 81.
14. Verbatim respondent 17.
15. Verbatim respondent 26.
16. Kellerman, *Bad Leadership*, 12.

access, we must open our spiritual doors—doors that invite and encourage his presence.[17]

This a significant tenet of faith; a deeply held belief that God is involved.

Dissonance appears to be pervasive, although in varying degrees of intensity. A respondent stated, "I am wrestling with how the church should approach gender identity and sexuality issues—this is not a safe discussion."[18] Sometimes this dissonance is internal to organizational situations, i.e., generated by practices and circumstances inside the structure of organizations. In other cases, this dissonance is external to the organization, including shifting marketplace attitudes and expectations, changing community structures, changing family characteristics, and changing approaches and attitudes to the concept of faith.

Several describe the stress of being self-employed and building a business. A respondent stated, "It can be scary at times."[19] This is a particularly unique phenomenon. Entrepreneurs, by nature, are resilient and hopeful, but the loneliness of leading a start-up can be overwhelming for them. New businesses are completely engulfing of the entrepreneur's time, resources, intellectual effort, emotional energy, self-esteem, and reputational credibility. Cash-flow concerns can occur daily. Sometimes these concerns reach crisis proportions. Family relationships can suffer. Community engagement outside of the enterprise can fall away entirely.[20]

A number of respondents affirm that their spirituality and faith carried them through difficult times. Respondents also discuss real joy derived from coming alongside others—providing help and guidance. They describe how they grew from such experiences. John Kuypers speaks to this. He suggests:

> We don't want inner peace first, we want results first. This is the stubborn human way that keeps us trapped in unhappiness for years over troubling issues. The first rule of inner peace is a mind-blowing paradox where we become spiritually powerful only after we become humanly powerless.[21]

---

17. Beckett, *Loving Monday*, 135 [emphasis original].
18. Verbatim respondent 1.
19. Verbatim respondent 8.
20. I recall many 2:00 AM moments wondering, painfully, how our little start-up would meet its next payroll obligation.
21. Kuypers, *The First Rule*, 107–8.

In other words, it is the inner peace of several respondents that sustains them in difficult times, and it is their love for others that urges them to find ways to help others find such peace. A respondent stated, "I was brought up to think that 'helping others' is what we're meant to do."[22] The *Golden Rule*, of course, pervades virtually all belief systems.

Some professions, such as teaching and nursing, appear to be circumstances where there are certainly stressors, but also where deep enjoyment of improving and shaping, sometimes saving, the lives of people is experienced. A respondent stated, "I work in the long-term care sector. I feel I have always been called to work with older adults."[23] Jennifer Worth affirms, "She was only a nurse and a social worker. What could she do? A calling from God is always hard and demanding, but it can never be resisted, whatever the cost to the individual."[24] Perhaps it is the nature of immediacy and urgency that caring for another as a medical provider or teacher in certain work situations simply cannot be deferred that makes the vocational call so strong that it cannot be missed.

Some express the notion that a sense of purpose has grown over the years. A respondent stated, "I have a sense of meaningfulness, but it is not deep and has grown over time."[25] Thus, for these individuals, their career has been a series of building blocks—a process of personal construction. This confirms that the seasons of a person's life have a bearing. As observed earlier, older respondents demonstrate a learned ability to cope and derive inner strength in the face of less-than-optimal workplace experiences. Career changes over time gradually help older workers to find work environments that are more in line with their values. Thus, for them, work-related dissonance is ameliorated.[26]

Some observe that personal economic successes provide opportunities for philanthropy. For example, wealth-creation leads to an awakening sense of accountability and purpose. A respondent stated, "We are able to contribute money to causes important to us."[27] In some cases this is the result of an expressed sense of community. In some cases, it is the

22. Verbatim respondent 10.
23. Verbatim respondent 20.
24. Worth, *In the Midst of Life*, 63.
25. Verbatim respondent 7.
26. My work with human resources counselling activity affirms that many individuals in forced career transition regularly find new and different roles that reflect the values they have come to embrace more clearly.
27. Verbatim respondent 17.

result of one's reflection on personal experiences of being economically challenged in an earlier period in one's life and being grateful to have achieved some business success. For some it is the response to one's faith calling that is manifest in the impetus to share one's gifts.

In several cases there is a clear sense of feeling adrift in the workplace—a loss of being secure in their expectation of return on the investment of one's labour relative to all the rewards one hopes to receive. A respondent stated, "Work does not satisfy my economic needs."[28] The 'gig economy' is a pervasive work construct in the postmodern environment, bringing with it a broad range of challenges, beginning with long hours commuting and/or on the job.[29] Nouwen writes, "If I were to let my life be taken over by what is urgent, I might very well never get around to what is essential."[30] Many are overrun by the urgent, yet the rewards may be modest, thus perpetuating the cycle.

A desire to help others is reflected by many respondents. One stated, "It is meaningful to me to work alongside people to help them explore their lives and life circumstances and how these things affect their wellbeing."[31] I believe that, for most, the need to feel needed is central. This may be among the most basic of human needs, and is at the very root of a caring environment. Nel Noddings writes, "[A]s I reflect on the way I am cared for, I see clearly my own longing to be received, understood, and accepted."[32] Whitehead and Whitehead add that this issue of needing to be needed is heightened in the middle years. These are often the most valuable years of one's career in terms of growth, progress, and self-actualization. They suggest:

> Psychologically the mid-years are marked by the dominance of three interwoven themes: personal power, care, and interiority . . . The middle-aged person wants to be, needs to be, effective in the tasks that define her or his work . . . The middle-aged person wants to be, needs to be, responsible for others . . . The outward movement of expanding responsibility in the mid-years

---

28. Verbatim respondent 1.

29. Gig Economy: A colloquial term that has become broadly used. People in the 'gig economy' are employed in multiple concurrent part-time jobs, or 'gigs.'

30. Nouwen, *Letters to Marc*, 3.

31. Verbatim respondent 12.

32. Noddings, *Caring*, 49.

is accompanied by a movement within. There is heightened sensitivity to the self and an increasing focus on inner needs.[33]

Thus, forced job change through layoffs in the mid years can be perceived as catastrophic.

Feelings of unfair or inappropriate treatment of self and others at work appear. A respondent stated, "Two males in same job before me [were] paid more!"[34] Such feelings are amplified by surprise and disappointment with failures of what should be automatic choices and decisions in a contemporary workplace. A perceived lack of justice in the workplace is articulated by several respondents. Gender income inequality, alternatively the sense of being passed over for opportunities that are viewed to be deserved, are described. There is disappointment over the perception that the needs of the organization take precedence over the needs of the worker, in some cases to the detriment of the worker. Once again, these experiences lead to dissonance. This dissonance presents as a lack of harmony and a lack of one's satisfaction in being fully aligned with organizational objectives.

A sense of calling or vocation, identified by a number as being divinely inspired, draws people to certain professions. A respondent stated, "I strive to be more like Jesus in the way I work and interact with my colleagues." [35] Economic needs lead some people to settle for less in terms of the achievement of meaningfulness.

Among the respondents, experiences of faith range from strong to non-existent. As will be seen, many assert a form of spirituality over traditional religious faith. People whose spirituality or faith is strong frequently struggle with their attempts to connect the tenets of their spirituality or faith with their decisions and choices. For the most part, respondents do not turn to their church, and sadly some even articulate observations of dissonance in their church environments.

There is anxiety over a lack of personal control and empowerment in many cases, both for self and for others in the workplace. Still, a number see their faith, or spirituality, as anchoring them, citing prayer as important in navigating through difficulties, especially in times of change. A respondent stated, "The industry changed and, in my view, became

---

33. Whitehead and Whitehead, *Christian Life Patterns*, 114.
34. Verbatim respondent 1.
35. Verbatim respondent 9.

less ethical."[36] Pattison presents that, "Change is extraordinarily painful; it often diminishes people's capacity to perform in an optimum way. It may bring increased illness within the workforce and affected communities and so contribute to making society less healthy."[37] By contrast, it is possible that when a core group values their work, others will begin to see work as having greater value. Engagement and commitment to community rises.

Changed Career Expectations

The Concept of a career-for-life appears lost for many. There appears to be a marked and profound change in the way people navigate careers. The one career for life expectation appears largely to be gone. Sometimes the result is a radical departure from what have been traditional career constructs, for example the rise of the 'gig economy,' where individuals see multiple, concurrent jobs as the norm. In other cases, it is a change in the ethos of a company or a particular industry that causes a person to move on. A search for greater purpose, sometimes resulting in the decision to become an entrepreneur, becomes the cause to move on. Wholesale organizational change leads to layoffs, sometimes for a small number of people, sometimes entire divisions.

Gender inequality encompasses not only compensation inequality, but also workplace practices and dynamics. To be perfectly frank, to continue allowing gender-based income inequality *delegitimizes* the role of women in the workplace. Norms that were tolerated, even accepted, in past eras, are no longer reasonable, but in many cases still knowingly practised. Behavioural characteristics that are commonly viewed as evidence of assertiveness are being viewed by women as archaic and deleterious. Compensation inequality appears across all sectors, including faith-based organizations. A respondent stated, "This is not how the body of Christ should behave. Males in same job before me [were] paid more!"[38] Being passed over for promotion opportunities is also a manifestation of inequality. The foregoing requires pause for emphasis. The complete and total recognition of agency and autonomy of all humans is foundational to the achievement of personhood. We might consider that

---

36. Verbatim respondent 3.
37. Pattison, *The Faith of Managers*, 127.
38. Verbatim respondent 1.

the emancipatory goals of postmodernism actually align completely with the Trinitarian activity found in the life of Jesus in his confrontation of systemic wrongs.

While faith in God is specifically referenced by many, a significant number make reference to a spirituality that is separate from any traditional faith orientations. A respondent stated, "I do not subscribe to an organized religion; however, I do hold to my own spiritual beliefs."[39] A number profess an atheist view. A respondent stated, "I am not a person of faith."[40] Another ignores the question. One person presents discomfort with the faith conversation, and another is wary of such conversations. Bell offers that, "Organizations . . . have an opportunity to help employees understand more about spirituality while building a work foundation that could potentially engage employees to search for new meaning in the workplace."[41] Hospitals have prayer facilities—they are not used solely by patients and families. Can we not expand their use?

Only one respondent specifically referred to a relationship with a mentor, stating, "I have sought out and found a mentor."[42] This apparent absence of mentorship may have the resulting development of attitudes of 'going it alone.' This may be the result of a decline in traditional middle management in organizational structure. It may also be the result of the rising gig economy and increased telecommuting. One respondent is critical of management engagement with particular issues, writing, "Many events have placed a sense of doubt in my job security. E.g., others not being supported; not being assigned to a position that I felt qualified to do; being assigned a role that suited the company, but which impeded my development. Being reprimanded for something I did not do."[43] An environment imbued with a culture of mentorship changes, positively, in many ways. An increased awareness of personhood pervades every action, every decision when mentorship and coaching are present.

Trust is sought but apparently hard to find. Several responses make it clear that people still care about one another, but are sometimes unsure of who to trust, or when to engage. A respondent stated, "My views, which stem from a deep-rooted belief in Christian life, are not popular

39. Verbatim respondent 5.
40. Verbatim respondent 19.
41. Bell, *Spirituality in the Workplace*, 3.
42. Verbatim respondent 6.
43. Verbatim respondent 22.

amongst peers. I feel quite powerless at times."[44] Another stated, "I have a quiet faith."[45] A number of responses suggest that these individuals are less than fully engaged emotionally in their work. A respondent stated, "I do not feel a high degree of meaningfulness—but to some degree, yes."[46] At the very least, this suggests that people approach deeper engagement with coworkers tentatively. At worst, people simply eschew engagement beyond the routine, practical requirements of the task at hand. In effect, full engagement is a function of deeper trust. A respondent stated, "I believe that we are all connected and that the energy we bring to our interactions affects the quality of connection, and other things, like loyalty, trust, etc."[47] Jack Barbalet asserts, "Trust is epistemic . . . trust entails a belief or feeling about the reliability of another, so that in depending on another through trust one expects not to be subject to incompetent support, or betrayal."[48] Indeed, there is a foundational element to trust. Barbalet underscores this, stating that "for a person to trust another person means the person they trust is reliable . . . trust, then, is by its nature, future oriented."[49] Kristine F. Hoover and Molly B. Pepper assert, "[C]ompanies not only need to manage levels of distrust, but actively work to achieve trust."[50] Creating an environment of trust, one might say, is a sacred obligation. Trust is paired with humility.

Where spirituality is expressed, there is evidence that views of work change. A few respondents expressed the belief that they were divinely designed, with a particular role in view. A respondent stated, "I believe that God has placed me where I am today."[51] Notwithstanding this, several circumstances were described as difficult to navigate or understand. A respondent stated, "There were times when the sense of being tested really could be borne through a sense of faith."[52] One response specifically articulated a view of the human condition of brokenness. Many express a sense of concern and disappointment, but accept situations as reality that

---

44. Verbatim respondent 6.
45. Verbatim respondent 21.
46. Verbatim respondent 32.
47. Verbatim respondent 4.
48. Barbalet, "The Experience of Trust," 15.
49. Barbalet, "The Experience of Trust," 14.
50. Hoover and Pepper, "How did They Say That?' 606.
51. Verbatim respondent 12.
52. Verbatim respondent 14.

must be managed or tolerated. The notion of faith in action is present, but only a few describe specific ways that they act on this imperative. Prayer for personal discernment and for others is noted.

Those affirming faith also affirm a sense of divine calling. Among those who do not affirm a personal faith within a religious paradigm, several nonetheless perceived a higher power—an energy that holds humanity together calling up motives of loyalty and mutual assistance, and of goodness. A respondent stated, "I believe that there is something higher, but not through the lens of religious faith."[53] In some cases, the faith call leaves unanswered questions as to right behaviour. A respondent stated, "I'm challenged. Do I take my son to church? Do we volunteer? Rather than church, I would rather be out there helping people."[54]

Regardless of faith or spiritual affirmation, respondents express a desire for belonging-ness, despite cynicism in some cases of the notion that good deeds would be reciprocated. A respondent stated, "I find myself more able to see the human side of issues. That does not always help."[55] Combined with this is the view that most are struggling, one way or another, to make the most of it at work. There is largely a sense that concerns and disappointments are facts of working life and are to be expected and coped with. A respondent stated, "I do not expect others to help me, but I do expect me to help others."[56] This appears to be an effort to compartmentalize or suppress one's own struggle, while still holding onto a sense of obligation to others.

Some are skeptical, even critical, of what they believe that religion has to offer, while others are cognizant of the role of Jesus as a model for them and felt divine direction in their lives and work. Thus, hope is stronger than lived experiences in many cases. A respondent stated, "I do have faith, but only [in the sense] that I believe there is something out there that we are all striving towards."[57]

Some have learned to bring faith into their workplace interactions, generally more by letting their faith show through in the way they treat others, rather than in explicit expression of faith precepts. A respondent

---

53. Verbatim respondent 4.
54. Verbatim respondent 29.
55. Verbatim respondent 18.
56. Verbatim respondent 16.
57. Verbatim respondent 16. A colleague spoke of hope as 'expectancy' rather than expectation. This wonderful statement suggests that hopefulness is an open-ended expectancy of a good future, where expectations may be more limited in nature.

stated, "My faith affects how I treat others. It deepens my perseverance to do the best I can do to glorify Him."[58] Others explicitly confirm strong avoidance of conversations regarding faith. Some foster an environment where views are welcome, as long as proselytizing does not occur. One respondent made the desire to discuss faith a condition of employment.

The question regarding discussion of work-related issues with a minister or spiritual counsellor drew responses that were largely in the negative or at best were tentative. Almost no one reported having work-related conversations with a minister or counsellor. Where positive responses were reported, feelings of empathy—a capacity for caring, being offered were reported. A respondent stated that a conversation with a counsellor "affirmed that things have a way of working out."[59] Offers of people being sounding boards were identified. A respondent stated, "I seek first if there is room for the conversation."[60] Where conversations with a counsellor were reported, they appear largely to have been episodic and incomplete.

As stated, many respondents spoke of peers as unique, equal, and connected. They also spoke of peers as extraordinary, unparalleled, or rare. People of confessed faith appear particularly to see their fellow human beings in this way. Seeing each other as uniquely designed by God brings a sense of experiencing interaction with others as a gift. One writes, "I am privileged to pave roads forward for others."[61] The notion of connectedness is asserted in many ways by people who identify as being of faith, or as being spiritual.

Respondents who are spiritual or affirm that they are people of faith frequently used such terms as steady, or humble. Respondents also use the words salvation, grace, and strength, to describe a divine source of strength in coping with their work. Grace in this context suggests receiving help or guidance from God—we are able to share that help (grace) with others. This echoes a number of respondents who assert that it is their overt action that counts in their efforts to bring grace into the workplace.

For emphasis, dissatisfaction with elements of work was a theme common to people of faith as well as those not of faith. A sense of calling was described by both groups also. Frequently, respondents knew, for

---

58. Verbatim respondent 32.
59. Verbatim respondent 13.
60. Verbatim respondent 6.
61. Verbatim respondent 1.

example, when they were not strongly called to the work they were doing. For respondents who do not describe themselves as people of faith, the word 'calling' appears to be used in the sense of an intellectual impulsion rather than a divine summons. The recognition of work trade-offs, for example longer hours or an unpleasant work environment in return for much-needed compensation, was clear. Conversely, respondents describe enjoying particular work for flexibility, freedom of choice, while acknowledging that they wished they could achieve a greater degree of financial reward.

It is clear that a sense of ethical behaviour and treatment of others is as critical among those who profess no faith as it is among those that do profess faith. An innate sense of justice is pervasive.

Among all the respondents, for the most part there is relatively little expression of how to change or improve their environments (although to be clear they were not asked to offer such perspectives). Fatigue and powerlessness were frequently linked to expressions of dissonance. Also evident was the sense of resignation that finding greater purpose required economic compromise. While some express expediency as a factor in their workplace endeavours and choices, ethical behaviour and correctness of behaviour are very much paramount. It is possible, even likely, that workplace demands create complexity in ways that are leading to greater dissonance.[62] Graham Stanton observes, "[C]omplexity renders the future fundamentally uncertain, and therefore unpredictable and uncontrollable."[63] Thus, environments which appear disorganized, or where clarity is lacking in terms of addressing rapidly unfolding situations create apprehension.

The issue of discussing faith at work drew varied responses, but broadly it drew caution. There is also the suggestion that when faith is brought up, the discussion is perceived as dogmatic and closed, rather than being presented as a means of open dialogue and discovery. Some say that they have learned to bring it up over time. Several make the point that they would rather let their actions express their beliefs. Two say that they actively seek to spread the gospel. Another says they do not want to be converted. There is also a view expressed by the respondents that peers are still searching for deeper purpose. The workplace has, generally,

---

62. Volatility, uncertainty, complexity and ambiguity are phenomena described by the U.S. Army War College in 1987. The acronym VUCA is frequently used in leadership journals.

63. Stanton, "A Theology of Complexity," 148.

become an environment where discussion of faith is avoided or considered unwelcome. It may be that spirituality, without reference to a specific faith orientation, may be broached, but generally *no* discussion is the standard. These responses lead to the assumption that most avoid the conversation, perhaps out of a desire to be polite, or of a sense of awkwardness, or a fear of conflict. The workplace, then, appears not to be viewed as a place for a discussion of faith. Nonetheless, most had a sense that their faith or spiritual orientation had bearing on their work, in the sense that they feel led to their work through their faith, or that the way in which they discharge their work duties and treat co-workers are guided by their faith.

Expressed in various ways there is a common voice from all these respondents. This voice asserts that work is vital. All respondents did—or if retired, have done—work that expresses their personhood, not only in the sense that it brings a degree of economic security but also as a means of putting intellect and learned skills to productive purpose. Virtually all respondents expressed a need for a work environment that provides a means of achieving some level of self-actualization and identity. A respondent stated, "I believe that my work's meaning is driven by my desire to contribute to others' growth and development. I am also deriving meaningfulness from volunteering."[64] Prayer regarding work and coworkers is referenced quite broadly. When personhood is not manifest in work, the worker moves on, or is left experiencing dissonance and withdrawal.

I want to draw particular emphasis to the issue of dissonance. Dissonance at work appears to be a very strong theme among the majority of respondents. Only six of thirty-two respondents describe working lives without referring to some form of dissonance. One respondent describes an early career that held considerable dissonance; however, this respondent's later career was enjoyable and without dissonance. The remaining respondents describe a workplace that held dissonance—a lack of harmony—that ranges from mild to severe as discussed below. Mild dissonance implies the presence of such emotions and realities as "feeling powerless,"[65] and dealing with others who do not share a focus on "good or skilled workmanship [sic]"[66] Several offered that they felt that co-workers did not share the same values or passion. Moderate

---

64. Verbatim respondent 5.
65. Verbatim respondent 6.
66. Verbatim respondent 16.

dissonance suggests a more troubling circumstance where co-workers do not "know how to get a deep sense of purpose."[67] Many in this category spoke to the view that they are not doing the work that they feel is their calling, or describe a financial cost to them to pursue their work. One specifically affirms "[My work is lacking] in terms of fully satisfying a sense of calling."[68] Several affirmed a lack of job-security and unreasonable compensation. Severe dissonance implies abuse. In two cases, the respondents perceived abuse from the perspective of gender income inequality, combined with a lack of recognition for their work. Several stated that they had no sense of fulfillment or vocation. Others perceived an increasingly unethical work environment. Several reported stress as a result of a lack of justice, combined with highly politically charged environments. One described the workplace as highly internally competitive; that everyone was out for personal gain, driven only by money.

For emphasis, some four fifths of the respondents expressed, through their comments, a view of work circumstances that range from moderately dissonant to severely dissonant. This is from an overall sample of individuals, supervisory and non-supervisory, that are in full time positions or have retired from full time positions. These phenomena suggest that the workplace is largely a place of dissonance in some degree, ranging from mild to severe.

The phenomenological observations that follow draw from particular anecdotes that bring deep insight into the lived experiences of the respondents. These offer a compelling understanding which will undergird both the grounded theory derived from this research and ultimately the leadership commentaries and recommendations that are offered later.

Several respondents appear to see beyond the challenges of their tasks. They describe God's very real presence in their lives. The word, 'justice' was used to imply a vision of appropriate organizational values and leadership behaviours. Concern for others is mentioned suggesting a desire for mutual self-fulfillment. This was manifest in the belief that peers want a deep sense of meaningfulness, but may not know "how to get it."[69]

The idea of meaningfulness—of having significance or purpose—was a view expressed by many respondents. Some said that meaningfulness went hand-in-hand with calling. One respondent described how

67. Verbatim respondent 2.
68. Verbatim respondent 17.
69. Verbatim respondent 2.

deeper meaningfulness has been perceived as they aged. A number of respondents describe inconsistency between the values they hold and the circumstances in which they work. This might be assumed to be a desire for an environment of rectitude, fairness, and soundness. A respondent described experiencing a stressful environment. Another respondent made the observation that they pay an economic price to achieve meaningfulness. While some stated they had achieved a sense of meaningfulness, in many cases, for these same individuals, it was accompanied by dissonance. The notion emerges that many have learned to compartmentalize their feelings of dissonance. These individuals chose to focus on those elements of the work that gave them meaning. For some, however, a state of meaningfulness was a yet unachieved aspiration. It was clear that several respondents have reached a place where they are content, at least to a degree, despite elements of their work that create dissonance.

For several, times of dissonance also brought forward a sense of spiritual presence and guidance. A respondent stated, "My faith keeps me steady when I don't see where next month's income will come from. My faith keeps me humble to know that I have something to learn from every client."[70] This notion of God leading them through specific challenges, and sometimes more broad conundrums, was evident. Prayer was mentioned both for personal guidance and on behalf of others.

Frequently appearing were the words, calling, and 'vocation' which seemed to have the same, or very similar, meaning. From the Latin *vocare,* to call, we get the term 'vocation'—interpreted as summons, or impulsion. In other words, an external demand is placed on us to commit ourselves and our labour to a specific occupation. The word *calling* also adds the dimension of inner urging. This sentiment was expressed by many respondents. What was also present was the suggestion that to respond to their calling brought both challenges and growth. In some cases, this resulted in a change to a different work environment—a completely new occupation. Such a change was required in order to find both peace and the opportunity to flourish.

A respondent discovered that a new business venture was the correct response to dissatisfaction with their present career. While in some cases the realization of a specific calling occurs prior to the change, for others there is a move to a new environment altogether, followed by a growing realization that the new environment brings a strong sense of

---

70. Verbatim respondent 6.

vocation. Several also commented that even though they shared the same work with others, their colleagues' sense of vocation did not necessarily seem pervasive. The terms, "ethics," and "purpose," were used quite frequently. These terms suggest standards of conduct, i.e., moral judgment and purpose—intention and determination behind an action or statement. When individuals use these terms in the context of describing their sense of calling and vocation, they describe the boundaries of behaviour and treatment that either keep a person within a realm of contentment with their circumstances, or they describe the type of situation that pushes them outside those boundaries, and therefore leads to dissonance and discontent.

Arriving at a Grounded Theory

The resulting output of analysis of the qualitative data derived from the research questionnaire supporting this work is a conceptualization of the lived experiences of the respondents. This conceptualization forms the emergent grounded theory upon which the perspectives and arguments presented are constructed. In particular, this emergent grounded theory crystallizes and reinforces the practices that will be argued as essential for transformational leadership. Elements of this emergent grounded theory will be prefaced by the term 'the findings of my survey indicate.'

Virtually every respondent articulated a desire for purpose and meaningfulness in their work, however this desire, for a significant number of respondents, is weakened, or rendered ineffective by a degree of dissonance in their experiences at work. For some this is a lack of harmony between their desire for meaningfulness and their comfort in expressing their complete personhood in their work. For others there is evidence of significant inconsistency between their values and their actual lived experiences in the workplace. For still others there is a cultural dissonance—the result of an inconsistency—wrought by a feeling of changing ethics in their chosen fields of endeavour.

Among respondents of professed faith or spirituality, there is a sense that their spirituality grounds them and strengthens them in uncertain situations, for example in navigating careers. Prayer is a frequently mentioned practice. A sense of hope is strong. Some express their work as an opportunity to be models of their faith.

Frequently there is a sense of resignation among respondents that finding greater purpose and meaningfulness requires economic compromise. Unfairness, inequity, and injustice, is experienced or observed in enough cases for it to be a significant issue. Stated examples are gender inequality, and being passed over for opportunities considered to be earned. This sense of resignation, which, it occurs to me, may be made worse by a loss of mentorship, frequently leads to eschewing achievement of purpose for an assurance of economic stability.

Although many stated that they act out their faith at work, people of professed faith or spirituality tended to avoid expressing their beliefs at work out of concern of feeling awkward, or finding themselves in conflict with others. People care about co-workers. Hope is manifest in many responses.

The majority of respondents have not had a conversation with a minister, pastor or counsellor regarding workplace challenges, though it is evident that there is a search for spiritual meaning. Several nuances in the responses suggest that there would be no perceived value in such a conversation. A respondent stated, "No. I don't want to be disrespectful."[71]

This research suggests that the specific elements and dynamics of the workplace experiences described can only be the direct result of leadership decisions and choices. Leaders hold charge of ethos, organization, and progress within the workplace. If there is dissonance, disappointment, injustice, and all the dynamics which lead to, or detract from, a depth of personal meaning, calling, and one's sense of flourishing at work, all of these phenomena, for better or worse, are in the hands of leadership.

Conclusion

Respondents in supervisory roles and respondents in non-supervisory roles offered similar comments in terms of the benefits of work and a sense of purpose. A number of individuals in both groups reported praying, and the view that God is involved in their lives. Those in non-supervisory roles had more to say in general, especially regarding stressors in the workplace. A retired respondent also lamented a loss of ethics in the workplace. Those who are self-employed expressed joy in helping others, and a strong sense of affiliation at work. The question regarding speaking

---

71. Verbatim respondent 26.

about faith in the workplace drew equally negative responses among supervisory and non-supervisory respondents.

What is clear is that there is a moderate-to-strong sense of dissonance at work. This lack of harmony between one's sense of purpose and the realities of workplace interaction can, and must be addressed by leadership. The research responses imply, collectively, that it is the ethos of leadership that is to be addressed in order to create a workplace that promotes flourishing. People want to have an impression that work is fair, ethical and meaningful in the fullest sense of a person's expectations. Further, those who express faith and those who do not, express a degree of passive acceptance, or acquiescence, about the apparent norms that they are required to conform to in order to make a living. Despite this, hope is expressed, particular by those who express spirituality or faith. A sense of caring about one's co-worker is strong.

It is possible that for many in society, the ability to reach a sense of flourishing may be at risk of disappearing altogether. Anne Snyder points out:

> Seven million prime-working-age American men [sic] sit at home, idle and unemployed. Neighbourliness is an increasingly rare experience, with only 31 percent of Americans socializing weekly with someone next door (down from 44% in 1974). More people live alone, eat alone, and displace real-time conversation with controlled (if frenetic) screen time than ever before. Moral depth and literacy have declined, while a 2017 Gallup poll found that Americans' views of the state of our moral values as a society are themselves at a nadir . . . The young express a crisis of purpose and moral direction.[72]

A significant number attest directly to what may be perceived as divine-human cooperation, even though they recognize that it is frequently fractured by their work environment. Others seek meaningfulness that is beyond economic security—for example, the simple satisfaction in a job well-done and to be recognized for good work by others.

It is likely that, post COVID 19, there will be an increasing number of people taking employment, out of necessity, that does not meet their sense of vocation.

---

72. Snyder, "Why Character," 44–45. This before the Covid 19 pandemic.

3

The Roots of the Contemporary Workplace

Also, a dispute arose among them as to which of them was considered to be greatest. Jesus said to them, "The kings of the Gentiles lord it over them; and those who exercise authority over them call themselves Benefactors. But you are not to be like that. Instead, the greatest among you should be like the youngest, and the one who rules like the one who serves. For who is greater, the one who is at the table or the one who serves? Is it not the one who is at the table? But I am among you as one who serves.

(LUKE 22:24 NIV)

ORGANIZATIONS ARE CONCEIVED, CREATED, structured, and shaped to achieve the goals and imperatives of the founders and stakeholders. Boards of Directors set the standards of governance and culture of service. Boards are accountable to the owners, or sponsors, of an enterprise for the ethical and efficient governance of the enterprise on behalf of all stakeholders. Once chosen, organizational structure in turn, effectively is the genesis of job descriptions, professional requirements, compensation structures, and career progress standards. Organizational structure dictates the nature, shape, and objectives of management hierarchy. Concepts of ethical norms pervade all organizations, as communicated and modelled by leadership.

With respect to for-profit enterprises, capital formation and the choice of funding models have a critical impact on the foregoing. In such organizations, stakeholder and shareholder expectations and demands create overarching expectations, with resulting, sometimes dramatic, impact on leadership imperatives. The emphasis of those expectations is communicated, generally, through compensation plans.

Enterprise clusters create social and community structure. In Ottawa, Canada and Washington D.C., for example, government and public service organizations are pervasive, leading to specific community and transportation hub creation. Organizational structures, while specific to the particular agency, have a significant number of commonalities across government and public service organizations in terms of compensation and benefits structures, career progress expectations, and so on. Communities reflect this.

Organizational structures are evolving, in some areas dramatically (supply chain constructs, for example) even while many enterprises employ as many as four generations. With these foundational imperatives and enterprise influences in view, I turn to a number of workplace dynamics as they influence human flourishing at work.

Guided by an established ethos, organizational structure, the establishment of hierarchy and the exercise of power all come together to create the organization's culture and, for better or worse, the achievement of human flourishing within the organization. Research respondent narratives expose many of the outcomes of the ways in which leadership power is exercised.

As will be discussed further, work-related dissonance—a lack of harmony between personal values and work imperatives—from moderate to severe, appears to be a significant inhibitor to human flourishing. This is manifest in a degradation of meaningfulness at work, frequently resulting in lost productivity, absenteeism and high employee turnover, in addition to lost business.

People care about their work and they care about their co-workers. However, they are concerned about a number of perceived challenges and inequities. Mentorship has declined, if not disappeared. Traditions are under duress. Career expectations have changed. Some experience isolation and loneliness.[1]

---

1. We can assume that under COVID 19 this worsened.

Models of leadership have evolved as organization structures and communication methods have changed. Some organizations have traditional, hierarchical structures while others are nodal in nature. In a broad number of structures, middle management ranks have declined or disappeared.

Following an analysis of the contemporary workplace, this chapter offers a view of leadership as theology in practice. Spirit-led leaders are conceptualized as shepherds, purveyors of hope and forgiveness as they innovate and adapt to changing workplace structures. Discussed also is the apparent rise in a post-religious spirituality.

Recalling my own history, in the 1960s "the job of sales clerk was considered a position to aspire to, requiring good arithmetic ability and communication skills. Indeed, more specialized work, for example the job of bank teller seemed unreachable to many."[2] Many sought such opportunities because they offered a reasonable and secure salary, frequently with appropriate benefits, plus good standing in the community. They could well become careers for life. Many of the financial institutions, as well as other employers, invested in considerable training programs for their employees—both for current and prospective roles. Much has changed indeed; many organizations seek 'just-in-time' expertise in the same way that they source 'just-in-time' materials.[3] Today, many commute long distances to their workplace, fracturing their sense of community. Long term career certainty is reduced, if it has not vanished for some. Somewhere along the way we stopped speaking about our faith at work as well. Jonathan Merritt confirms, "An overwhelming majority of people say that they don't feel comfortable speaking about faith, most of the time."[4] A respondent notes, "Faith is rarely discussed in a workplace—as such this is awkward and I rarely, if ever, begin it."[5] In 2005, Helen Cameron et al suggested that, "There appears to be little scholarly dialogue between the fields of management studies and theological studies."[6] This does appear to be changing. As suggested earlier, many

---

2. Bates, *Sales Force Management*, 79.

3. Just-in-Time (JIT) inventory management aligns the supply of raw materials with production cycles in a manufacturing situation, thus reducing inventory costs and improving efficiency.

4. Merritt, "It's Getting Harder," [n.d.].

5. Verbatim respondent 18.

6. Cameron et al., *Studying Local Churches*, 68.

leading business schools, including, for example, Harvard, are exploring the question of whether there is a place for spirituality in the workplace.

Foundational to organizational formation and the imperatives of management is the economic concept of scarcity. Economic imperatives drive the science of the conception of goods and services, together with the manufacture, distribution and ultimate consumption of those goods and services. Nobel Prize winner in Economics Milton Friedman presents a strong opinion on "the role of competitive capitalism—the organization of the bulk of economic activity through private enterprise operating in a free market—as a system of economic freedom and relying primarily on the market to organize economic activity."[7] Specifically, management must choose among a restricted set of potential alternatives in setting a path forward for the enterprise. James Gwartney and Richard Stroup suggest, "Since scarcity prevents us from having as much as we would of economic goods . . . we are forced to choose among a restricted set of potential alternatives."[8] This is a critical matter in the decision to add or remove resources to an enterprise. Most organizations grow (or decline) in a linear fashion. However, the decision to add or remove resources, particularly large capital resources as well as human resources, is one that might be described as a *step function*. The timing of such decisions can have major implications on cash flow, for example. Indeed, a series of timing missteps of investments can be financially jarring. At worst, missteps may result in insolvency.

The choice of incentives is a critical executive leadership decision. How should employees be paid, both in sum and in structure? This is tied to what economists describe as monitoring, which is focussed to an extent, on the concern that unmonitored employees will shirk. Gwartney and Stroup describe shirking as, "Working at a less than normal rate of productivity thus reducing output."[9] This contemplates the notion that, left to their own devices and without the right resources and incentives, workers slack off. A key economic concept, which leads to organization theory, is the study of productivity and choice of specialized skills. Again, this a cost/output dilemma that leadership must resolve.

---

7. Friedman, *Capitalism*, 4.
8. Gwartney and Stroup, *Economics*. 5.
9. Gwartney and Stroup, *Economics*. 499.

Organizational Theory

Fundamentally, organization theory focuses on acquiring and structuring the physical, technical, and workforce attributes necessary for success. Nancy Langton et al. assert that:

> There are six elements that managers need to address when they design their organization's structure: work specialization, departmentalization, chain of command, span of control, centralization and decentralization and formalization [of the decision-making process].[10]

To these we add the specific requirement of sustaining a work environment that promotes the physical and mental health of employees.

Critically it is the community of effort, and that community's engagement with the world, that must be created and nurtured in order to achieve and sustain the goals of the enterprise. Hatch and Cunliffe present critically important social and organizational changes in perspectives that distinguish the postmodern era from the modern era. Their work begins with a summary of the "key philosophical differences constituting the modern, symbolic and postmodern perspectives and their implications for organizational theory."[11] Of particular interest are perspectives on the structural choices for organizations, as well as the issue of internal competition. Both of these elements of the postmodern organization have bearing and will be discussed.

The ages of the respondents to my research survey supporting this book range from mid-twenties to mid-seventies. Thus, the contrasting perspectives offered by Hatch and Cunliffe are important. They write:

> Because humans belong to many different communities of practice, each having their own ways of talking that produce a context for local meaning making and identity construction, an organization's social structure can embrace multiple communities of practice, each emerging spontaneously in response to particular interests, needs, desires, or problems. Communities of practice can cross boundaries drawn between business units and project teams, hierarchies, or any other dimension of social structure.[12]

---

10. Langton et al., *Organizational Behaviour*, 502.
11. Hatch and Cunliffe, *Organization Theory*, 14.
12. Hatch and Cunliffe, *Organization Theory*, 14.

When we are reminded that as many as four generations of workers occupy the same workplace, these observations gain considerable heft. Organization structure dictates the enterprise's approach to the way human talent is identified, chosen, located, organized, trained, and remunerated. Organizations are *enabled* by the structure and resulting effect of management.

Management Theory

Understood at its most fundamental level, management is involved with the structuring of work—to conceive of, develop and direct the appropriate apparatus and expertise for the task at hand, in the most cost-effective manner possible. Peter Drucker writes:

> Within the life-span of today's old-timers, our society has become a 'knowledge society,' a 'society of organizations,' and a 'networked society.' In the twentieth century, the major social tasks came to be performed in and through organized institutions—business enterprises, large and small; school systems; colleges and universities; hospitals; research laboratories; governments and government agencies of all kinds and sizes; and many others. And each of them in turn is entrusted to 'managers' who practise 'management.'[13]

Knowledge, organization, and networking could well describe the critical intellectual factors for virtually every enterprise. It is the theory, structure, and processes of management frameworks that create the environments for, as well as the demands that are placed upon, leadership. I suggest that the ultimate critical success factor may be teleological in nature. Hoover and Pepper offer that, "Many American managers have used utilitarianism, [a form of teleological ethics] as a framework for decision-making."[14] In simple terms, we might consider the questions where are we going? What route will we take? and how will we know we have arrived? The answers to these questions knit together knowledge, organization, and networking in a way that leads to the deeper question: 'Are we flourishing?' Thus, and I suggest unavoidably, there becomes a spiritual dimension to this deliberation.

---

13. Drucker, *Management*, 1.
14. Hoover and Pepper, "How Did They Say That?" 608.

Michael Keren offers some valuable thoughts regarding Moses, whom he describes as, "the 'ideal' type of visionary realist."[15] Keren writes, "The visionary realist recognizes ethical limits and does not forget that when these are overlooked, the original goals cannot be fulfilled."[16] Keren also ascribes two qualities, displayed by Moses, that are crucial to the visionary realist. He presents, "The first is a sense of determination that leads him to continue the task even if the people do not appear to match expectations. The other is simple human compassion for the sufferings of those led towards the grand visionary goals."[17] Here we have a portrayal of a humble person, called, inspired and equipped by God to bring his people out of slavery and into flourishing nationhood. Moses is given a task that is extraordinary, one that any one of us might understandably shy away from. Moses has to keep his nation moving forward toward their goal.

Mintzberg writes, "Study after study has shown that [a] managers work at an unrelenting pace; [b] their activities are typically characterized by brevity, variety, fragmentation and discontinuity; and [c] they are strongly oriented to action."[18] No wonder, then, leaders, especially front-line leaders, risk getting caught up in the minutiae. Time for reflection is clearly at a premium, particularly when leaders are focussed on, often largely remunerated by, achieving relatively short-term shareholder expectations. Indeed, of critical importance for the management hierarchy is the adherence to and achievement of the set of quarterly and annual performance metrics deemed essential for the enterprise.

The tangible goal of workplace efficiency is measurable output, whether it be social or economic. Ever since the Dutch East India Company allowed the public to invest in its business in 1602, for those enterprises focussed on economic returns, the tangible measure is profit. Getting the best possible return for stockholders may, however, require a deeper understanding of, and possible investment in, the development of greater purpose among employees. This may include working with those employees on community initiatives not necessarily tied directly to the organization's core products and services. Such initiatives tend to appeal to a worker's spiritual orientation. This coincides with the findings of

---

15. Keren, "Moses as a Visionary Realist," 71.
16. Keren, "Moses as a Visionary Realist," 71.
17. Keren, "Moses as a Visionary Realist," 77.
18. Mintzberg, *Managing*, 19.

my survey which indicate that for most there is an expression of faith or spirituality. However, explicit expression of faith appears broadly, by the research respondents, to be perceived as unwelcome in the workplace. Efforts to find resolution to this dilemma may yield an increase in employees' sense of flourishing.

Tyler J. VanderWeele writes:

> Flourishing itself might be understood as a state in which all aspects of a person's life are good . . . most would concur that flourishing, however conceived, would, at the very least, require doing or being well in the following five broad domains of human life: (i) happiness and life satisfaction; (ii) health, both mental and physical; (iii) meaning and purpose; (iv) character and virtue; (v) close social relationships.[19]

If human flourishing in the workplace dimension of one's life is achievable, arguably increased productivity is the outcome. Increased productivity inevitably leads to increased customer satisfaction, and business profitability. Drucker adds:

> To know what a business is, we have to start with its *purpose*. Its purpose must lie outside of the business itself. In fact, it must lie in society, since business enterprise is an organ of society. There is only one valid definition of business purpose: *to create a customer*.[20]

To have a customer is relational—it creates a community. Creating a customer requires engagement. Certainly, there is economic reward in building a strong customer base, but is passionate action that initiates the entire process across an enterprise. Simon Sinek crystallizes the point, "Great leaders . . . are able to inspire people to act. Those who are able to inspire give people a sense of purpose or belonging that has little to do with any external incentive or benefit to be gained."[21] Such people find their reward *within* themselves, finding joy in their acts of service. Such leaders and their organizations create a lasting customer relationship.

Creating a customer requires a relationship of trust. Trust is essential to community. Critically important to Drucker's statement is its corollary: individual purpose. Organizational purpose is manifest when the purposes of the individuals *within* the organization become manifest. It is safe

---

19. VanderWeele, "On the Promotion of Human Flourishing," 8149.
20. Drucker, *Management*, 97–98 [emphasis original].
21. Sinek, *Start With Why*, 6.

to assume that when purposeful work is absent, employee turnover rises, resulting in impaired, even neglected relationships with customers; thus, reducing customer loyalty.[22] A respondent stated, "In terms of my spiritual beliefs, I believe that we are all connected and that the energy we bring to our interactions affects the quality of connection, and other things like loyalty, trust, etc."[23] Trust is personal. By contrast, my grounded theory suggests that it is evident that several respondents resign themselves to the perspective that finding greater purpose requires personal economic compromise. Dissonance is the result. Drucker points out:

> We do not learn anything about the work of a heart specialist by being told that he [sic] is trying to make a livelihood, or even that he [sic] is trying to benefit humanity. The profit motive and its offspring maximization of profits are just as irrelevant to the function of a business, the purpose of a business, and the job of managing a business . . . The first function of a business is marketing. The second function is innovation.[24]

When someone perceives that they are contributing to an innovative enterprise—that their contribution is part of that innovation, it is enlivening. By contrast, where there is dissonance, innovative spirit is dampened, even quashed. A respondent stated, "I changed careers 16 years ago to start a business. It has become my calling. It can be scary and overwhelming at times. All my efforts and funds go into the business. My workers and family are my peers."[25] Another respondent stated, "The industry changed and, in my view, became less ethical. I joined a small firm owned by a gay Christian man, who is on the same page as me in terms of ethics and purpose."[26] Thus, short-term return of profit to a shareholder may have far broader ethical implications than the mortgaging of next quarter's returns. Regulatory hearings are littered with proceedings emanating from decisions that are rooted in short-term expediency.

---

22. In recent experience, I have noted that some companies seem to focus their sales efforts on customer acquisition, to the exclusion of customer retention. I do not know if this is related to the circumstances described above. In any event, this must have a significant effect on specific investment decisions, together with profitability in the long term.

23. Verbatim respondent 4.

24. Drucker, *Management*, 97.

25. Verbatim respondent 8.

26. Verbatim respondent 3.

Organization culture can be impacted, even dominated by the business funding model. A significant development in the formation of capital markets in recent decades is the rise of venture capital. These are pools of money raised with the purpose of higher risk investments in start-up or early-stage enterprises that may be unable to raise capital through borrowing or through issuing shares directly in the stock markets. H. Ooghe et al. write:

> Companies with high-risk projects cannot raise finance from conventional funding sources . . . The venture capitalist provides mostly equity capital . . . Another aspect of importance for the venture capitalist are the exit mechanisms as he [sic] wants to sell his [sic] participation after five or ten years with the hope to realize capital gains.[27]

When start-up businesses are funded by venture capitalists, generally the venture capital provider is not a passive lender. Substantial investors demand positions on the board of the investee company. They frequently impose their own values, performance benchmarks and timelines on the investee organization. They become involved in the governance and strategic imperatives of the enterprise. Sometimes this is valuable, and sometimes it is stressful. Selznick writes, "Perhaps the most obvious indicator of organizational character as a palpable reality is the abandonment of old organizations and the creation of new ones when changes in general orientation seem required."[28] Venture capital objectives can, and often do, crowd out all aspirations of the business, save for those of the venture capitalist. Employees of these enterprises may feel adrift in terms of understanding the values and ethos of their employer.

The findings of my research suggest that, rather than proselyting, acting our faith—being guided by faith, may be the most important way to bring faith into the workplace. This finding coincides with research by James Butler, who describes acts of "non-heroic faith."[29] Butler continues, "For many of the participants in both congregations [which participated in his research] faith was primarily practical and participative."[30]

Considering the biblical call to hospitality, it seems certain that the workplace can be enhanced by an active effort to increase diversity in

---

27. Ooghe et al., "Venture Capital," 29–30.
28. Selznick, *Leadership in Administration*, 41.
29. Butler, "The 'Long and winding road' of Faith," 277.
30. Butler, "The 'Long and winding road' of Faith," 281.

the workforce. A pronounced example may be implied by the situation described by Israel Drori et al. who write:

> Transnational entrepreneurs are individuals who migrate from one country to another, concurrently maintaining business-related linkages with their countries of origin and with their adopted countries and communities. By travelling both physically and virtually, transnational entrepreneurs engage simultaneously in two of more socially embedded environments.[31]

Thus, these transnational entrepreneurs gain insights that others may not be aware of. As a result, they adapt and respond easily to multiculturalism. We can learn from this unique adaptive capability.

This observation leads me to think of the notion of positive deviants. Sara Parkin describes a positive deviant as a "person who does the right thing despite being surrounded by the wrong institutional structures, the wrong processes and stubbornly uncooperative people."[32] This situation seems to be echoed by a respondent who stated "Even though I worked under great distress and pressure I felt this was my calling."[33] Parkin uses the term 'positive deviant' specifically in connection with those who champion issues of sustainability. However, others use this term in consulting situations where significant change is being sought in organizations where the right person to bring about change may not be part of the management structure of the organization.[34] Positive deviants frequently find themselves in conflict with prevailing ethical values in an organization. Positive deviants, when supported and encouraged, can influence the ethical values of an organization in a positive way. Arguably, it is particularly the forgiving nature of Spirit-led leadership that brings forward the deeply adaptive capacity needed to seek out and engage with positive deviants in the organization. Writing in the time of COVID 19, Ed O'Malley offers this:

> At the very time when we need a spirit of experimentation to learn our way forward, the pressure on those in authority to

---

31. Drori et al., "Researching Transnational Entrepreneurship," 3.
32. Parkin, *The Positive Deviant*, 1.
33. Verbatim respondent 21.

34. During a consulting assignment in Latin America, I learned that finding and engaging a positive deviant would prove to be a critical element of change leadership. This discovery may have accelerated the adoption of new approaches by months, if not years.

solve problems if off the charts. Certainty isn't always helpful, and if we're honest, in 'normal' times it's always more of a chosen perception that a reality. Leadership in this unmasked era needs to be experimental. That means trying things, failing, learning, trying something else, bringing in unlikely suspects to shine light on surprise pathways.[35]

Adaptive capacity has resilience at its core. Punit Renjen underscores this, writing, "In times of crisis, it is essential to recognize the impact that uncertainty is having on people."[36] I add that forgiveness and resilience are paired qualities. The story of Jesus' encounter with the woman at the well (cf. John 4: 4–26), and its aftermath, may be considered through this lens. It occurs to me also that the Book of Acts gives us, in a sense, the perspective of an adaptive 'organization' emerging from a fledgling group of believers from different circumstances; coalescing around a central, powerful calling.

Effective leaders imbue an organization with a culture of responsibility. Robert Gibbs lays a foundation for the praxis of leadership that this book seeks to explore. Gibbs offers a series of questions, the responses to which press us to consider all human responses to critical issues. He puts forward:

> An ethics of responsibility, arises out of the need to think: to give an account to others of why we should respond for other people. Having found itself in question, philosophy requires an ethical justification through an ethics—an extreme ethics for thinking that has so much to answer for today . . . This [work] offers an ethics whose center is responsibility and not principles of autonomy or rational deliberation or optimal benefits. I distinguish here between the ethical exigency of bearing a *responsibility* and the corresponding *responsive* performance in the following manner: I can be responsible for doing something, even when I fail to act responsibly. Responsiveness is thus the fulfillment of a responsibility, but my bearing of that responsibility is independent of whether I act ethically or not.[37]

Among many human dilemmas, Gibbs discusses Jesus' instruction in the Sermon on the Mount that no one can serve two masters (cf. Matt 6:25ff). From the perspective of vocation this presents a dilemma that can only be

---

35. O'Malley, "Leadership in Uncertain Times," 68.
36. Renjen, "A Guide to Resilient Leadership," 43.
37. Gibbs, *Why Ethics*, 3 [emphasis original].

resolved, I would argue, when we recognize work as a contribution to the Kingdom—that work is eschatological. Ethics, and perceptions of ethical behaviour and norms pervade our politics and culture. A respondent stated, "I know that all work, regardless of its value on Earth, should be done with the same passion as if working for Jesus directly."[38] Another writes, "My role is fulfilling. I was raised to believe that kindness to one will be passed on to another. I have seen how a calm approach can spread with others in the room. I'm not sure if my coworkers share the same views."[39] This suggests that these respondents broadly recognize the presence or absence of positive, and constructive ethical values and standards.

The findings of my research indicate that dissonance, mild to severe, is a frequent theme among respondents. Class structure, merit-based or socially-based, is an element of economics and in turn organizational structure and behaviour. Joyce Mercer discusses practical theology's turn to class and economics. She suggests:

> Historically sociology has been a primary academic location for studies of the relations between social groups, including economic systems and class relations . . . As scholars of pastoral care gradually shifted their attention more fully to groups, communities, organizations and congregations, sociology achieved a wider embrace, particularly among those practical theologians searching for theoretical frameworks and research methods more adequate for making sense of social relations between groups . . . A second influence on practical theologies turn to economics and class relationships has to do with current global economic conditions. There is a sense of urgency to understand and account for the role of the economy in human experience.[40]

My thesis argues that secularization in our economic endeavours, the distancing of work from its spiritual value, and the decline in attendance at a place of worship as a part of the rhythm of life, all come together to leave arguably important conversations incomplete.[41] Mercer writes:

> [A] definitive aspect of practical theology is its transformational impulse: practical theology is concerned not simply to describe reality and to make sense of it, but to seek transformation

38. Verbatim respondent 7.
39. Verbatim respondent 7.
40. Mercer, "Economics, Class, and Classism," 435.
41. At the invitation of a colleague, I attended an Orthodox Jewish service, to learn that members of their community attend Temple daily.

The Roots of the Contemporary Workplace 69

> toward the love and justice of God for all people . . . Practical theologians must address economic and class-based contexts in which people are embedded, as part of the normative dimension of our work.[42]

This describes a desire, and an effort, to steer an organization's culture from what *is* to what *could be*. Being spiritually anchored, I suggest, is foundational to resilience, in the sense that this anchoring gives us the ability—courage even—to experiment. Carl Folke et al. assert that, "Adaptability is part of resilience."[43] It may be that efforts in activism in the community, sponsored by the organization and undertaken by employees indeed may bring deep reward. Joining with others in activist endeavours in the community creates strong new bonds upon which deeper conversation may begin—ultimately perhaps leading to greater diversity in the workplace. Activism can be community-based or workplace based. Richard Osmer writes:

> Phenomenological research seeks to describe the essence of a particular type of event or activity for a group of people. For example, it might ask: Among hospital patients, what is the essence of their experience of a caring interaction with a nurse? A guiding assumption of phenomenology is the 'intentionality' of consciousness, that is, that consciousness is always directed toward an object. Researchers attempt to bracket out their own preconceptions and to allow individuals' lived experience (their consciousness) of events of activities to disclose themselves. After gathering many instances of lived experience, they then analyze them to identify their common structure or 'essence.'[44]

Activism is an example of intentionality of consciousness which may be as straightforward as doing one's job with all the determination and care that one can muster. Analysis of the lived experiences of research respondents provides rich information for activism. A respondent stated, "I would rather be out there helping people."[45] Exploring such views provides a strong field for social activism and engagement.[46] Adapting

---

42. Mercer, "Economics, Class, and Classism," 436.
43. Folke et al. "Resilience Thinking," 20.
44. Osmer, *Practical Theology*, 52.
45. Verbatim respondent 29.
46. I have witnessed workplace-based community activities, such as the *United Way*, effectively become community wide activism efforts. Habitat for Humanity is another example.

to new environments alongside colleagues may, in addition to increased diversity, build adaptive capacity.

Organizations such as local Boards of Trade offer myriad opportunities through networking events and special purpose committees. Becoming involved in such networks will provide broad and rich knowledge of community issues and will lead to opportunities for activism. VanderWeele suggests, "If it is the case that the family, work, education, and religious community are important determinants of various aspects of human flourishing, as indeed they seem to be, then this has profound implications for societal organization and resource allocation."[47] This observation underscores not only the leader's role in the enterprise for which she or he is responsible, but adds the call for engagement in civil society at large.

As stated earlier, the 'one-career-for-life' expectation appears to be gone completely, sometimes resulting in a radical departure in mid-career. By example, the rise of the gig economy is where individuals have come to view multiple concurrent jobs as the norm. Treated as independent contractors, individuals such as ride-sharing drivers can find themselves, overnight, without compensation; as we have learned through the Covid 19 Pandemic.[48]

Design and governance of organizations must include a consciousness of the promotion of personhood. A stark example is workplace privacy. William Brown writes:

> In addition to issues such as technology enabled worker surveillance, current practices such as drug and alcohol testing, computer-aided credit checking, AIDS testing, genetic screening, overall healthiness screening, on-and-off duty conduct regulation (e.g., company monitoring of worker behaviors such as political activities, gambling, lifestyle preferences ...) are the subject of hotly contested debate.[49]

Max Depree, founder of Herman Miller, asserts, "In addition to all of the ratios and goals and parameters and bottom lines, it is fundamental that leaders endorse a concept of persons."[50] This may be one of the most

---

47. VanderWeele, "On the Promotion of Human Flourishing," 8153.

48. The post Covid 19 environment could see a rapid increase in contract labour over permanent salaried positions as organizations seek greater flexibility in labour costs.

49. Brown, "Technology, Workplace Privacy and Personhood." 1237.

50. Depree, *Leadership Is an Art*, 9.

tangible ways that leaders can act out their faith in the workplace—simply engaging with, and upholding colleagues.[51] In the postmodern era, when virtually everything is questioned, this may be more critical than ever. Nicholas Rescher writes:

> Thought-implementation—the capacity to act in response to and under the direction of thought—is the crux of personhood ... Persons are first and foremost cognitive agents ... Persons are bound to have beliefs about how matters stand in the world ... Persons are intelligent beings who see themselves—reciprocally—as having the capacity for self-controlled choice-implementation and who insist on viewing themselves as something other than robots or mere naturally evolved mechanisms without the ability of choice or self-inaugurated agency.[52]

My grounded theory asserts that there is an awareness that spirituality has a role to play in terms of a person's sense of purpose and thus, personhood. In a moving commentary, a respondent stated, "Because I work with palliative patients, I find myself asking why these people are suffering. On the other hand, I feel my faith has been strengthened because I don't know all the answers and find myself praying."[53] For this person, their feeling of shortcoming is strengthened by a reliance on prayer. Another respondent stated, "I don't feel a high degree of meaningfulness—but to some degree, yes."[54] Depree adds, "For many of us who work, there exists an exasperating discontinuity between how we see ourselves as persons and how we see ourselves as workers."[55] The economic impact of this internal tension is potentially staggering. The loss of human dignity is greater. Ronald Heifetz writes, "[L]eadership engages our values ... When we call for leadership in our organizations and politics, we call for something we prize."[56] That something, I suggest, is dignity. Dignity is at the heart of personhood.

---

51. I visited a call centre in San Antonio, Texas, where workers were situated in groups. At the centre of each were boards covered in photos of family and community gatherings.
52. Rescher, "Personhood," 173–74. Taking a look at one's self in the mirror is a good habit.
53. Verbatim respondent 30.
54. Verbatim respondent 31.
55. Depree, *Leadership Is an Art*, 32.
56. Heifetz, *Leadership without Easy Answers*, 13.

We grow into personhood as our true calling emerges. A respondent stated, "[My] first career gave a sense of deep meaningfulness. Able to leverage my gifts and honouring a family career tradition. Second career—what I am meant and called to do."[57] People will change careers to reach a deeper sense of flourishing. Against this, my grounded theory suggests that structural changes in society have narrowed workplace discussion primarily to economic output and success against tangible metrics. Heifetz demands a broader dialogue, writing:

> Authorities commonly have the power to choose the decision-making process. In essence, they must decide on the presence and relevance of conflict, and whether and how to unleash it. Deciding which process to use—autocratic, consultative, participative, or consensual—requires judgment . . . Where the authority has the expertise to define and solve the problem, people generally opt for autocratic or consultative decision making . . . Adaptive situations, however, tend to demand a more participative mode of operating.[58]

The choice of approach is a complicated matter, however. These choices rest with those in leadership roles, as they should. In a participative work environment everyone grows, not least the leader.[59]

Distinct from hierarchical organization structures, networked environments, including research conglomerates and consulting consortia, are now a significant organizational structure. Leadership among peers is the model for these structures. Heifetz writes:

> Because we are not used to distinguishing between leadership and authority, the idea of leadership without authority is new and perplexing. As a result, the person without authority gets few relevant pointers from scholarship. Analysts have generally neglected the distinctive problems and opportunities of mobilizing work from positions of little or no authority.[60]

It is leadership as partnership that is required. In effect, this is *paracletic* leadership.

Several research responses imply that traditions that influence our workplace expectations appear to be under duress, in some cases extremely

---

57. Verbatim respondent 15.
58. Heifetz, *Leadership without Easy Answers*, 121.
59. Volunteer work is a strong example.
60. Heifetz, *Leadership without Easy Answers*, 184.

so. Butler Bass speaks of people experiencing "cultural distortion."[61] In other words, lived reality is grossly out of line with expected norms. A respondent stated, "The industry changed and, in my view, became less ethical."[62] Peter Drucker offers, "The first sign of the decline of an industry is its loss of appeal to qualified, able, and ambitious people . . . [We must ask] what must our job parameters consist of to attract and hold the kind of people we need and want?"[63] This may be a factor in the determination by business schools to pursue studies in spirituality.

As industries become altered in terms, for example, of employee benefits, workers apprehend significant changes in the perceived ethical traditions, for better or worse, of their profession. This is an exceptional change in tradition.[64] An example is the rise in meal delivery enterprises. Like the ride-sharing business, in jurisdictions that permit it, such companies frequently treat delivery personnel as independent contractors rather than employees, frequently eschewing employee benefits of any kind.

In other situations, the adjustment to new societal norms can bring tension as new traditions of community, gender identity, and faith expression come alongside, sometimes challenging, even upending existing traditions. When such changes are rapid, particularly in a workplace that involves several generations, such tensions can be extreme, requiring great care on the part of leadership. Adjusting to multiculturalism and other community dynamics is occurring at a time when mentorship appears to be declining.

A decline in mentorship creates a new form of loneliness. A respondent stated, "I spoke with a supervisor—very loving, trusting and humble."[65] Such views were not expressed by the majority of the respondents. There appears to be a decline in the existence of institutionalized mentorship, with the resulting development of attitudes of 'going it alone.' The elimination of middle management in a number of organizations brings significant reduction in mentorship. Mintzberg asserts:

> The overriding purpose of managing is to ensure that the unit serves *its* basic purpose, whether that be to sell products in a

---

61. Butler Bass, *Christianity after Religion*, 33.
62. Verbatim respondent 3.
63. Drucker, *Management*, 109.
64. To complicate this, some organizations have preserved certain benefits for long-standing employees while offer minimal benefits to new employees.
65. Verbatim respondent 7.

retail chain or care for the elderly in a nursing home. This, of course, requires the taking of effective *actions*. Mostly other people in the unit do that, each a specialist in his or her own right. But sometimes a manager gets close to this *action*. More commonly, however, the manager takes one or two steps back from the action. One step back, he or she encourages other *people* to take action—the manager gets things done through other people by coaching, motivation, building teams, strengthening culture, and so forth. Two steps back, the manager gets things done by using information to drive other people to take action. He or she imposes a target on a sales team, or carries a comment from a government official to a staff specialist.[66]

Written just a decade prior to the writing of this work, this model appears to assume that some form of mentorship is in place, perhaps underscoring the changes that have occurred since Mintzberg's book was published. As stated, institutionalized structural, effective and pervasive mentorship may no longer be the norm. In particular, Mintzberg's model alludes to the value of what I describe as *curbside coaching*; providing in-the-moment discussion and feedback on practices.

My grounded theory asserts that the desire for interaction with others that is ethical and caring is pervasive. Organizations must nurture this.

We must seek ways to provide reasonable compensation and meaningful benefits to workers. Jeffrey Pfeffer writes:

> Some of the most problematic, stress-causing aspects of work environments include low wages, shift work, and the absence of job control. For example, low wages produce stress from having to survive with little income. Not surprisingly, a number of research studies find that low wages predict obesity, anxiety and depression, low birth weights, and hypertension.[67]

The findings of my survey indicate that in some cases, finding greater purpose required economic sacrifice. This suggests evidence of resignation in the face of failure to find greater purpose in addition to reasonable remuneration. A respondent stated, "In terms of fully satisfying a sense of calling, that is more difficult. I'm still trying to figure it all out."[68] There is tension here. Tension can lead to fatigue and withdrawal.

---

66. Mintzberg, *Managing*, 49 [emphasis original].
67. Pfeffer, *Dying for a Paycheck*, 10.
68. Verbatim respondent 17.

Richard Booth offers the perspective that, "Loneliness occurs when a person's network of social relationships is small or less satisfying than the person desires."[69] At the heart of this network is, for many, one's professional association and network. A loss of mentorship may destroy a worker's sense of rootedness in the organization. They become "lost in the system."[70]

The findings of my survey indicate that there is dissonance in the workplace. Sometimes this dissonance is internal to organizational situations, i.e., generated by practices and circumstances embedded in the structure of organizations. In other cases, this dissonance is external to the organization (for example global restructuring of supply chains), including shifting marketplace attitudes and expectations, changing community structures, changing family characteristics, and changing approaches and attitudes to the concept of faith. Pfeffer writes:

The *American Institute of Stress* has collated numerous studies of stress. Some highlights from these data are:

- Job stress is far and away the major source of stress for American adults and . . . it has escalated progressively over the past few decades.
- 80 percent of workers in the Attitudes in the American Workplace survey reported feeling stress on the job.
- Two separate studies reported that about 10 percent of employees said there was physical violence or an assault in the workplace because of job stress.[71]

---

69. Booth, "Toward an Understanding of Loneliness," 116. Harriet Ekperigin writes, "I believe that the definition of loneliness has evolved. Loneliness is now considered as the feeling of being alone, regardless of the amount of social contact. While social isolation is a lack of social connections. Social isolation can lead to loneliness in some people, while others can feel lonely without being socially isolated. 'Centre for Disease Control and Prevention, 2020.'

70. Booth, "Toward an Understanding of Loneliness," 116.

71. Pfeffer, *Dying for a Paycheck*, 13.

Stress may be extreme.[72] A respondent stated, "Some co-workers are driven only by money, lifestyle, or power."[73] Giving the sense that such coworkers appear to care little for their colleagues, this is certainly at odds with an environment of collaboration and collegiality. While this, at first blush, may not seem like an extremely stressful situation the lack of a perceived path to resolve the anxiety-causing phenomenon results in deeper stress, potentially rising to extreme levels—particularly if the situation persists. Pfeffer writes, "[T]he adverse effects of work environments on people's health may be getting worse. One reason is the changing nature of work and specifically the rising prevalence of precarious employment—the contract and freelance work of the so-called gig economy."[74] People are putting in long hours, often at multiple jobs. Yet, productivity may be waning and home life fractured.[75]

If dissonance and its concomitant state, unhappiness, are as broad as my research suggests, then dissonance—in this context a mild to severe state of mental discord or conflict—could be construed as an *economic agent*. I.e., dissonance is an agent acting upon the worker. Thus, dissonance counteracts feelings of achievement and fulfillment, negatively impacting the output of the worker. Output becomes less than optimal. Gwartney and Stroup state, "Economics is about people and the choices they make."[76] They also go on to affirm that "economic theory [is] developed from basic postulates of human behaviour."[77] Gwartney and Stroup assert, "Economics deals with people as they are—not as we would like to

---

72. Funded by Health Canada, the Mental Health Commission of Canada is providing workplace volunteers with Mental Health First Aid training. The training is designed to recognize and provide help to a person developing a mental health problem or experiencing a mental health crisis. Just as physical first aid is administered to an injured person before medical treatment can be obtained, Mental Health First Aid (MHFA) is given until appropriate treatment is found or until the crisis is resolved.

73. Verbatim respondent 29.

74. Pfeffer, *Dying for a Paycheck*, 14.

75. Some years ago I witnessed a moving speech. A middle school principal implored the men in the audience to devote volunteer time to reading to young boys in her inner city school, due to the fact that these boys were often being brought up by single mothers who were holding down two or three jobs in order to make enough to support their family; leaving their sons without home schooling time. In addition, a lack of male influence in their sons' lives, was perceived as significant. These single mothers face a stress-inducing choice. They must choose between time with their children or giving that time to multiple jobs in order to make ends meet financially.

76. Gwartney and Stroup, *Economics*, 4.

77. Gwartney and Stroup, *Economics*, 7.

remake them. Should people act more charitably? Perhaps so. But this is not the subject matter of economics."[78] Perhaps it is, or should be. Turning specifically to behavioural economics, James Allison forms much of his work on the *contingency rule*: "Event *B* will occur only if event *A* occurs beforehand."[79] Allison uses a well-known colloquial expression heard in academic circles to illustrate: 'Publish or Perish.' In other words, "if the newly hired university instructor wishes permanent employment in the form of academic tenure, the instructor must start a program of research and publish its results in the scholarly press."[80] Allison concedes, however, "Perhaps we face a difficulty in predicting the behavior of the factory worker, the grocery shopper."[81] Indeed, Allison appears to leave morality as a factor in behaviour to one side. Betsy Stevenson takes a deeper behavioural approach. She states:

> Economists are concerned with human welfare. For a very long time, we believed the best thing to do was just look at what people do and infer their preferences from their behaviour. But we've started to learn that there are some domains where that is hard to do, and simply asking people about their well-being can shed light on the situation . . . I think one of the richest potential areas for happiness data is in the area of behavioural economics—in situations where the way people behave may not actually reflect their true, underlying preferences . . . perhaps we're missing a sense of greater purpose or fulfillment.[82]

Self-fulfillment, or a lack thereof, *is* an economic agent. This is critical. The findings of my survey indicate that desire for interaction with others that is ethical and caring is quite pervasive. We do not appear to be responding fully to this fundamental desire, and yet the economic impact of failing to do so could be substantial.

78. Gwartney and Stroup, *Economics*, 12.
79. Allison, *Behavioural Economics*, 5 [emphasis original].
80. Allison, *Behavioural Economics*, 5.
81. Allison, *Behavioural Economics*, 194.
82. Stevenson, "What are the Economics of Happiness?" [n.d.].

Meaningfulness

A respondent asserts, "My work does provide a deep sense of meaningfulness. I find it very satisfying to know I had a positive impact."[83] Abraham Maslow asserts the importance of motivated people. He writes, "Almost every leader we interviewed made mention of the competitive advantage that lies within the people of an organization."[84] This becomes a poignant observation when viewed in the light of the dissonance experienced by the respondents to my research questionnaire. For emphasis, note that four fifths of the respondents expressed work circumstances that range from moderately dissonant to severely dissonant. Annie McKee writes:

> Happy people are better workers. Those who are engaged with their jobs and colleagues work harder—and smarter. And yet, there is an alarmingly high number of people who aren't engaged. According to a sobering 2013 Gallup report, only 30% of the U.S. Workforce is engaged. This echoes what I've seen in my work. Not many people are truly 'emotionally and intellectually committed' to their organizations. Far too many couldn't care less about what's happening around them. For them, Wednesday is 'hump day' and they're just working to get to Friday. And then there's the other end of the bell curve—nearly one out of five employees is actively *disengaged*, according to the same Gallup report.[85]

This is one of the most puzzling elements of my research. It seems clear that a high level of engagement delivers high output, yet so many organizations seem to fail to fully grasp the gravity of this, or to fully react to it. A respondent states:

> I actually need to feel a deep sense of purpose. I want to pay my bills but I also have a deep sense of justice. My 'calling' has changed a lot. I feel called to this time and place for a reason. He is still revealing. I think my peers and coworkers want that deep sense of meaningfulness, but I'm not sure everyone knows how to get that.[86]

Another respondent stated, "I am blessed to continually receive what I need. [However], many events have placed a sense of doubt in my job

---

83. Verbatim respondent 13.
84. Maslow, *On Management*, 99.
85. McKee, "Being Happy," para. 2–6.
86. Verbatim respondent 2.

security; e.g., others not being supported."[87] As meaningfulness wanes, loneliness ensues, deep engagement and productivity declines.

A respondent stated tentatively, "I feel secure for now."[88] Responding to changing marketplace values is neither new nor novel—it is the quality of the depth and breadth of response that is key. A lack of feeling secure can result in real loneliness. This requires being centred in our values while at the same time coping with loneliness and what can be profound uncertainty, yet without mentorship this could be unresolved. This is particularly relevant for those in leadership positions during times of change and inflection.[89] Heifetz asks:

> Why is it lonely on the point? Because those who lead take responsibility for the holding environment of the enterprise. They themselves are not expected to be held. They do the holding, often quite alone. They run the risk of moral regret.[90]

This is a very real issue. People, especially leaders, going through such times search for sources of hope, frequently without a satisfying answer. The Spirit-led leader has found a source of hope. A respondent stated, "I no longer fear the unknown and feel confident that spiritual guides as well as the support network I have in my life will help me reach my goals. I will be ok no matter what."[91] This is a truly moving declaration of hope. The findings of the research indicate that hope is stronger than lived experiences in many cases. The findings of the research indicate also that among people of professed faith or spirituality there is a sense that their spirituality anchors them and strengthens them; providing them with meaningfulness, vocational fulfillment, and joy, thus counteracting isolation. It is important, also, to note the importance of spiritual guidance and fellowship in securing and upholding the person, particularly during times of stress and distortion.

As stated, the findings of my survey indicate that there appears to be a decline in the existence of mentorship. This lack of mentorship—the loss of a caring agent who has intimate knowledge of the workplace

---

87. Verbatim respondent 22.

88. Verbatim respondent 7.

89. My first corporate presidency occurred following a stock market crash. I spent many sleepless nights wrestling with strategic choices being contemplated to preserve profit for the company. It was a time of loneliness.

90. Heifetz, *Leadership without Easy Answers*, 250.

91. Verbatim respondent 28.

with whom to discuss workplace challenges—erodes a person's ability to maintain hope and momentum. A lack of mentorship also erodes one's sense of fulfillment and may lead to deep loneliness. A respondent stated:

> My career was stressful and at times very political and demanding. I was compensated well but job security was not guaranteed. Performance was key. Even though I sometimes worked under great distress and pressure I felt that this was my calling. I believe I was a strong but compassionate leader. I don't believe my coworkers shared my views. Competition was their belief [in terms of the path] to success.[92]

Working in an environment where competition between workers is significant brings loneliness and isolation. Human resources consulting firm, Mercer states:

> In our latest norms, we found that just 67% of leaders and managers think the level of stress they experience at work is manageable; the other third was unsure or overwhelmed. A similar percentage said they struggle to maintain work-life balance. Just half of leaders and managers feel they have enough time to do a quality job, and only 48% feel they can detach from work. These results suggest that anywhere from a third to a half of leaders and managers are struggling to cope with the challenges of their job.[93]

These are astonishing observations. Loneliness is, arguably, exacerbated when people are not aware of the opportunity or value of speaking with a counsellor regarding workplace challenges.

Power, and its Abuse

If the workplace is rife with interpersonal competition, then power is a dominant element.[94] On the phenomenon of power, Mary Jo Hatch and Ann Cunliffe offer:

> [P]ower is always exercised in the context of relationships between actors. Power never resides in actors; it is always relational . . . formal authority is only one source of individual level power and the others do not work in strictly top-down ways, they also

---

92. Verbatim respondent 21.
93. Mercer, "Leadership, Stress, and the Importance of Self-Care," [n.d.].
94. I have witnessed occasions where inappropriate power, even control, was being exercised by a superior over a subordinate.

work up the hierarchy, laterally, or cross-organizationally, and may work in all directions at once.[95]

According to this research, the inappropriate exercise of power negatively impacts industry, government, the not-for-profit sector, and, indeed, the church. A respondent working in a faith-based environment writes, "This is not how the body of Christ should behave."[96] Maslow turns to the perversion of leadership by the drive for power.[97] He writes:

> [T]he one who seeks for power is the one who is just exactly likely to be the one who shouldn't have it, because he [sic] neurotically and compulsively needs power. Such people are apt to use power very badly; that is, use it for overcoming, overpowering, hurting people, or to say it in other words, they use it for their own selfish gratifications . . . the one who is therefore most selfless in the situation—just that person, because by definition he [sic] is psychologically healthier, gets absolutely no kick out of being able to order people around or to boss them.[98]

Most of us will recall a time when a superior, feeling that we have expressed views of disagreement, perhaps in a meeting, will seek an act of reprisal, or retaliation. A respondent asserts, "I find it hard to have honest, open conversations without fear of reprisal."[99] This is significant when we consider the view of the postmodern organization as a "site for enacting power relations."[100] Generally, we cannot easily escape the inappropriate exercise of power. Jacques Ellul states, "Never before has the human race as a whole had to exert such efforts in its daily labors as it does today as a result of its absorption into the monstrous technical mechanism."[101] This brings to mind the environment of near drudgery that we will find on the floor of an assembly plant or the parcel shipping floor of a distribution centre. This may be an emerging factor also for people who telecommute; spending most of their time working at home, alone. A respondent stated, "I am not [currently] doing the work that

---

95. Hatch and Cunliffe, *Organization Theory* 231.
96. Verbatim respondent 1.
97. A student once commented to me that he 'couldn't wait to have people under' him.
98. Maslow, *On Management*, 155.
99. Verbatim respondent 1.
100. Hatch and Cunliffe, *Organization Theory*, 15.
101. Ellul, *The Technological Society*, 319.

I would feel is more my calling."[102] There is distortion here. Can it be resolved through a new leadership approach? Perhaps, but first a leader must be aware of the condition.

Abuse of power by superiors, as well as peer-to-peer aggression, may lead to burn-out. We are, clearly, witnessing increased absenteeism. Statistics Canada reports that total days lost per worker in a year were 10 in 2018, up from 8.8 in 2014. Some regional data were dramatically worse. R. H. Hall discusses the relationship between job satisfaction and absenteeism. Hall writes, "[A]mong workers who are most likely to exhibit absenteeism (young workers for example), the more satisfied workers will be absent less frequently than the less satisfied workers."[103]

The findings of my survey indicate that among people of professed faith or spirituality there is a sense that their spirituality grounds them and strengthens them; providing them with meaningfulness, vocational fulfillment and joy. Thus, a strong sense of flourishing leads inexorably to improved productivity.

Leadership

Warren Bennis' work on leadership became a reference source for aspiring leaders in virtually all fields of endeavour. It is frequently a starting point for other authors on the topic of leadership. Bennis focuses particularly on the leader's task in situations of change. He writes:

> Leaders are, by definition, innovators. They do things other people have not done or dare not do. They do things in advance of other people. They make new things. They make old things new. Having learned from the past, they live in the present, with one eye on the future.[104]

By implication, leadership involves participating in and frequently introducing a degree of disruptive challenge into the environment. This may involve leading a discussion of a potential risk or shortcoming that others have ignored or minimized. Bennis offers that "one of a leader's principal gifts is to grow in office."[105] This suggests that leadership

---

102. Verbatim respondent 4.
103. Hall, *Dimensions of Work*, 93.
104. Bennis, *On Becoming a Leader*, 35.
105. Bennis, *On Becoming a Leader*, 138.

involves, by definition, a significant degree of "pain and reflection"[106] if there is to be growth. Bennis lays an important foundation for understanding and interpreting the dynamics of the workplace. This leads to an articulation of several critical elements of behaviour if leaders are to be broadly effective. These will be explored in chapter 4.

A respondent stated, "It is meaningful to me to work alongside people to help them explore their lives and life circumstances and how these things affect their well-being."[107] Most leadership situations require constant study—in particular deep domain knowledge and experience from industry 'insiders.' Other situations require expertise in bringing insights from non-related settings. A lack of fundamental, circumstance-specific, knowledge on the part of the leader can lead to indecisiveness and stuck-ness. Such phenomena can stultify an enterprise, even result in disaster. Frost suggests:

> The pain that incompetent managers create takes a number of forms. Some vacillate too much, driving staff 'up the wall' with their inability to make a decision or to stick to one once they have made it. Managers' indecisiveness can leave staff exasperated and even immobilized.[108]

Critical are openness and discretion in conversations. A respondent stated, "I find it hard to have honest, open conversations without fear of reprisal."[109] This is a loss of opportunity. Closing down situations of encouragement for dialogue is another example of creating severe dissonance. If this phenomenon is broadly repeated in an organization the economic loss could be major; the impact on psychological wellbeing worse. This is important. Clive Boddy points out:

> Affective, emotional or psychological well-being is a state where a person is content and happy with their life and with their work, home, emotional and spiritual lives. Such a state promotes a healthy and stable society. At work it helps promote a stable and efficiently functioning organisation.[110]

---

106. Bennis, *On Becoming a Leader*, 138.
107. Verbatim respondent 12.
108. Frost, *Toxic Emotions*, 39.
109. Verbatim respondent 1.
110. Boddy, "Corporate Psychopaths," 109.

Leadership, almost by definition, brings change. Indeed, change might be vitally important. Marketplace situations are never static—response is required. Change, however, can bring destabilization, sometimes pain, sometimes violence. The findings of my survey indicate that there is dissonance in the workplace. Peter Frost writes:

> Pain is a fact of organizational life. Companies will merge, bosses will make unrealistic demands, and people will lose their jobs. The pain that accompanies events like these isn't in itself toxic; rather, it's how that pain is handled throughout the organization that determines whether its long-term effects are positive or negative. What turns emotional pain into toxicity, especially in organized settings, is when others respond to that pain in a harmful, rather than healing, way.[111]

A respondent stated, "I earn a very good living, but ... job security is always an issue."[112] This may not affect everyone in the same way.[113] Frost writes:

> [A]n unfeeling response [from a superior] undermines people's confidence, esteem, dignity, and sense of connection to others. It *disconnects* them from the capacity to respond competently to their painful situation. It removes the desire and the ability to do their jobs. Perhaps most problematic, a toxic response decreases people's sense of hope—a critical component in feeling connected to life around them.[114]

It is important to reflect on the reality that leadership actions and decisions may not be the direct cause of pain. Frequently in today's organizational structure, it is peer-to-peer competition and aggression that creates pain. In times of rapid transition to an environment of multiculturalism, it is possible that racial micro-aggression may occur.[115] It is the leader's task to recognize such phenomena and to respond appropriately. My research findings indicate that dissonance, mild to severe, is a frequently experienced phenomenon. Some simply live with it, some compartmentalize it. Some seek a completely new environment where they can experience the

---

111. Frost, *Toxic Emotions*, 12.

112. Verbatim respondent 29.

113. I spent many decades in the capital markets. I accepted this environment knowing the personal insecurity of the capital markets industry.

114. Frost, *Toxic Emotions*, 18.

115. There are many examples of racial micro-aggression. One example is assigning intelligence to a person of colour on the basis of their race, using such expressions as, 'You are so articulate.'

environment they truly sought. Frost writes, "Other sources [of toxicity] can be traced to a company's policies and practices; sometimes there's a direct connection between how individuals create toxicity and the way the corporation conducts its business."[116] The findings of my survey indicate that desire for interaction with others that is ethical and caring is quite pervasive. People watch how leaders respond to situations that require correction. They will emulate the behaviour they observe.[117] Frost writes:

> Some bosses develop grudges toward particular individuals and direct most of their vindictiveness to encounters with them. A manager may not like a staff member who has been transferred into his [sic] unit, even if highly recommended. The staff member may find herself [sic] picked on, her [sic] performance criticized at every turn.[118]

Correction of gender inequality, and indeed all forms of inequality, should be first-order leadership actions. A respondent stated:

> Many events have placed a sense of doubt in my job security. E.g., others not being supported; not being assigned to a position that I felt qualified to do; being assigned to a role that suited the company, but which impeded my development; being reprimanded for something I did not do.[119]

Regular employee engagement surveys would help to ameliorate such circumstances.

In language that has become vernacular to some workplace environments Kim Scott introduces the concept of *Radical* Candor. Scott asserts, "Radical Candor is what happens when you put 'Care Personally' and

---

116. Frost, *Toxic Emotions*, 35.

117. In my own experience I recall a time when I discovered that, when dealing with a client complaint letter, some investment brokerage firms would send a stern legalistic letter worded in such a way as to encourage the client simply to drop their complaint. I instructed our team to assume that the client was telling the truth. The way that our team responded to clients became a truly effective client retention effort, and I believe strengthened the way that our customer care team viewed themselves and their work. I also advertised that I would sit on the trading desk at a certain time each week to take calls directly from clients. Interesting, while some calls were to register a concern with me, the vast majority of the calls yielded wonderful ideas for new services.

118. Frost, *Toxic Emotions*, 36.

119. Verbatim respondent 22.

'Challenge Directly' together."[120] The goal of Scott's book, essentially, is to show us how to bring about change in behaviour. Scott presents some valuable situational leadership observations and suggestions, particularly the need to care for a subordinate as precursor to candid feedback. We need to go further, however. Scott seems to present this pairing of care and candour in an almost transactional sense. I suggest that caring and candour cannot be paired in a transactional manner. Caring and candour must be viewed as elements of a deliberate transformational process, for both subordinate and boss. Transformational experiences take time, sometimes months. My research findings emphasize acting our faith over professing our faith. *Offering candid feedback, if it is actually to be useful, requires earning the right to be candid.* Earning that right can take multiple cycles of deeply caring interaction. Picture an upward evolving spiral, with each upward iteration marked with a caring exchange that earns the right to move to a deeper conversation. This caring effort is by its nature intensive, requiring a level of engrossment in the aspirations, concerns and values of a subordinate colleague that we may not realize. There is another critical element of earning the right to be candid: we need to prove that we actually know what we are talking about. We all have witnessed new managers wading into their work with surprisingly little effort actually to understand the dynamics of the environment and the critical success metrics for their unit.

To take this to a higher plane, we may be well reminded of the exhortation found in Prov 9: "The fear of the Lord is the beginning of Wisdom." Bartholomew and O'Dowd state:

> Wisdom and knowledge are indeed the product of a human search, but one conducted in a deep communal and spiritual abiding in God . . . Wisdom is concerned with the general order and patterns of living in God's creation . . . Wisdom provides discernment for the particular order and circumstances of our lives.[121]

My research findings indicate that it is possible that an epistemological social foundation is emerging. In other words, a spiritual perspective upon which one forms a view of the world and one's engagement with the world. This spiritual perspective may not be associated with what we may consider a traditional religious perspective. Most appear to seek

---

120. Scott, *Radical Candor*, 9.
121. Bartholomew and O'Dowd, *Old Testament*, 25–27.

to fulfill a deep sense of spiritual purpose in their work. A respondent stated, "Everyone wants to feel 'needed' at their workplace."[122] Earnest workers sacrifice much in order to build their career—contributing to their employers and to society. This requires our recognition. Wayne Alderson and Nancy McDonnell offer:

> What is so right about valuing another person? Every person has the need to be valued . . . There's not a person in any organization—executive, manager, supervisor, worker—who doesn't have that need. We generally don't, however, recognize that everybody has certain intangible, emotional, human needs, or admit them openly to one another. [These are] love, dignity, and respect.[123]

The Anglican *Book of Alternative Services* (BAS) includes Jesus' admonition to "love thy neighbour as thy self."[124] This is an admonition that reaches back to ancient times. To be sure, leadership often requires corrective, even disruptive, conversations. Jesus' ministry is clear evidence of this (cf. John 8). However, charging into a radically candid feedback session can be catastrophic. Alderson and McDonnell state, "Subordinates who may actually know more about the critical success metrics for their unit, grounded in a more developed understanding of the fundamental mission of the enterprise than the manager are going to leave."[125]

Incompetent supervisors frequently cover their incompetence by taking credit for a subordinate's work. A respondent stated, "[I feel] that I have been put in a position of being taken advantage of."[126] This is an example of severe dissonance. To be taken advantage of while being compelled to carry out specific tasks is abuse. It can get worse. Repeated abusive behaviour is malice. Frost underscores this, writing:

> The purpose of malice is to deliberately harm someone else. Its reasons are many and varied: a need to control or dominate; a dislike of individuals from a particular gender or ethnic background; past experiences with staff who were themselves painful, leaving the abusive boss distrustful of his [sic] current staff. Or the malice may stem from a belief that this is how to motivate people and get the best out of them. Whatever the reason, the typical

---

122. Verbatim respondent 9.

123. Sitting on the commuter train and listening to conversations has provided insight into numerous such blunders. Sometimes it is more than blunder.

124. Anglican Book of Alternative Services, 231.

125. Alderson and McDonnell, *Theory R Management*, 54–55.

126. Verbatim respondent 22.

emotional response from those on the receiving end of malicious behaviour are fear, anger, confusion, and resentment.[127]

My research findings indicate that among people who expressed meaningfulness, vocational fulfillment and joy, there was also expression of a degree of fatigue and powerlessness. Such phenomena are a net cost to organizations and are debilitating to employees. Inflicted pain may not be deliberate, but rather circumstantial. A respondent stated, "My chosen industry was not at all secure."[128] Industries can be in flux for many reasons. Consider the airline industry during Covid 19. Structural change can impact entire workforces. Investing in the development of adaptive capacity is critical. It is the adaptive leader who can respond quickly to adversity.

Adaptability

Leadership, indeed at its core, is a profession of adaptability. Bennis writes, "[U]nless the leader continues to evolve, to adapt and adjust to external change, the organization will sooner or later stall. In other words, one of a leader's principal gifts is the ability to use his or her experiences to grow in office."[129] While Bennis does not make the connection explicitly, it is my view that prayerful contemplation strengthens adaptive capacity. One respondent details a decision to leave an organization due to its perceived negative change. A Canadian Broadcasting Corporation (CBC) investigation exposed a significant issue for bicycle food delivery personnel and workplace injury protection. The news story reads:

> On any given day in downtown Toronto, you'll see a flurry of bike couriers pedalling their way through traffic, bags strapped to their backs, on their way to deliver your next meal. Food delivery apps operate in nearly every Canadian city and they're changing the way we eat by offering convenient access to a wider range of takeout options. A few taps on your phone and food from your favourite restaurant will be delivered to your door. But if those couriers get hurt on the job, a [CBC] Marketplace investigation has found their eligibility for work-related

---

127. Frost, *Toxic Emotions*, 37.
128. Verbatim respondent 3.
129. Bennis, *On Becoming a Leader*, 137.

compensation depends on the province they work in and which app they deliver for.[130]

Thus, the food delivery service company provides workers' compensation insurance coverage only when explicitly required by law. Where is empathy in this situation? Bing Feng et al state, "Many organizations fail to make behaviour change happen due to a fundamental empathy gap."[131] These organizations apparently do not build into their ethos mechanisms for a sharing of emotions, hopes, and aspirations. The findings of my survey indicate that hope is stronger than actual lived experiences, yet hope may be harder to cling to in some sectors of today's work environment. Bennis writes:

> A major challenge that all leaders are now facing is an epidemic of institutional malfeasance, as we read nearly every day in the news. And if there is anything that undermines trust, it is the feeling that the people at the top lack integrity, are without a solid sense of ethics. The characteristics of empathy and trust are reflected not just in codes of ethics, but in organizational cultures that support ethical conduct.[132]

Humanity has long been aware of the temptation to choose the wrong path. Aristotle wrote:

> Men [sic] do wrong when they think it can be done by them; when they think that their action will either be undiscovered, or if discovered will remain unpunished; or if it is punished that the punishment will be less than the profit to themselves or to those for whom they care.[133]

There is, however, the narrow road that Jesus implores us to take. The narrow road is the road that calls for conduct becoming the leader with integrity. Jesus made it clear that there may be few who choose the narrow road (cf. Matt 7), and those that do may suffer ridicule.

Adaptability requires paying attention, beginning with *intensive listening*. This is hard intentional work. Leading will be made more effective

---

130. Ghebreslassie et al., "Ontario Workplace Safety," para. 1.

131. Feng et al, "Harnessing Behavioural Insights," 7.

132. Bennis, *On Becoming a Leader*, 155–56. This challenge was evident in the many tribunals that I participated in as a securities regulator. I have witnessed egregious and deliberate actions whereby principals of enterprises enriched themselves while blatantly ignoring the wellbeing of employees.

133. Aristotle, *The Art of Rhetoric*, BI, xii.

through focussed listening. It takes precious time and the ability to shut out everything but the conversation.[134] Relevant and non-threatening questions will lead to deep conversation regarding shared concerns. By example, Dykstra and Bass write:

> Both individual and human failings and unjust social structures set countless obstacles in the way of practices that are good for all people. Moreover, in history and in the present day, practitioners who bear the name of Christ have participated in shared activities that are distorted, damaging, and manifestly not embodied responses to the active presence of God for the life of the world. Egregious examples leap to mind, but the quieter damage that can be wrought in the course of everyday life also evokes this problem, as people who bear the name of Christ fail to practise forgiveness, discernment, or hospitality.[135]

What we say in the boardroom must be mirrored by how we behave in the hallways. We must move to *radical engagement*, founded in a deep awareness of lived experiences.[136] This can only happen when we see the other fully, even as we offer to the other that new approaches are required. Being present, and straightforward is key. When information ceases, gossip begins. Without constant communication of factual information, rumours abound and take root. Conspiracies blossom. Today, social media is a significant issue in terms of misinformation. By example, Tom Nichols writes:

> Did you know that chocolate can help you lose weight? Sure, you do. You read it in the paper. In fact, you might have read it in several papers, and woe to any expert, including a doctor, who might have told you otherwise. After all, hiding the miraculous weight-decreasing qualities of the tastiest thing in the world is just the kind of thing experts would do. Thankfully, a German scientist, Johannes Bohannon of the Institute of Diet and Health, wrote a paper that was published in a journal and then joyfully covered in press throughout the world, and he verified what we have all suspected all along: chocolate is really good for

---

134. I have interacted with nine billionaires during my career. While all different, what I observed that they have in common was this extraordinary ability to focus in on a conversation; turning everything else off while they listen.

135. Dykstra and Bass, "A Theological Understanding," 27.

136. I recall standing beside a co-worker and listening to our superior giving a speech. My colleague pointed at him and turned to me saying, "I've worked for that guy for ten years and he couldn't pick me out of a lineup."

you. Except Johannes Bohannon doesn't exist. Neither does the Institute of Diet and Health.[137]

In a world where we are witnessing a crescendo of misinformation, when leaders stop communicating truthfully, regularly and completely, dis-organization emerges, and internal politics begins. Social media and gossip fill the space left when deep, relevant, and timely communication is lacking.

New forms of supervision emerge where leadership without conferred authority is required. Richard Pascale and Jerry Sternin state:

> Some business problems—employees working at half their potential, endlessly escalating health care costs, conflicts between departments—never seem to get fixed, no matter how hard people try. But if you look closely, you'll find that the tyranny of averages always conceals sparkling exceptions to the rule. Somehow, a few isolated groups and individuals, operating with the same constraints and resources as everyone else, prevail against the odds . . . There are people in your company or group who are already doing things in a radically better way. The process we advocate seeks to bring the isolated success strategies of these 'positive deviants' into the mainstream.[138]

Heifetz writes that, "Leadership is dangerous, with or without authority, because the stresses of adaptive work can be severe."[139] This is particularly true when individuals offer leadership without authority, because they are stepping outside the hierarchy of authority within their environments, frequently placing themselves at great risk of retaliation, even dismissal. Here is the reality, however; senior leaders must, in fact, seek such individuals out and find ways to support their efforts within the organization's structure. We may tie this directly to flourishing.

Flourishing

If one accepts the premise that human flourishing positively impacts productivity and profitability, then human flourishing, on its grandest economic scale, affects a nation's gross domestic product.[140] Leadership

---

137. Nichols, *The Death of Expertise*, 134.
138. Pascale and Sternin, "Your Company's Secret Change Agents," para. 2.
139. Heifetz, *Leadership without Easy Answers*, 235.
140. Gross domestic product is a monetary measure of the market value of all the

resulting in a workplace that nourishes human flourishing, therefore, is nation building. This call should be responded to. Speaking specifically of the United States, Bennis states:

> Since the organization is now the primary social, economic, and political form, and since business is a dominant cultural force in America, organizations in general and business in particular [must respond to sweeping changes in society] ... Clearly it is time for a [new] transformation, and the key to such a transformation is the organization's attitude toward its workers. Because the organization is the primary form of the era, it is also the primary shaper. The organization is, or should be, a social architect—but this means that its executives must be social architects too.[141]

Our ambitious focus should be on achieving pervasive flourishing—growing, succeeding, thriving, and prospering.[142] These descriptors apply to one's emotional and psychological wellbeing as well as one's economic wellbeing. As a result, we ask, what can we do in terms of influencing organizational structure and leadership methods that will be *catalytic* in promoting vitality and flourishing? If we consider that a sense of *vocation* is linked to flourishing, what can we do to enhance/equip employees' identification of their vocation and their progress toward the feeling that they are achieving their goals and desires as related to vocation? Mary Grey writes:

> If we are to nurture (and resource) the spirit, a renewal of hope is needed. Hope stretches the limits of what is possible. It is linked with that basic trust in life without which we could not get from one day to the next ... Conversely, to be without hope is to be trapped. It is to be helpless, to have no sense that it is worth getting out of bed, taking a decision.[143]

Hope, then, is at the heart of flourishing. Hope must be nourished through the posture of leadership.

A respondent stated, "I truly experience and enjoy a sense of deep meaningfulness at work. I feel trusted. My views, which stem from a

---

final goods and services produced in a specific time period, usually annually.

141. Bennis, *On Becoming a Leader*, 173–74.

142. I have brought forward the notion of setting 'flourishing' as the goal of an organizational human resources strategy, to find that this goal seemed too lofty to achieve. It is absolutely achievable.

143. Grey, "Survive or Thrive?" 396.

deep-rooted belief in Christian life, are not popular amongst peers."[144] Colleen Capper explores a multitude of epistemologies which may have bearing on workplace dynamics. In the preface to her work on organization theory, Capper writes:

> [T]his text addresses a range of critically oriented epistemologies, including critical theories; Critical Race Theory and Black Crit; LatCrit, Asian, Tribal Crit; Disability Studies theories, feminist theories, Queer Theory, poststructural epistemology, feminist poststructuralism, and theories of intersectionality . . . This book also considers how these critically oriented epistemologies can inform fresh theorizing about organizations and leadership toward equitable ends.[145]

Capper covers an appropriately broad range of organizational issues, including perspectives on leadership, motivation, plus specific implications for such areas as sensitivity training. However, there appears to be little essential discussion of faith or spirituality as a critical epistemology to be explored from an organizational and leadership point of view. Perhaps it is time for broader dialogue. The findings of my survey indicate that there is an expression of spirituality in the lives of the majority of respondents.

Recognizing that behaviour may be undergirded by spirituality is critically important. This cannot be overstated. As suggested by Souba earlier, ontological perspectives—views of reality regarding ethics espoused by medical professionals may be under siege. Their purpose, the reason they responded to their vocational call, whether consciously spiritual in nature, may be overwhelmed by the structure and nature of their environments.[146] Clearly this is alluded to in several respondent narratives. This is foundational. As stated, research findings suggest that for most respondents there is an expression of faith or spirituality. This appears to be significant. A statement by Miroslav Volf underscores this. He writes, "The significance of secular work depends on the value of creation, and the value of creation depends on its final destiny. If its destiny is eschatological transformation, then . . . we *must* ascribe inherent value to human work." [147] This requires emphasis. If work is to be considered as

---

144. Verbatim respondent 6.

145. Capper, *Organization Theory*, x.

146. Sadly, the COVID 19 pandemic brought home the dire predicament and resulting frustration surrounding the sourcing of Personal Protective Equipment (PPE).

147. Volf, *Work in the Spirit*, 93 [emphasis original].

eschatological, then human flourishing must be the goal of the workplace. If human flourishing is the goal, then organizations that focus solely on material output irrespective of this deeper imperative are simply missing the mark: beyond loss of potentially significant economic return on an organization's endeavours, this would be unethical, even negligent.

People Seek an Ethical Workplace

Employees know when a workplace lacks an ethos of flourishing. A respondent stated, "I used to wear rose-coloured glasses and then get crushed when people weren't as justice minded or compassionate as I was."[148] The findings of my research indicate that desire for interaction with others that is ethical and caring is pervasive. Bennis continues:

> Since the release and full use of the individual's potential is the organization's true task, all organizations *must* provide for the growth and development of their members and find ways of offering them opportunities for such growth and development. *This is the one true mission of all organizations and the principal challenge to today's organizations.*[149]

While Bennis appears not to link mission to spiritual purpose, Volf goes straight to the point. He writes, "I believe that it is possible to align desires, commitments, talents, and efforts with God as revealed in Jesus Christ no matter what situation we find ourselves in."[150]

Taken together, these statements from Bennis and Volf are unequivocally powerful. *They are saying that if we can recognize the spiritually gifted talents and potential of our employees, and create an environment where those employees are guided, empowered and given permission to perform at the peak of their ability, the results will be astonishing.*

Leadership as Spirituality in Practice

I offer that Leadership may be viewed as spirituality in practice. My work emphasizes and calls for the recognition that it is the supremacy of the Spirit over the temporal and mundane that truly enables leadership. In

---

148. Verbatim respondent 2.
149. Bennis, *On Becoming a Leader*, 184 [emphasis added].
150. Volf, *Flourishing*, 17.

terms of concepts of spirituality in the workplace, Ian Mitroff and Elizabeth Denton write:

> 'Spirituality' is defined as 'the basic feeling of being connected with one's complete self, others, and the entire universe.' If a single word best captures the meaning of spirituality and the vital role that it plays in people's lives, that word is 'interconnectedness.' Those associated with organizations they perceived as 'more spiritual' also saw their organizations as 'more profitable.' They reported that they were able to bring more of their 'complete selves' to work. They could deploy more of their full creativity, emotions, and intelligence; in short, organizations viewed as more spiritual get more from their participants, and vice versa.[151]

It was this statement which inspired the choice of research questions posed for my study.

A respondent speaks of being taken advantage of, thus reducing their drive and loyalty. While this experience may be disappointing. Situations can become far worse. *Incivility can quickly descend into significant aggression.* However, if the workplace can be a place of aggression, then it is also a place to practise forgiveness (cf. Matt 5:7). Forgiveness is a critical practice, leading to restoration, trust and inclusiveness. Leaders can model this. A respondent stated, "I believe that we are all connected and that the energy we bring to our interactions affect the quality of connection, and other things like loyalty, trust, etc."[152] David Whyte states:

> Forgiveness is a heartache and difficult to achieve because strangely, it not only refuses to eliminate the original wound, but actually draws us closer to its source. To approach forgiveness is to close in on the nature of the hurt itself, the only remedy being, as we approach its raw centre, to imagine our relation to it.[153]

In forgiving we must understand the fragility of the situation. It can be a process of sorting through many layers. It is also forgiveness, however, that heals. Perhaps it is *only* forgiveness that heals. Appropriation of the Spirit, suggests L. Gregory Jones, "invites us not to forget the past, but to remember it well so that we can envision and embody a future different from the past. In that sense, we need the Spirit both to return us to our

---

151. Mitroff and Denton, "Study of Spirituality," para. 5.
152. Verbatim respondent 4.
153. Whyte, *Consolations*, 67.

memories and also to enliven our imagination."[154] Change happens in an organization, resulting in job loss, fear and anger, sometimes together with an entrenched sense of being wronged by a former employer. This can be overwhelming, and can result in a massive personal challenge that can take many years to cope with, hence Jones' admonition above. Indeed, sometimes the best we can do is to compartmentalize the issue, and set it aside. Some have carried such compartments for a very long time.[155]

Every workplace reflects the makeup of the community around it. Kyle Patterson asserts, "Leaders work together to restore families, churches, cities and communities."[156] Our workplaces are diverse in every possible way. Capper develops a broad dialogue in the areas of equity and diversity. While focused on leadership in the education environment, her views have meaning for all workplace circumstances. Capper writes, "While the structural functional epistemology focuses on how organizations operate with a goal of efficiency, interpretivists are concerned mainly with how people experience the organization with a goal of understanding."[157] There are complexities here. This is an emerging leadership skill discussion. Capper states:

> Educators who adopt the interpretivist epistemology posit that schools as organizations are socially constructed and exist only in the perceptions of people. Individuals are viewed as interdependent, dependent on one another, dependent on others.[158]

People need their organization. Organizations need their people. Matching is critical for both to succeed. It is through the discernment of gifts that this matching succeeds. A respondent stated:

> I work in the long-term care sector. I feel I have always been called to work with older adults. I have dedicated my life to working with this demographic in NFP organizations. I started

---

154. Jones, *Embodying Forgiveness*, 149.
155. I know that I have.
156. Patterson, *Transformational*, 106.
157. As stated, epistemology seeks to distinguish belief from opinion, i.e. the nature, sources, and limits of knowledge. Structural functionalism is a sociological theory that offers an explanation of the functioning of society by focussing on the relationship between social institutions as defined historically. Interpretivism in epistemology considers knowledge as a social development involving many points of view and influences of various types of meaning determining the subject's knowledge of reality which is then an interpretation of reality, not a strict definition of reality.
158. Capper, *Organization Theory*, 55.

working directly with patients, and now I find I miss the patient interaction. I feel a very deep sense of intrinsic meaning.[159]

Our interaction with the world in adulthood, potentially in large part, is derived from actual workplace experiences, which create for us an interpretation of reality. This interpreted reality shapes our approach and response to situations beyond the workplace. The manner in which we treat others at the grocery store or on the commuter train is influenced by the treatment we receive at work.[160] Capper writes:

> Leaders leading from an interpretivist epistemology emphasize personal awareness, the significance of relationships, and having a purpose or mission. From the interpretivist epistemology, the education leader serves as a facilitator and collaborator . . . Other leadership practices aligned with the interpretive epistemology include the work on emotional intelligence, distributed leadership, *spirituality and leadership*, the reflective practitioner, leading for learning, and the learning organization.[161]

Leaders operate within a structure, even when they have little control over that structure. However, they always have control over themselves. For example, an attitude of forgiveness and a willingness to support and come alongside colleagues and subordinates will develop skills as well as trust and commitment. Capper writes:

> The differences between the interpretivist epistemology and critically oriented epistemologies . . . These may be summed up by the phrase 'Charity, not justice.' As such, educators with an interpretivist epistemology focus on charity and sympathy but not on changing the systems and practices [that might prevent or change situations].[162]

Leadership, by contrast, cannot be satisfied with a focus solely on charity and sympathy, but must be prepared to lead effective change of systems and practices *while* acting charitably and sympathetically.

159. Verbatim respondent 30.

160. As I was walking across the walkway between a parking area and a local grocery store, a person drove right into my path, causing me to have to jump out of the way. Shaking my head I continued to the store, when the driver rolled down their window and yelled at me," You need to calm down!"

161. Capper, *Organizational Theory*, 59 [emphasis added].

162. Capper, *Organizational Theory*, 59. Capper offers that theories of social justice, equity, and critical qualitative research methods originate out of critical theory (a philosophical approach that confronts social, historical, and cultural ideologies).

Jesus presents the role of shepherd as loving, caring, and trustworthy (cf. John 10:27). I offer that leaders are called to be shepherds; hence the title of this book. They are called not only to lead, but to tend to, and care for followers.

Philip Selznick states:

> Group leadership is far more than the capacity to mobilize personal support; it is more than the maintenance of equilibrium through the routine solution of everyday problems; it is the function of the leader/statesman [sic]—whether of a nation or a private association—to define the ends of group existence, to design an enterprise distinctly adapted to these ends, and to see that that design becomes a living reality.[163]

At times of inflection in an organization or, indeed, in an entire industry, this can be especially difficult. Entrenched individuals perceive a loss of control.[164] A respondent stated:

> It was as a leader that I gained most satisfaction: working with colleagues to improve the institution. I believe that I built bridges. If I am honest, there was no sense of vocation in the early days. It has grown, almost imperceptibly.[165]

This is painstaking work. It is no light commitment. Much time is required to articulate vision, and the path toward that vision. Time is, indeed, of the essence.

Post-Religion Spirituality

The findings of my research indicate that it is possible that an epistemological social foundation is emerging from several among my research respondents. This emerging phenomenon appears to be a thirst for spirituality that eschews traditional religion. A respondent stated, "I believe that there is something higher, but not through the lens of religious faith."[166] Another writes, "I do not subscribe to an organized religion; however, I do hold to my own spiritual beliefs. I believe that my

---

163. Selznick, *Leadership in Administration*, 37.

164. Consider the polarized response to the remedies offered for the control of COVID 19 spread.

165. Verbatim respondent 14.

166. Verbatim respondent 4.

work's meaning is driven by my desire to contribute to others' growth and development."[167] Reggie McNeal writes:

> Spiritual leaders exercise a significant stewardship in their response to culture. Through their choices, they instruct those they lead. What they accept, their followers accept. What they reject, others do too. What they change casts their shadow, through others, through history . . . Understanding the role of culture in the heart-shaping process involves more complex analysis than merely treating the culture as something outside the leader to be accepted or rejected. It also involves learning to appreciate the gifts of culture as one of the forces God has used and continues to use in forming the leader. Ultimately, leaders integrate these insights into their life mission.[168]

We do not need dogma; we need love. This is leadership as caring and nurturing—responding to peoples' search for calling and connection. It is pervasive and long-term in nature. It is transformational, not transactional. It requires awareness. The findings of my research suggest that the person and model of Jesus is valued by many. One might say that the tempter offered Jesus transactions: In return Jesus offered transformation (cf. Luke 4). It is reasonable to believe that people of faiths other than Christianity find their values to be central also. All give a sense of belonging and of being needed. A respondent stated, "Everyone wants to feel 'needed' at their workplace."[169] Our need for acceptance and belonging, to be believed in and valued—these are root elements of meaningfulness and fulfillment. We crave this in our home and community lives, and we crave it at work. McNeal explains:

> People are increasingly engaged in a search for meaning, purpose, love, self-worth, compassion, dignity, and transcendence, a sense of unity with others and with the universe, along with a means to express these things . . . To assume that people are not in church because they are not interested in spiritual truth demonstrates denial regarding attitudes about spiritual matters . . . Post moderns can speak about spirituality without ever mentioning God . . . The challenge for the church involves helping spiritually hungry people speak with church leaders about *their*

---

167. Verbatim respondent 5.
168. McNeal, *A Work of Heart*, 75.
169. Verbatim respondent 9.

lack of cultural relevance rather than an accurate reading of people's experience of classic Christian truth.[170]

I have already argued that organizational mentorship appears to be in decline. A significant percentage of respondents to the research questionnaire express faith or spirituality yet a very small percentage confirm that they have spoken with a minister of spiritual counsellor regarding workplace issues or challenges. For example, one respondent stated, "I pray most nights that I am making the right/best decisions."[171] However, this same respondent's reply to the question, 'Have you ever spoken with a minister or counsellor?' is simply, "none."[172] When we stand at a crossroad, we may need someone to give us direction, yet few of the respondents affirmed discussion with a minister.

A respondent stated, "I believe that God has designed each person uniquely with a role to play."[173] For a significant number of respondents, work is biblical, yet they are reticent to raise this in the workplace. We must seek appropriate methods to respond. Goran Agrell affirms:

> What is the relationship between 'man [sic] works' and 'man [sic] serves God? In a number of [Hebrew] texts, it is held that man's [sic] work is part of God's created order, or derives its strength and inspiration from God. To say that man [sic] is appointed to rule the rest of creation (Gen 1:26–28; Ps. 8:7–9) is not a clear statement that work is a divinely appointed task, but it can certainly be given that interpretation . . . According to the wisdom poem in Isa 28:23–29, the farmer is taught by the Lord so that he [sic] can carry out his [sic] various tasks in the right order . . . But 'man [sic] serves God' includes as well such things as restrictions on work. The Sabbath command (Ex 20:8–11; Deut 5:12–15) shows this. It states that all work is to be conducted on six days of the week.[174]

Work brings toil and exhaustion, yet work also calls for stewardship, creativity, pride and enjoyment in a craft well completed. Work provides the means for sustenance, and work also provides for the joy

---

170. McNeal, *A Work of Heart*, 80–81.
171. Verbatim respondent 18.
172. Verbatim respondent 18.
173. Verbatim respondent 1.
174. Agrell, *Work, Toil and Sustenance*, 16.

of caring for another.[175] Work frequently weaves joy and angst together. A respondent stated:

> I experience very deep joy and meaningfulness in my work. In my mid-thirties I followed God's leading toward a career using more of my gifts and a desire to help/serve. My views, which stem from a deep-rooted belief in Christian life, are not popular amongst peers. I feel quite powerless at times. I have chosen to work in a non-Christian environment where I can model Christ.[176]

The majority of respondents confirm a view that spirituality in some form pervades their life and work. Volf asserts, "In the past few centuries Christian theologians have come to view human work as cooperation with God."[177] A respondent stated, "We have been called upon to use our talents to the best of our ability."[178] It is unclear whether leaders actually notice this depth of calling among their co-workers. Research suggests that it is lacking.

Agrell writes:

> Many [Hebrew Scripture] texts express the thought that it is the Lord's blessing and man's [sic] work which together provide man [sic] with his [sic] sustenance. In Gen 8:21ff., it is ordained that the Lord, by his [sic] promise never again to curse the earth, will allow sowing and harvest to remain and the changes of the seasons always to continue.[179]

We should seek to re-introduce a biblical rhythm of work, rest, play, worship. This is not simply an exhortation to individuals, but also to communities. God calls for Sabbath rest. God also provides for relaxation and festivity! That said, work will never be easy. Agrell continues:

> Work for a living is, according to the [Hebrew Scripture], most often toil, involving such suffering that man [sic] even needs rest

---

175. I viewed my role as Dean of a Business School, in a small way, as shepherding role for our students. It brought great joy, made all the more intense as the years have passed and I receive emails and messages from former students as they tell me about their unfolding careers—around the globe.

176. Verbatim respondent 6.

177. Volf, *Work in the Spirit*, 98.

178. Verbatim respondent 9.

179. Agrell, *Work, Toil and Sustenance*, 16. I wish to add here that Agrell and many other Christian theologians use the initials 'OT' to refer to the 'Old Testament.' For Jews these sacred texts are not old, but living. I prefer that we call them what they are. On my bookshelf is the *TANAKH*: the holy scriptures of the Jewish faith.

> from it and comfort for being compelled to do it. Especially slave labour is seen as painful, since it is done under compulsion, is hard, yields poor results or results the worker cannot enjoy, and since it can keep the worker from believing in the possibility of liberation from slavery . . . But the [Hebrew Scriptures] can also look on work more favourably. Work done for oneself, yielding results the worker himself [sic] enjoys, is something positive, blessed, a cause of joy for the worker.[180]

Toil does not involve purely physical demands and exhaustion. Toil will also bring emotional and psychological stress, even pain. The findings of my survey indicate that people care about one another, but are sometimes unsure of who to trust, or when to engage. This suggests a fragility in terms of true security in the workplace. This fragile sense of feeling secure may be exacerbated by two conditions of work today. One is the growing need for more than one job in order to meet personal and family economic needs. In this circumstance one is exposed to, and required to navigate, sometimes very different workplace cultures which confuse the worker and distance them from deep engagement with each workplace.[181] The other is the situation of the telecommuter—the worker who rarely physically enters a traditional workplace where co-workers are gathered together. This worker operates primarily at home and is culturally distant from others working for the same organization, notwithstanding available communications technologies.[182]

The findings of my survey indicate that desire for interaction with others that is ethical and caring is quite pervasive. This is particularly evident among respondents for whom faith, or spirituality, is declared. We should find ways to introduce, or reintroduce, the biblical notion of work and calling, regardless of the label we give it. God acknowledges that work brings toil. However, as Frederik Schiotz states, "The God who works, commissions man [sic], his creature, to work."[183] Thus toil is an element of vocation. The Apostle Paul is the model for evangelism and ministry combined with carrying out a task aimed at sustenance. Paul

---

180. Agrell, *Work, Toil and Sustenance*, 31.

181. Consider the revelations, during the Covid 19 Pandemic, of healthcare workers working in multiple long term care facilities.

182. This is yet another phenomenon that we are learning about more due to the COVID 19 Pandemic.

183. Schiotz, "A Christian Concept of Vocation," 3.

adds, however, the critical element of God's call for all work to be done for the Kingdom. Agrell writes:

> Paul's only real teaching on work is found in 1 Thessalonians 4: 9–12... The Thessalonians are urged to conduct their lives even more assiduously according to what Paul has taught them... Paul exhorts the Thessalonians not to exploit their brothers [sic] in matters of business... [Believers] are to maintain a positive contact with the world.[184]

There is pride in a job well done particularly when we recognize the divine value of work. We just have to notice and acknowledge it.

Peace and security are themes in the Hebrew Scriptures (cf. Jer 33:6). Today, as we have seen, job security is far from certain. A respondent stated, "Many events have placed a sense of doubt in my job security."[185] Another respondent stated, "Job security is always a concern."[186] Hatch and Cunliffe add:

> A growth strategy for an organization leads to increases in size and differentiation... If growth involves mergers, acquisitions, or joint ventures, then adaptation to new units and the cultures they bring with them will put strains on the organization that can lead to conflict. Strategies involving downsizing contribute to conflict by creating the perception of shrinking resources, which provokes competition over what remains to be divided. When jobs are on the line, competition becomes fierce.[187]

Trust does not have to be lost during times of inflection. Indeed, it must be preserved and strengthened. This is a critical task of leadership. Robert Hurley states:

> [A] distrustful environment leads to expensive and sometimes terminal problems. We hardly need reminding of the recent wave of scandals that shattered the public's faith in corporate leaders. And although you'll never see a financial statement with a line item labeled 'distrust,' the WorldCom fiasco underscores just how expensive broken trust can be.[188]

---

184. Agrell, *Work, Toil and Sustenance*, 103–4.
185. Verbatim respondent 22.
186. Verbatim respondent 29.
187. Hatch and Cunliffe, *Organization Theory*, 258–59.
188. Hurley, "The Decision to Trust," para. 4.

The findings of my survey indicate that among people of professed faith or spirituality there is a sense that their spirituality grounds them and strengthens them. This grounding provides them with meaningfulness, vocational fulfillment, and joy. David McLean states, "Relational resonance, intentionality, and agility co-existed [in the stories he heard in his research]."[189] These are gifts which are honed and shaped over time. We can respond by inspiring environments with a culture that will allow this to occur. Wilfred Drath writes:

> The tasks of leadership [may be] articulated as setting direction, creating and maintaining commitment, and facing adaptive challenge. It is the need to accomplish these tasks that call forth leadership based on whatever principle people in the community or organization hold in common.[190]

Engaged, passionate and connected leaders hold people together in times of deep inflection, or turning points. However, this ethos has to exist long before inflection is encountered. While detailed and constant communication is critically helpful, there is not always an easy solution to workplace dilemmas. As stated earlier, a respondent stated:

> I learned a 'trade' but learned it is so much more than that. People rely on a person's expertise. Money was what drove me at first, but then I realized a sense of helping others in need. I have noticed lately that people are losing their sense of good or skilled workmanship [sic]. Instead, it's all about speed and price.[191]

This is a particularly poignant situation. Here is a self-employed craftsperson wrestling with changing marketplace perceptions of value. Such professions may no longer have a 'guild' that they can turn to for guidance and discussion. This presents a loss in terms of securing what could be valuable mentorship from fellow crafts-persons.

Where are we today in terms of spiritual conversations? The findings of my survey indicate that, largely, people are not aware of the opportunity or value associated with speaking with a minister or advisor regarding workplace challenges, or/and minsters do not approach people with offers of such conversations. Perhaps they lack the lexicon to have such a conversation. One respondent stated, "[I have had] annual visits

---

189. McLean, "Understanding Relational Agility," 90.
190. Drath, *The Deep Blue Sea*, 18–19.
191. Verbatim respondent 16.

with our church elders. These conversations help with applying our faith to our everyday lives."[192] Another respondent stated, "I can't say that I've had a conversation with a spiritual advisor that I can remember. I've studied a lot of spiritual material."[193] Largely, it seems, these conversations are few and far between. Meeks offers this:

> No household will survive without work. Unless what is necessary for human life is made available by human effort we cannot even speak of an economy. Work, moreover, far from being simply the means of producing what is necessary for life, is also a means of access to household and a means of shaping the household. Thus, a community constitutes itself in answering the questions, who gets what kind of work? Who owns the tools and product of work? . . . Some say that work is the deepest satisfaction of their lives and has made them who they are; others say that work has destroyed their health and their family life. Some say technology has overcome back-breaking work; others say machine work and the division of labour have caused social fragmentation and boring and demeaning work.[194]

What Meeks is getting at here is the type of conversation that might be approached from a spiritual perspective. If work is central to our lives, and those in ministry wish, indeed, to bring the message of the Gospel as a central element of our lives, then these elements must be connected explicitly, either through the messages delivered through our sermons, or through forms of workplace-related chaplaincy and ministry, perhaps especially to young adults. Other methods include activism, direct involvement with communities, for example engagement with LGBTQ+ groups or recent immigrant communities. Simple fellowship can be the starting point for deeper conversation. A respondent stated, "We are all broken. We are all in need of salvation. I'm able to give a little more grace to people and a little more grace to myself."[195] The findings of my survey indicate that acting our faith—being guided by our faith, may be the most important way to bring faith into our workplaces. Volf states:

> We will have to insist (against Thomas Aquinas, for instance) that perfect happiness does depend on the resurrected body. And if the concept of 'body' is not to become unintelligible by

---

192. Verbatim respondent 9.
193. Verbatim respondent 17.
194. Meeks, *God the Economist*, 127–28.
195. Verbatim respondent 2.

being indistinguishable from the concept of the 'pure spirit' we must also insist that 'external goods' are necessary to perfect happiness. The resurrection of the body demands a glorified but nevertheless material environment. The future *material* existence therefore belongs inalienably to the Christian eschatological expectation.[196]

Do leaders contemplate this eschatological dimension of work? A respondent cites a verse from Paul's letter to the Colossians (Col 4:24) and offers "My life is one of witness and testimony."[197] Scriptural accounts suggest that Paul, both before and following his experience on the road to Damascus, had always worked hard. Post his transformation he worked with new purpose. Work is part, arguably a critical part, of creation. Darrell Cosden writes:

> A theology of work is not merely a discussion of how one should carry out work, or a discussion of how to resolve specific difficulties and problems faced in the working world. This would essentially be an ethics of work. Nor it is a theology of work satisfied with only making theological comments about work as they arise within a discussion of some other point of doctrine. This would constitute a theological reflection on work. A theology of work is a much broader concept. It is a recent methodology developed for comprehensively exploring the phenomenon of work itself as part of created reality.[198]

So here at approximately the centre of this book we come to assert the heart of this work. Our gifts are divinely given—loaned to us if you will—and we are inspired to carry out the work that we are called to, with skills divinely loaned to us. Leadership is one of those gifts which we are called to perform virtuously, studiously, and compassionately. Volf confirms this when he writes, "Since a theology of work has normative ethical implications, its task is not merely to interpret the world of work in a particular way, but to lead the present world of work toward the promised and hoped-for transformation in the new creation."[199] This is a critical theological metanarrative that appears to be largely missing, or at least avoided, in postmodern environments. Yet, leadership is stewardship. Cosden writes, "A fundamental question is whether the gifts and

---

196. Volf, *Work in the Spirit*, 95 [emphasis original].
197. Verbatim respondent 27.
198. Cosden, *A Theology of Work*, 5.
199. Volf, *Work in the Spirit*, 82.

talents used by everyone in ordinary work are really the same as the specifically 'spiritual' gifts in the New Testament."[200] I believe they are. This was Moses' task. It was God's call that resulted in the enactment of Moses' practice of leadership. His was a practical theology. So it was also for Paul following his dramatic conversion. So it is now, for us. Craig Dykstra and Dorothy Bass write:

> Awareness of the possibility of a way of life shaped by a positive response to God pervades the Bible and Christian history—as do examples of the human tendency to fall short of God's invitation to such a life . . . It is vital that those who seek to walk in such a way learn to recognize the lived wisdom of Christian people over time and across cultures as a constructive resource.[201]

This walk, when fully understood and embraced fills us with the strength and encouragement of all the saints that walked before us. With a foundational premise of work as a response to God's call, and for leadership to be an enabler and facilitator of work as service to the Kingdom, leadership is a theological practice.

Focus on the Worker

Organizational humanism in the second half of the twentieth century, according to Wren, emerged to bring a "new focus on man [sic] and his [sic] varied needs, on work as a means of fulfillment, and on the process rather than the structure of activities."[202] Thus, by the 1960s, great thought was developing in terms of the *psychic* income of the worker. This issue of psychic income is significant. Lea Zagorin's research argues:

> [E]vidence to support that the residents of Chapel Hill, NC receive a positive psychic income from Carolina Athletics. Of particular interest is that psychic income sub-categories [included] pride from increased visibility, opportunities for social bonding, [and] civic pride . . . In conducting this study, I would suggest that the term 'psychic income' be renamed 'emotional impact.'[203]

---

200. Cosden, *A Theology of Work*, 5.
201. Dykstra and Bass, "A Theological Understanding," 16.
202. Wren, *Evolution of Management*, 445.
203. Zagorin, "Beyond Economic Impact," 49–52.

While Zagorin's research is focussed on the 'emotional impact' on a community of having a successful sports team, her work has relevance. Zagorin gives voice to the breadth of psychic income—emotional impact not only for the direct participant in a given endeavour, but to the entire community at large. Arguably, this concept holds true also for an emotionally healthy worker, in a respected enterprise, which in turn positively impacts an entire community. Hope becomes infectious.

A respondent stated: "I used to wear rose-coloured glasses and then get crushed when people weren't as justice minded or compassionate as I was."[204] Another respondent stated, "I have a quiet faith and hope I am humble in all my actions."[205] My research findings suggest that hope is stronger than lived experiences. Spirit-led leadership, both through words and actions, will give others freedom to explore and be guided by their own spirituality. Faithful contemplation will bring insight, and will lead us to the focal calling of leadership. Gene Veith writes:

> [O]ur relationship with God has nothing to do with our works, good or bad, and is, indeed, totally God's work, St. Paul continues, 'For we are his workmanship, created in Christ Jesus for good works, which God prepared beforehand, that we should walk in them' (2:10). By virtue of our creation, our *purpose* in life is to do good works, which God Himself 'prepared' for us to do... Our relationship to God, then, has nothing to do with our works. Our relationships to other people, though, in the world that God has placed us in, *do* involve our works.[206]

While I am not sure that I fully agree with everything Veith says, I accept his emphasis that God is always the first mover. The findings of my survey indicate that acting our faith and being guided by faith, rather than proselytizing, may be the most important way to bring faith into the workplace. A number of respondents echo the desire to bring their faith into their workplace, but may not know how to do so. Veith discusses the notion of giving and receiving in God's economic design when he writes:

> [I]f it is true that we are supposed to be dependent on other people, it is also true that other people are supposed to dependent on us. [This is] an active exchange: my gifts for yours; my

---

204. Verbatim respondent 2.

205. Verbatim respondent 21.

206. Veith, *God at Work*, 37–38 [emphasis original]. Harriet Ekperigin writes, "I see this as a very strict and unrealistic view and I am not entirely in agreement."

> vocation for your vocation. This is why St. Paul could make the seemingly harsh statement, 'If anyone is not willing to work, let him [sic] not eat' (cf. 2 Thess. 3:10).[207]

In simple vernacular language, Paul is saying, 'you have gifts; use them!' Leadership involves interdependency. This is what allows the leader to delegate. Veith points out that, "Our vocation is not one single occupation; we have callings in different realms—the workplace, yes, but also the family, the society, and the church . . . Callings change . . . Vocation is in the here and now.[208] This is a valuable statement, suggesting that 'calling' is not static but evolving. This is evidenced by several of the research respondents.

Spirituality in the Workplace

Maslow turns to the issue of spirituality in the workplace. He writes:

> Enlightened management is one way of taking religion seriously, profoundly, deeply and earnestly. Of course, for those who define religion just as going to a particular building on Sunday and hearing a particular kind of formula repeated, this is all irrelevant. But for those who define religion not necessarily in terms of the supernatural, or ceremonies, or rituals, but in terms of deep concern with the problems of human beings, with the problems of ethics, of the future of man [sic], then this kind of philosophy, translated into the work life, turns out to be very much like the new style of management and of organizations.[209]

The findings of my survey indicate that there is a wide range of perspectives in terms of what it means to be spiritual. A respondent stated, "I believe that my work's meaning is driven by my desire to contribute to others' growth and development. I am also deriving meaningfulness from volunteering.[210]

Ellul writes, "Man [sic] was made to do his [sic] daily work . . . but see him [sic] now, like a fly on flypaper, seated for eight hours, motionless

---

207. Veith, *God at Work*, 41.
208. Veith, *God at Work*, 47–49.
209. Maslow, *On Management*, 83.
210. Verbatim respondent 9. My own sense of meaning has been greatly shaped by volunteer work.

at a desk.[211] While working life, thankfully, may seldom be as dramatic or severe as Ellul portrays, often we are indeed captive to our circumstances. My research findings indicate that introducing places for interfaith dialogue and spiritual practices to occur may be useful. Miller and Ngunjiri write, "As a part of spirituality at work, corporate chaplaincy can be considered an extension or articulation of organizational leaders' perspectives on the integration of faith and work."[212] Simply providing an interfaith prayer room will make a difference. The Interfaith Room located in McMaster University's DeGroote School of Business' Ron Joyce Centre in Burlington, Ontario, Canada is a well-used facility by students of all faiths. It is a place for quiet contemplation and prayer, and I believe it brings a valuable message to future business leaders. Ellul writes:

> I believe in God's secret presence in the world. God sometimes leaves us in silence, but God always tells us to remember. That is, God recalls us to the world which God has spoken and which is always new if we rebuild the path from the word written to the world lived out and actualized. God is a God incognito who does not manifest in great organ music or sublime ceremonies but who hides in the surprising face of the poor, in suffering (as in Jesus Christ), in the neighbour I meet, in fragility.[213]

To this I would add the person on the subway, in the elevator, and across the hall. Many respondents expressed their belief in God and sought greater purpose in their work. At the same time, finding greater purpose frequently required economic sacrifice.

Cosden explores a threefold nature of work. He writes:

> [T]he normative theological understanding of work is best construed threefold as a dynamic inter-relationship of instrumental, relational, and ontological aspects. In fact herein lies a double hypothesis. The first part says that truly human work, i.e. work as it ought to be, is constituted with each of these three aspects (instrumental, relational, and ontological). They exist together in a mutual and interdependent relationship . . . The second part of the hypothesis, the part that will require particular attention theologically is that work is, and must be construed as, ontological.[214]

---

211. Ellul, *The Technological Society*, 322.
212. Miller and Ngunjiri, "Leadership View," 131.
213. Ellul, *Essential Spiritual Writings*, 21.
214. Cosden, *A Theology of Work*, 5.

From the beginning of recorded time, we know that to be human is to be a worker. We are anatomically and intellectually constructed to be workers. Instrumentally, work is designed around a product, either a profit-related product or a public good product. The relational element of work centres on the creation of a community, while the ontological element of work centres on the achievement of meaning and purpose.

Finding a way to bring spirituality to the workplace conversation, I argue, results in bringing everyone to their best. Thelma Hall writes, "Prayer can never be dissociated from our everyday life."[215] Many respondents confirm this. A respondent stated, "I believe that I am doing good works, utilizing God-given talents."[216] Another respondent stated, "We have been called upon to use our talents to the best of our ability."[217]

The platonic perspective is that, metaphysically, work—as a fundamental component of our worldly activities—is focussed on ends or purposes. With this in mind, this I argue that work is, indeed, teleological in nature. It is, in effect, relational, i.e. it has a future-oriented purpose, in other words the improvement of life. Thus, ontologically what may be viewed as the daily carrying out of our work has a teleological trajectory. Cosden argues for a more explicit and theologically shaped ontology of work. To work is a central part of our nature of being, and relationships are generally central to our nature of existing, therefore our work. There are very few professions that occur outside of relationships. Steven Covey affirms:

> There is one thing that is common to every individual, relationship, team, family, organization, nation, economy and civilization throughout the world—one thing, if removed, will destroy the most powerful government, the most successful business, the most thriving economy, the most influential leadership, the greatest friendship, the strongest character, the deepest love . . . On the other hand, if developed and leveraged, that one thing has the potential to create unparalleled success and prosperity in every dimension of life. Yet, it is the least understood, most neglected, and most underestimated possibility of our time . . . That one thing is trust.[218]

215. Hall, *Too Deep for Words*, 33.
216. Verbatim respondent 8.
217. Verbatim respondent 9.
218. Covey, *Speed of Trust*, 1. Harriet Ekperigin writes, "I 100% agree . . .as I read this quote, I was hoping that he had it right and that his conclusion was 'trust'. Thankfully, he did not disappoint."

Thus, while talent is critical to the success of any enterprise, it is trust—the ability to rely on, and relied on by, co-workers—that allows talent to be employed. This is a critical statement, as will be seen below.

Trust

Trust is both central and essential to relationship. There is at least one talented person that you have encountered that you do not trust.

How can this be remedied? Covey answers, "We *can* increase trust—much faster than we might think—and doing so will have a huge impact, both in the quality of our lives and in the results we're able to achieve."[219]

Trust is a foundational requirement for people to achieve meaningfulness. A respondent stated, "My work does provide a deep sense of meaningfulness. I find it very satisfying to know I have had a positive impact."[220] People will disagree. Sometimes disagreement is irreconcilable, arguably however, trust does not have to be lost. Disagreement does not have to descend into bitterness. Covey writes, "The number one reason people leave their job is a bad relationship with their boss."[221] Generally this is a trust issue. Such unsatisfactory relationships, frequently, are the catalyst for entrepreneurship. In other situations, a divine encounter strengthens a person and sustains them. A respondent stated, "I have a sense of meaningfulness, but it is not deep and has grown over time. I also experienced a stressful environment. As I walked into the fog and did all I could, God met me and journeyed with me." [222]

Trust in others can ameliorate stress. Groups of workers that act together as teams with a common goal overcome stress. Trust is an outcome of an environment that is ethical, caring and responsive.[223]

---

219. Covey, *Speed of Trust*, [emphasis original] 3.
220. Verbatim respondent 13.
221. Covey, *Speed of Trust*, 12.
222. Verbatim respondent 7.
223. As I write this, I read the story of Vancouver-based social media company *Hootsuite* which has backed out of a business relationship with the U.S. Immigration and Customs Enforcement (ICE) agency in response to vocal disagreement by a significant segment of the company's employees.

Wisdom and Divine Inspiration

Isaiah 11 presents wisdom and understanding as gifts of the Spirit. Contemplating wisdom as a divine endowment. Robert Sternberg offers this:

> [Wisdom is] the application of intelligence, creativity, and knowledge as mediated by values toward the achievement of a common good through a balance among (a) intrapersonal, (b) interpersonal, and (c) extrapersonal interests over the (a) short- and (b) long-terms, in order to achieve a balance among (a) adaption to existing environments, (b) shaping of existing environments, and (c) selection of new environments.[224]

Applying Sternberg's lens, we observe an entirely different perspective of a functional, Spirit-led leadership. It provides a constant process of guiding both individuals and groups from the present to the future, shaping both anticipation and preparation together with eagerness to move forward. Here then is another view of the characteristics of adaptive capacity, seen starkly in one respondent's description of changes in their given profession. This respondent stated, "I have noticed lately that people are losing their sense of 'good' or 'skilled' workmanship—instead it is all about speed and price."[225] Traditions are being eroded. It can be difficult to cope with the changes wrought. While the circumstance above may seem mundane, one may quickly realise that this observation goes to the heart of the respondent's sense of worth and purpose. Structural changes in society have pressed, at least for this respondent, workplace discussion toward narrow economic output (price) and success against narrow tangible metrics (speed). Here is an example where expectations are for a payoff resulting from gaining expertise in a craft appear unrealized in the way hoped for. These phenomena lead to the theory that most avoid a conversation regarding deeper matters, perhaps out of a desire to be polite, or of a sense of awkwardness, or a fear of conflict. The workplace generally, then, is not a place for a discussion of faith. It does not have to be this way. The findings of my survey indicate that introducing 'places' for interfaith and spiritual practices to occur may be useful, together with broad communication of recognition of multiple faith events. This may

---

224. Sternberg, "Foolishness," 331–52.
225. Verbatim respondent 16.

produce the impetus for broader discussions and sagacity around our responses to a changing marketplace.[226]

Henri Nouwen's entire corpus centres human engagement with the divine. He is focussed not only on his own travails, but also on those of whom he encounters. In a number of his works, Nouwen offers to us that his own faith walk often seems barren. Although his domain is quite different, he is contemplating circumstances that are similar to that of our contractor above. Nouwen's letters are to his nephew, who at the time of writing his work, was an eighteen-year-old. In these seven letters to Marc, Nouwen is, at the same time that he is assisting and nudging his nephew to find a moral compass in faith, exposing his nephew Marc—and us—to his own challenges in maintaining a strong and assured faith walk. Nouwen affirms:

> The spiritual life has to do with the heart of existence. This is a good word. By heart I do not mean the seat of our feelings as opposed to the seat of our thoughts; I mean the center of our being, that place where we are most ourselves, where we are most human.[227]

Nouwen is situating his ministry to Marc in the context of this young man's life. He is acting out his calling as a shepherd and as a spiritual guide to Marc in his affirmation that it is at the contemplative centre of our existence that we will find Jesus. It is at this contemplative centre that we will find our calling.

Nicholas Harvey offers insight into this. In the context of Moses' encounter with God in the burning bush, Harvey writes that, "Revelation opens up a new dimension of consciousness, while contemplation of the mystery makes it possible to live in that dimension."[228]

Nouwen is also asserting that prayer is the means of moving to this centre. Nouwen is encouraging his nephew to spend time secretly in the presence of God to allow his faith to mature away from the world. These pieces of advice are strongly reminiscent of Nouwen's use of polarities: in the world but not of the world, of downward mobility, of withdrawal and solitude. Nouwen is urging Marc to eschew the temptation to become

---

226. I recently spoke with a minister who is a retired long distance truck driver. He now spends a significant amount of his time at truck stops chatting with drivers about their challenges as their industry unfolds.

227. Nouwen, *Letters to Marc*, 5.

228. Harvey, "Revelation and Contemplation," 153.

well-known too quickly; risking hubris over humility. We may well ask whether humility is a leadership virtue at all when contemplated theologically. At Numbers 12:3, we read, "Now Moses was a very humble man, more humble than anyone else on the face of the earth." Many interpret this passage narrowly, suggesting that Moses is presented as humble *before God*, rather other humans. This does cause us to ask whether we can view humility as a leadership strength or a weakness. There are differing views on this. Some argue that in the canonical Hebrew Scriptures, the notion of humility was indeed defined in the narrow sense of humbling oneself before God, and not lowering oneself before others. Daniel 10:12, for example, presents the words of the Angel speaking to Daniel, saying, "Do not be afraid, Daniel. Since the first day that you set your mind to gain understanding and to humble yourself before your God, your words were heard, and I have come in response to them." It is argued by some, however, that the virtue of humility, prized in later Judaism and early Christianity—the lowering of oneself before an equal, does, indeed, find its roots in the Hebrew Scriptures. Sara Rushing emphatically states, "I argue that humility is a crucial political virtue that fortifies us and helps us resist disillusionment."[229] I agree with this perspective. We do know that Paul, in his first letter to the Corinthians, wrote, "For I am the least of the apostles and do not even deserve to be called an apostle, because I persecuted the church of God. But by the grace of God I am what I am, and his grace to me was not without effect. No, I worked harder than all of them—yet not I, but the grace of God that was with me." (1Co 15:9 NIV) Magnus Frostensen offers that, "humility involves joy in other peoples' success."[230] These are critical perspectives upon which to contemplate the deep value of developing leadership practices that are Spirit-led. This is mentorship.

Each of the thirty-two respondents who completed the questionnaires that, together, are critical to this work are very much normal individuals, in a range of professional pursuits in three countries. Each response reflects careers of earnest endeavour, fulfilling a goal for themselves, their loved ones, for the enterprises they are working with, for their communities and for civil society. Lyotard proposes:

> [N]o self is an island; each exists in a fabric of relations that is now more complex and mobile than ever before. Young or

---

229. Rushing, "Comparative Humilities: Christian, Contemporary, and Confucian Conceptions of a Political Virtue," 198.

230. Frostensen, "Humility in Business," 92.

> old, man or woman, rich or poor, a person is always located at 'nodal points' of specific communication circuits, however tiny these may be. Or better: one is always located at a post through which various kinds of messages pass. No one, not even the least privileged among us, is ever entirely powerless over the messages that traverse and position him [sic] at the post of sender, addressee, or referent.[231]

Lyotard's analogy of each 'self' being located at a nodal point is apt. The research respondents, like all of us, work in networks of communication pathways, reporting relationships, and shared tasks. They also are located in a network of shared hopes, fears, ambitions, needs, and aspirational goals. We each are enmeshed in numerous networks—they exist inside one's employment environment, one's family, one's community, one's professional affiliations, and so on. Each brings different and sometimes conflicting sets of hopes, fears, ambitions, and needs. A respondent stated, "I believe that God has designed each person uniquely with a role to play."[232] It is the task of leadership to *fit* a person in the role that allows them to fulfill their vocational call.[233] This can only be done if the leader truly knows each person.

Looking to a higher plane, society, in effect, is the cumulative result of the vocational endeavours of every one of its constituents. In the broadest sense, society functions on the backs of its workers. As Y. R. Simon writes:

> The daily life of man [sic] is composed of things whose meaning is in the mystery of their familiarity. Work is one of these. Other examples would be love, companionship, sincerity, honour, sport, ennui, and community-feeling.[234]

Each element of our existence both affects and is affected by the other. Flourishing, or the lack of flourishing, in one sphere affects the extent of our flourishing in all elements. Flourishing at work cascades to our entire existence. The converse is also true.

231. Lyotard, *The Postmodern Condition*, 15.

232. Verbatim respondent 1.

233. Harriet Ekperigin writes, "This reminds me of my role at a consulting firm 12 years ago where the endless possibilities were sold to me prior to accepting the job. Upon starting there, I was given meaningless work to do. My constant push for work that aligned with my skills, calling, and the promises made fell on deaf ears. I lasted a year and left when my soul couldn't bear anymore."

234. Simon, *Work, Society and Culture*, 1.

We have evolved to our current situation. Anthony Kenney and Geraldine Smyth observe that, "The century of the reformation . . . [Was] succeeded by two centuries of secularisation."[235] We can assume that secularization in the workplace followed this trend. It was science and technology that spawned a wave of industrial progress. Consider Johann Gutenberg's achievement in the development of the first metallic moveable type for a printing press.

Critical for my enquiry is the denouement of the substitution of machine power for human power in industries from hay-baling to robotic surgery; ushering in the era of economics, financial modelling, and capital formation together with management theory, and leadership as a profession. Wren points out:

> Pre-industrialized societies are characterized by low per capita income, economic stagnation, dependence on agriculture, a low degree of specialization of labour, and a widespread geographical integration of markets.[236]

These environmental changes brought about changes in society. Wren describes the emergence of "a willingness to innovate, to place trust in one's own capacity. And to perceive oneself as a thinking and emotion-feeling organism."[237] Concurrently, the farmer-entrepreneur was becoming the owner of a larger enterprise, requiring delegation of the oversight of the enterprise to professional managers. Efficiency, productivity, sound use of capital and profitability were the new overarching requirements. By the early nineteenth century, Britain saw the emergence of texts devoted to management theory. These texts focussed on maximizing quantity and quality of work, repairing equipment and managing costs. Wren points out that a new challenge quickly emerged. He states, "The Labour problem . . . broadly [has] three aspects: recruitment, training, and discipline."[238] Customs of craft were being replaced by "punctuality, regular attendance, supervision, and the mechanical pacing of work effort."[239] The beginning of the erosion of long-standing traditions was under way. This may be more extreme today. A respondent stated, "I have noticed

---

235. Kenny and Smyth, *Secularism and Secularisation*, 317.
236. Wren, *Evolution of Management*, 37.
237. Wren, *Evolution of Management*, 39.
238. Wren, *Evolution of Management*, 47.
239. Wren, *Evolution of Management*, 50.

lately that people are losing their sense of good or skilled workmanship [sic]—instead it's all about speed and price."[240]

Interestingly, in the early years of the industrial revolution in Britain, a key method for creating a new workplace ethos was the *in-situ* teaching of religious morals and values. Wren writes:

> The encouragement of moral education, even on company time and in early company towns, reading of the 'good book,' regular church attendance, and exhortation to avoid the deadly sins of laziness, sloth, and avarice were methods of inculcating in the working population the right habits of industry.[241]

We could argue, however, that these efforts were aimed less at the promulgation of human flourishing, but more at the assurance of discipline on the shop floor. Of further interest is that some argued against buying the most expensive machines while hiring the cheapest labour, making virtually no investment in the human resources of the enterprise.

By the middle of the twentieth century, several voices were being raised in criticism of the "neglect of a focus on the nature of work and the satisfactions in work for man [sic]."[242] While some articulated a "*Protestant ethic* [that] saw work as an end in itself, not necessarily to be enjoyed but to serve as a sign of election and a means to achieving the grace of God."[243] It appears that Wren suggests an interpretation of 'toil' as the path to salvation, rather than seeing our work as a contribution to God's Kingdom. Critics such as Karl Marx had seen the industrial revolution as an "imposition of power of the exploiting capital class upon the working class."[244] The emerging modern era developed a "view of work, of man [sic], and how to achieve organizational harmony by designing organizations to allow expression of what was assumed to be a natural urge to find satisfaction in work."[245] Thus, this was a realization that people need to be motivated. According to the results of my survey, however, conversations of faith appear unwelcome. A respondent stated: "I seek first if there is

---

240. Verbatim respondent 16.
241. Wren, *Evolution of Management*, 52.
242. Wren, *Evolution of Management*, 444.
243. Wren, *Evolution of Management*, 444 [emphasis original].
244. Wren, *Evolution of Management*, 444.
245. Wren, *Evolution of Management*, 445.

room for the conversation, [but] I barely hear the word God, let alone discussion about who Jesus is."[246]

Conclusion

This chapter has examined and drawn from the fields of economics, organization theory, ethics, pastoral theology and leadership theory both from an historical and contemporary perspective. These fields are viewed through the lens of societal change, and dramatic change in workplace structure. There has been a deliberate interpretation of the interdisciplinary dynamics that have shaped and continue to shape the workplace, in the sense that the instruction given by one domain of practice has been interpreted through the language of another field of study. The interaction between these domains, woven together with the grounded theory developed by the qualitative research undertaken, has resulted in a specific, adaptive, framework for Spirit-led leadership. Thus, what will be harnessed in the next chapter will be leadership practices that are the encompassing engagement of multiple techniques—methods of procedure in planning, equipping, executing, motivating, assessing, rewarding and correcting that comprise the task of leadership.

This examination captures leadership fully within a spiritual construct that creates a cohesion between workplace behaviours and those moral principles that should govern and inspire such behaviours. Power becomes yoked with nurturing. Work becomes joyful, even when it involves toil. From this an assertion is made that leadership should be perceived as having the spiritual depth required to imbue an organization with its ethos—the organization's ethical and distinguishing characteristics. Work is restored as a part, perhaps the central part, of God's created order.

---

246. Verbatim respondent 6.

4

Spiritual Leadership in a Secular World

The greatest among you will be your servant. For whoever exalts himself will be humbled, and whoever humbles himself will be exalted.

(MAT 23:1 NIV)

ORGANIZATIONAL LEADERSHIP IN THE postmodern era appears to be focussed significantly, but not only, on the expedient imperatives of organizational structure; driven by output-related metrics. As Gustafson writes, "[T]he postmodern ethicist does not spend so much energy coming up with a universal system of ethics as with coming up with local rules that can work and be agreed to."[1] I do believe there is risk that leadership may be frequently lacking what is right or effective in terms of creating broadly an environment for human flourishing. Stott writes, "Our model of leadership is often shaped more by culture than by Christ. Yet many cultural models of leadership are incompatible with the servant imagery taught and exhibited by the Lord Jesus."[2] This observation is certainly underscored by many of the testimonies provided by research respondents presented here, together with several perspectives offered by those who have kindly reviewed this work prior to its publication.

---

1. Gustafson, "Making Sense of Postmodern Business Ethics," 652.
2. Stott, *Basic Christian Leadership*, 113.

Spiritual Leadership in a Secular World

This chapter presents a practice of leadership that reflects Jesus' message to his disciples. Shaped by research, I assert that leaders who are of Christian faith must be leaders of people of all faiths as well as those of no professed faith. These are what Thiessen calls "religious nones,"[3] a term which I do not perceive as pejorative, but rather a reflection of reality. The common ground is modelling and assuring ethical behaviour: deeper engagement with, and care for the other person. Leaders can make a massive difference simply by assuring an ethical, responsive and caring workplace. The foundation for such behaviour is love. Paul Ramsey states:

> Christian love is the source from which men [sic] learn to *attribute* value to human persons. From Christian love, men [sic] have life and have it abundantly (John 10:10). The creation and preservation of community is in fact the same thing as persistent attribution of worth to another human being.[4]

To underscore a point already made, management is about organization of work, assignment of work, selection of the worker, communication of tasks, and measurement of the results of work. Leadership; more acutely Spirit-led leadership, may well include all these roles but, above all of them, leadership is about *ethos*. Miller and Ngunjiri assert:

> Spiritual leadership taps into the fundamental needs of both leader and follower for spiritual survival so they become more organizationally committed and productive . . . This entails creating a vision where organizational members experience a sense of calling, and establishing a social/organizational culture based on altruistic love whereby leaders and followers have genuine care, concern, and appreciation for both self and others.[5]

This chapter is about practices of Spirit-led leadership. In this chapter I bring into focus a number of leadership activities and imperatives. These are enumerated under the key elements of my grounded theory articulated earlier, as follows:

Responding to Desire for Purpose and Meaningfulness; Leaders Should:

- Be focussed on ethos.

---

3. Thiessen, *Meaning of Sunday*, 94.
4. Ramsey, *Basic Christian Ethics*, 246 [emphasis original].
5. Miller and Ngunjiri, "Leadership View," 131.

- Be forgiving.
- Be trustworthy.
- Maintain high levels of communication.

Recognizing the Person; Leaders Should:

- Recognize the ways that work impacts lives.
- Nurture workers.
- Be mentors.
- Recognize and celebrate good work.

Upholding Values and Lived Experiences; Leaders Should:

- Have the words of their mission and values in front of them every morning.
- Encourage dissenting views.
- Align work expectations with values.
- Exercise discernment.
- Focus on legacy.

Responding to Changing Ethics; Leaders Should:

- Identify Power Dynamics
- Advocate for workers.
- Be students of organizational structure.
- Build community.
- Respond to disruptive market forces.

Espousing Spirituality and Hope; Leaders Should:

- Respond to errors in a way that is restorative.
- Create conversations.
- Choose words prayerfully.
- Allow faith to guide.
- Retain humility.
- Be present.

Promoting Fairness, Equity, and Justice; Leaders Should

- Reflect constantly on the assurance of justice and fairness.
- Recognize and correct corrupt behaviour.
- Be hospitable.
- Confront destructive situations.
- Consult, and then act.
- Remove inequities.

These topics are about the obligations and challenges of leadership. These are all elements of *Spirit-led* leadership.

I begin by offering that *the right to spiritual fulfillment in one's labour is a social justice issue*. Ruth Yeoman declares:

> Work is either a source of expressive human action . . . fulfilled in a correctly ordered society which enables all persons to do decent, humane and dignified work; or it is an experience of oppressive degradation, from which we must escape . . . Meaningful work is a fundamental human need because it satisfies our inescapable interests in being able to experience the constitutive values of autonomy, freedom and dignity.[6]

Leadership, if it is about ethos, must champion and exemplify social justice, specifically fair and just treatment for all. Drath introduces a particularly important principle. Drath asks:

> When there is shared work among people who make sense of that work from differing worldviews, how can those people accomplish the leadership tasks while holding their differing worldviews as equally worthy and warrantable?[7]

Drath's answer to this question includes the requirement that "Differing worldviews are held as equally worthy."[8] At its core this admonition is an exemplification of the demand for social justice in the workplace. This is missional. Achieving purpose and meaning in the workplace will change entire communities. Phipps writes that God is "nudging us into alertness, to take notice and respond."[9] Dietrich Bonhoeffer lays it bare

---

6. Yeoman, "Conceptualizing Meaningful Work," 235–36.
7. Drath, *The Deep Blue Sea*, 125.
8. Drath, The Deep Blue Sea, 131.
9. Phipps, *God on Monday*, 27.

when he writes, "One is distressed by the failure of *reasonable* people to perceive either the depths of evil or the depths of the holy. With the best of intentions they believe that a little reason will suffice them to clamp together the parting timbers of the building."[10] We need to be cautious that we may be taking an early step onto a slippery slope in the decisions and choices that we make. In other words, *the words of our mission and values should be in front of us every morning* to remind us of our fundamental obligation to see that the values and mission that underpin our actions and decisions will be pristine. A respondent stated, "I changed careers 16 years ago to start a [new] business. It has become my calling. It can be scary and overwhelming at times. All my efforts and funds go into the business. My workers and family are my peers."[11] This straightforward statement represents the pinnacle of ethics-driven leadership. We are exhorted to be a light to the world (cf. Matt 5:14–16). We are called to let our faith be experienced by others through our actions, decisions, and by the way we come alongside them as we move forward together.

Badrinarayan Shanker Pawer discusses Southwest Airlines' initiative to adopt spiritual values in its culture. Pawer provides:

> [T]he relationship between employee experiences of altruistic love which includes spiritual values and resulting development in the employees of the aspects of spiritual leadership can also suggest that spiritual values of an organization can induce positive or spiritually oriented behaviours from employees in the organization.[12]

The majority of respondents to the research questionnaire supporting this work make reference to faith or spirituality, and go on to articulate how their faith orientation is interwoven with their work and their feelings about work. Those respondents who assert having no faith orientation also articulate a focus on ethics and care for others. So it must be. They seek meaningfulness in their work. They seek avoidance of conflict. They value the opinions of others. Grenz offers:

> For Christians, faith is by nature immediate. It arises out of the human encounter with the person of God in Christ, mediated by the community's testimony to the divine revelation in Jesus. Personal faith, therefore, is our response to the call of God,

---

10. Bonhoeffer, *Ethics*, 67 [emphasis original].
11. Verbatim respondent 8.
12. Pawar, "Leader Spiritual Behaviours toward Subordinates," 42.

which involves participation in the believing community. Personal faith extends to all aspects of our psyche. It includes our intellect. In the faith-response we accept as true certain assertions concerning reality, and as a result we view the world in a specific way. Faith includes our will. It entails the volitional commitment of ourselves to another—to the God revealed in Jesus Christ—and consequently we enter into a commitment with the disciples of Jesus. And faith includes the emotions, for it is the heartfelt love for the one who saves us, which translates into affection for others.[13]

This affection is offered unconditionally. Grenz affirms that for people of expressed faith, there is a vocational imperative in the way that they carry out their work, and treat their co-workers. Grenz also speaks of volition and emotion. We experience distortion when we perceive a lack of alignment between our values and our lived experiences. This is evident in the narratives presented by the respondents to my research questionnaire. Such experiences call for us as leaders to invest ourselves completely in the work that we do. I present leadership as both a divine gift and a sacred obligation to be exercised in a demeanour of servanthood. A critical element of this is the *recognition of persons*. We are called to create an environment where people will flourish, and where applicable, enable people of faith to experience harmony between their faith and their work. If people deepen their faith as a result of their work experiences, that is the work of the Spirit. Ira Sankey writes a wonderful story which illustrates this:

> One day, while the children in a Mission Chapel were singing 'One more day's work for Jesus,' a woman passing by stopped outside to listen. She went home with this words fixed in her mind. The next day, the words of the hymn came to her again and aroused the question, 'Have I ever done one day's work for Jesus in all my life?' That marked the turning point. Then and there she began to work for Jesus . . . A new light came into her life.[14]

For me, the poignancy of this story is that the children singing in the church were not even aware of the woman's existence. It was the Spirit that used their work to reach this woman. So it will be with our leadership as the Spirit moves. This is crucial. This wonderful, simple story exemplifies

---

13. Grenz, *Theology for the Community of God*, 8.
14. Sankey, *Sankey's Story of the Gospel*, 160.

the mystery of God's action. Paul Johnson introduces a fictional situation in which the Holy Spirit enters the life of a corporate CEO. He writes:

> Rare were the times when you actually listened to your workers. At Board of Directors meetings you looked at those around you. They were all men. You gave the impression of listening to them, but you knew what you wanted to do before the meeting began. You had already decided . . . Apparently you really listened to the lunchroom group . . . Most employees 'worked' for you, but after listening to the folks at the lunchroom table you felt you were actually working with them to solve a problem.[15]

To paraphrase Johnson, Grace had entered the room, just as Grace entered the life of the woman in Sankey's story. God calls to us in the secular world—the temporal earthly world. Grace *demands* that we do what is right and proper. This is not a negotiation. It is an absolute requirement. Phipps writes:

> [Moses] goes away to Midian, and there a whole welter of experiences is churning in his mind—a sense of social responsibility, a sense of despair at those for whom he feels responsible, a realisation that he has set about it wrongly . . . Though he is not yet aware of it, in and through all that is pressing upon him, God is *speaking*, raising his awareness. Thus, when he goes off into the desert and comes upon the burning bush, he is already alerted and aware. Here, a purely secular phenomenon arrests his attention. 'I will turn aside,' he says, 'and see this great sight.' God called him out of the bush, 'Moses, Moses.' Alerted by the secular to its inner significance—the ethical outrage of his people's bondage, and his own responsibility in the face of it—he is now ready for God's personal call.[16]

As alluded to earlier, this is divine revelation leading to contemplation, in this case contemplation of what will culminate in the leading of a people in bondage to nationhood.

---

15. Johnson, *Grace for the Workplace*, 43.
16. Phipps, *God on Monday*, 19.

Justice and Fairness

Jesus said, "Blessed are those who hunger and thirst for righteousness."[17] A critical early step in Spirit-led leadership is espousing Justice and Fairness. A respondent stated, "I have always questioned my salary. I have been put in a position of being taken advantage of, reducing my drive and loyalty."[18] The assurance of justice and fairness is critical. Its absence has a direct, negative effect on productivity. Justice requires confronting corrupt behaviour. Among the various interpretations of the word 'corrupt' are: to break; change from a sound condition to an unsound one; spoiled; contaminated. If an awareness of the spiritual dimension of one's daily economic endeavour has been lost, a restorative response is required. Restorative effort should begin by understanding the root causes of corruption of the environment in which we find ourselves. Restoration brings new hope.[19] The findings of my survey indicate that hope is stronger than actual lived experiences.[20] Ignoring people does not just dampen hope. It is a fundamental injustice. Gerald Blakely et al. assert:

> Organizational Citizenship Behaviours may include helping a co-worker who has been absent from work, volunteering for extra duty when needed, representing the company enthusiastically at public functions, and acting in ways that improve morale, and resolving unconstructive interpersonal conflict . . . Perceptions of fairness tapped into employee beliefs about the fairness of [employees'] social and economic exchanges with organizations. If exchanges were deemed fair, the employees

---

17. Matt 5:6.

18. Verbatim respondent 19.

19. Thus, while restitution may be required, it is *restoration* that is preeminent.

20. A poignant example of this occurred at the end of a lecture that I had given to a second year undergraduate commerce class, just about two weeks before exams. There were some two hundred and fifty students seated in a steeply banked auditorium. The goal of the lecture, among other things, was to inspire these young people to be encouraged, dedicated in their studies, and prepared for the world. The lecture continued as an encouragement to seek one's own path, concluding by affirming that every human being is a unique and special person. My time came to an end and I made my way out of the auditorium, looking at my watch and thinking about where I needed to be next. As I made my way to the exit, a student moved into my path and asked me a question. The student went on to say that she did not feel very special, and became quite emotional. I knew right away that nothing else in my day mattered more than stopping to talk with her. I saw her. We stood there together in the entrance to the lecture hall for some time. She told me about her studies, her aspirations, and her challenges, for which I shall always be grateful.

would be more likely to reciprocate the fairness by performing in ways that benefit the organization.[21]

Thus fairness engenders *hope*. Hope is ignited when we notice people. Buber writes:

> When I confront a human being as my You and speak the basic word I-You to him [sic], then he [sic] is no thing among things nor does he [sic] consist of things. He [sic] is no longer He or She, limited by other Hes and Shes, a dot in the world grid of space and time, nor a condition that can be experienced and described, a loose bundle of named qualities. Neighbourless and seamless he [sic] is You and fills the firmament. Not as if there were nothing but he [sic]; but everything else lives in his [sic] light.[22]

I think that Buber is saying, fundamentally, that when we see another person as a whole, uninjured, sound, complete, human being—truly an entire person rather than an object—they *become* a whole person: an 'I' rather than an 'it.' Butler-Bass provides an important addition to the concept of wholeness.[23] She writes that that the Latin root of the word salvation is "*salvus*, meaning 'whole,' 'sound,' 'healed,' 'safe,' 'well,' or 'unharmed.'"[24] These are the outcomes of being seen—being raised to full personhood. Thus *seeing* people is a critical and fundamental act of leadership. It is, perhaps, among the first acts of leadership. When another person realizes that we have seen them, we are going to notice an overwhelming, and almost instantaneous, change in that person's entire demeanour. I invite you to try this today. Robert Gibbs introduces a powerful additional thought here. He writes, "To become 'I' is to become responsible."[25] What Gibbs may be suggesting is that as we *recognize* someone, we also draw them into full stature. In so doing we equip, and at the same time *obligate*, them to be in full participation with us as-co-leaders. They become fully accountable. Thomas Hobbes essentially underscores this when he asserts, "A person is he [sic] whose words or

---

21. Blakely et al, "The Moderating Effects of Equity Sensitivity," 259–60.

22. Buber, *I and Thou*, 59.

23. Tim Arnill writes, "A core part of Verity's service philosophy is that every person who walks through our doors has their own story to tell and it is incumbent on us to help them build and tell that story. You cannot accomplish this if you do not truly 'see' the other person."

24. Butler Bass, *Christianity after Religion*, 183.

25. Gibbs, *Why Ethics*, 331.

actions are considered as his [sic] own."[26] We may interpret this as inferring that to be a *person* is to be responsible.

In fully seeing, as leaders we are also uplifted by the testimony of those we encounter. We learn to listen deeply to testimonies, and to respond to them with affection and intensity.[27] We are reminded that everyone has a story, and every story deserves to be heard.[28] In a world where we seem to have little time to engage in a conversation, *hearing* is paired with *seeing*. A respondent stated, "I don't offer my opinions unless asked, but will discuss my viewpoints openly."[29]

Here is another outcome of learning to see whole people. The people that we see, as they become whole people in front of us, take up space in our lives that we may have previously risked filling with our own self-importance. We act our faith. As the findings of my survey indicate, acting our faith—being guided by our faith, may be the most important way to bring faith into the workplace. When we exercise *discernment*, though we may not articulate it, we bring our faith to work. In simple terms, we lead by our example. Rosemary Vogt adds another dimension of the impact of *seeing* people. She writes emphatically:

> Spiritual well-being and loneliness are easily overlooked by supervisors . . . Now there is a growing body of empirical research showing spiritual approaches can influence the workplace, impacting employee well-being, organizational performance and profitability.[30]

Simply seeing people fully; acknowledging them and recognizing their work, leads to uplifting restoration of purpose and, indeed, being. This is at the heart of the 'master-apprentice' relationship, where the master craftsperson instructs, guides and works alongside the apprentice, until

---

26. Hobbes, *Leviathan*, 126.

27. Harriet Ekperigin writes, "My last name 'Ekperigin' literally means 'a story to tell' I am reminded of this when I meet new colleagues and they are intrigued by my last name, it often leads to us sharing stories about the paths we have taken to get to where we are now. This always opens an opportunity to build relationships."

28. When told this, a student once said to me, "Oh come on; not everyone's story is worth listening to!"

29. Verbatim respondent 22. Tim Arnill writes, "perhaps one of the misconceptions in business is that your relative position on the organization chart does not determine your value as an employee or your worth as a human being. Seeing everybody in the organization as equal human beings goes a long way towards creating an environment where individuals can flourish."

30. Vogt, "Workplace Loneliness," 24.

that apprentice is ready, in turn, to become a master craftsperson in their own right, and the cycle repeats itself. Pawer adds a broader perspective, stating that, "Spiritual values of an organization can induce positive or spiritually oriented behaviours from employees in the organization."[31]

If we are to spend the greatest portion of our days at work it is impossible to separate the various purposes for which we work from our fundamental cooperative role in the narrative of redemption. A respondent stated, "I learned a 'trade' but learned that it is so much more than that." [32] Work experiences impact our lives.[33] When work is aligned with one's values, these experiences have forceful positive effect.

Leadership will sometimes involve saying no, regardless of the cost. However, it does not require belligerence. Jesus says, "Let your word be 'Yes, Yes' or 'No, No.'" (cf. Mt. 5:37). Leadership requires no oaths, rather it calls for deep contemplation of potential outcomes of one's considered actions and words. We must *exercise discretion*. Prayerful choice of words is paramount. Rowan Williams offers this:

> We haven't understood Jesus' warning that we shall be called to account for every word we waste (Matthew 12:36)—which presumably means every word that does not in some way contribute to the building up of myself and my neighbour as persons maturing in the life of grace.[34]

---

31. Pawar, "Leadership Spiritual Behaviours Toward Subordinates," 442.

32. Verbatim respondent 17.

33. During the writing of this work, I received a telephone call from a colleague and former student who is agonizing over the manner in which his employer recently terminated a fellow employee—in a way that the person's self-esteem was left in shreds. We cannot run away from these situations. The findings of my survey indicate that dissonance; mild to severe, is a frequent theme. Here is a situation where this individual is completely arrested by what he has witnessed. I learned that Leaders need to correct missteps. As a securities regulator, participating in adjudicative panels, I found, with a reasonably high degree of accuracy, that my colleagues and I could work our way backwards through the financial transactions given in evidence in cases of alleged malfeasance, to arrive at the specific moment when the wrong path was taken. Our task then was to determine the cause for the path taken from that point forward to the issue that brought the respondent in front of the tribunal. Had this been a deliberate act? Had it been negligence, or a really bad, unfortunate, error? Why had someone in the organization not played out in their minds the probable outcome from the path that was being chosen? This may be an example of malfeasance through disengagement or ennui.

34. Williams, *Silence and Honey Cakes*, 76.

Capital markets regulators speak of the *guiding minds* of an organization. These minds are there to guide! Guiding calls for a discipline, figuratively, of 'standing' some significant amount of time beyond a critical decision before it is made. We can ask ourselves 'is this still making sense?' This is a time of fundamental opportunity to reflect and to *uphold our values*. Yet we see, time after time, the evidence that this really important work is not done. People stumble from one bad decision to another when foresight is missing. The result is confusion and lost direction.

For the most part there is little expression from the respondents on how to change or improve their environments, although they were not specifically asked for such commentary. There are occasions when concern is expressed by someone further 'down' in an organization, but they do not speak up for whatever reason, sometimes fear, or simply the view that no one will listen. Frequently it is simple disengagement that causes people not to speak up. It can take courage and the inspiration to act. We should be willing to draw out and embrace contrary perspectives around the table when key decisions are being contemplated. We must seek out the positive deviants, and invite their action in solving an issue. Bennis writes, "Leaders embrace error; Leaders encourage reflective backtalk; Leaders need people around them who have contrary views—who can tell them the difference between what is expected and what is really going on."[35] By *encouraging dissenting views* we can move toward resolution of dissonance.

We often describe those that have a laser-like vision on a future unseen by others as brilliant, or visionary. Leonard Doohan describes this as, "seeing beyond the immediate."[36] This may be a *learned* brilliance through the practice of *discernment*—recognizing new approaches through contemplative practice. This practice can be institutionalized. The work of the Spirit may bring forward the courage to be brilliant (cf. Matt 5:14–15). A respondent stated, "Most people either believe in nothing, or believe in something so rigid and prescriptive that there is no point in discussing it."[37] If we are to invite discussion, we must choose our words prayerfully. A nurturing approach opens the possibility for meaningful dialogue, and for brilliance. This also deepens the opportunity for dialogue regarding factors of work that encourage perceptions of meaningfulness. Further, such dialogue amplifies awareness and

---

35. Bennis, *On Becoming a Leader*, 190–91.
36. Doohan, *Spiritual Leadership*, 85.
37. Verbatim respondent 24.

cognizance of the spiritual orientation of coworkers. A respondent stated, "My faith enables me to see all as equals, full of potential gifts that need to be exercised in order for them to find deeper reward."[38]

Sooner or later, a great number of us seek to answer the questions: How might we know what to do with the days that have been given us? May we find sanctification in our work? In what way will we be held to account for that work? What will be our *legacy*?[39] Some find these questions daunting, because deep reflection is required.

Deep Focus on Ethos

Maintaining a focus on the ethos of the organization in all situations leads to even-handedness and ultimately greater trust. Ethical considerations become strategic. Tracy Wilcox writes:

> Within organizations, accounting and financial control systems are seen as the legitimate definers of reality. The logic of accounting can be seen to dominate organizational thinking, and ground much of management action. It is embedded in organizational life to the extent that it is rarely questioned. One of the more significant manifestations of this changing set of values is the growing short-term imperatives faced by many managers. In corporations, this has risen partially in responses to demands from increasingly influential investors, as well as fears of hostile takeovers. For public sector organizations, this short-termism has reflected political considerations and shifting ideologies. Within organizations themselves, new ethical issues have arisen. These include the dilemmas associated with downsizing, executive remuneration, the outsourcing of work, the employment of contractors, [and] sourcing of materials.[40]

Resulting dilemmas have consequences. A respondent stated, "I was given HR responsibilities that afforded me the opportunity to learn and grow. It also means firing people although it was always difficult. It was done as kindly as possible."[41] Change is, by design, disruptive, sometimes to the point of fracture. Our personal reputations as leaders will be built, or destroyed, at points of inflection—moments when we must respond

---

38. Verbatim respondent 6.
39. The concept of legacy, for me, has become an overarching imperative as I age.
40. Wilcox, "Ethics as Strategic Thinking," 75–76.
41. Verbatim respondent 3.

to, and sometimes introduce, disruptive events.⁴² Inflection is described as a turning point. Turning points come in many forms—some chosen, some imposed. These moments can occur in the form of turning back when we realize that we are on the wrong path and need to get back to the place where the decision was made so that we can choose the right path (cf. Jer 6:16).⁴³ Such times frequently require separating ourselves in order to spend time in deep reflection. Leadership decisions become clear in solitude. Jesus chose solitude many times. Stepping aside to find time for *reflection* is critical.

Inflection points may require us to be a change agent. This is a frequent demand on leaders. Change can bring violence, either in the form of an inward struggle to cope with change, or sometimes an outward violence⁴⁴ that seeks to halt, or reverse the change.

Change, especially significant change, can be perceived as a betrayal of a psychological, if not a real contract. Elizabeth Wolfe Morrison and Sandra L. Robinson describe this. They write:

> Psychological contracts, made up of employees' beliefs about the reciprocal obligations between them and their organization, lay at the foundation of employment relationships (Rousseau, 1989; Schein, 1965). Yet a variety of trends—restructuring, downsizing increased reliance on temporary workers, demographic diversity, and foreign competition—are having profound effects on employees' psychological contracts.⁴⁵

Thus, while legally contractual elements of the employer-employee relationship may be unaffected, "perceived promises . . . where a *promise* is defined as any communication of "future intent"⁴⁶ may be considered as violated. Thus a perceived reduction or removal of "socioemotional elements such as loyalty and support"⁴⁷ could be viewed as a betrayal. Organizational changes that encompass degrees of restructuring, even

---

42. A colleague who had a long career in her chosen vocation, described being let go by her employer. She described the dark day when she was handed an envelope and told that, after some three decades, her services were no longer required. My colleague handled that day with grace and dignity.

43. In my experience, these 'wrong-path' realizations usually occur around two A.M.

44. This can bring deep division, sometimes devolving into threats and bullying.

45. Morrison and Robinson, "When Employees Feel Betrayed," 226.

46. Morrison and Robinson, "When Employees Feel Betrayed," 228.

47. Morrison and Robinson, "When Employees Feel Betrayed," 229.

those which we may consider minor, require that *we must focus on ethos, maintain high levels of communication, and retain humility.* Even with such deep focus, encamped points of view may emerge. Micro-aggression may develop and escalate into full-blown intimidation.

Times of inflection can be searing experiences. They can also require what is perhaps a key cognitive discipline upon which self-awareness grows. This discipline is reflection and contemplation. Hall writes, "*Contemplation* is variously described as a 'resting' in God, or a loving gaze upon him, or a knowing beyond knowing, or a rapt attention to God."[48] Contemplative practice may be a path to a deeper understanding of the ethos we are called to uphold. Our language, demeanour, tone and cadence are all outward manifestations of our inner self-regulation and reflection. A respondent states, "I find myself challenged from time to time on specific incidents, and I pray most nights that I am making the right/best decisions."[49] Spirit-led leaders that navigate through inevitable inflection points by using this mechanism of self-regulation, founded in prayer, will be noticed for their caring, moral judgment and stability (cf. Neh 8: 9–12). They will be followed.

If we accept that leadership is, before anything else, about ethos, can we tie our analysis of corporate financial results to ethos? Financial analysts can find trace evidence of concern about ethos in elements of the valuation of corporations. There are many approaches to enterprise valuation, many of them building off the standard discounted cash flow model—in other words, what are the future returns from the enterprise and how should those returns be valued in today's dollars? This is known in financial terms as calculating 'Net Present Value' (NPV). Analysts look at stock price to book ratios, price to earnings ratios, price to sales ratios, price to earnings before interest, taxes, depreciation and amortization (EBITDA) ratios, *beta*[50] comparisons and price to you-name-it ratios. Studying the difference between the accounting enterprise value of a publicly traded company and its total market capitalization, investors make buy or sell decisions based on a perceived future that is better (or worse) than the present situation of a company. Responsible Investing (RI) adds a dimension to this. RI is a movement that espouses the incorporation of environmental, social and governance factors and embeds

48. Hall, *Too Deep for Words*, 9.
49. Verbatim respondent 18.
50. Beta is a measure of a stock's volatility relative to the market.

these criteria in investment decisions. Thomas Berry writes, "[The] dominant profit motivation of the corporation endeavour [must] be replaced with a dominant concern for the integral life of a community."[51] Arguably, primary focus on community will bring in its wake reasonable and deserved profits.

In effect, the analytical approach used by the RI community creates what we might call a *value to ethos ratio*. Such analysis shines a light, in effect, on the enduring ability of leadership to make the proverbial whole bigger than the sum-of-the-parts. We can find evidence of this when the current market price seems to elude all of the tried-and-true valuation calculations, for better or worse. There is an improvement, or deterioration, in value that we cannot fully explain mathematically. How the company conducts itself may provide the answer.

As leaders rediscover the importance of faith as a centering of understanding of their calling and, in turn its effect on ethos, a new epistemology becomes apparent. Indeed, Mitroff and Denton assert that "at our current stage of human development, we face a new challenge. We have gone too far in separating the key elements. We need to integrate spirituality into management. No organization can survive for long without spirituality and soul."[52] *Advocacy*, at its most foundational level, is a critical underpinning of Spirit-led leadership. Deepening employee participation is advocacy. Creating teams, supporting those teams with budgets to undertake community initiatives that are both internally and externally focussed, and then incorporating the products of those initiatives into business strategy, is advocacy.

A focus on ethos involves myriad elements of work. Thus leadership involves complexity. Complex challenges require complex thinking. Roger Martin writes:

> As comforting as simplification can be, however, it impairs every step of the integrative thinking process. It encourages us to edit out salient features rather than consider the question of salience broadly. Editing, in turn, leads to unsatisfactory resolution of the dilemma that business throws at us . . . Simplification makes us favour linear, unidirectional causal relationships, even if reality is more complex and multidirectional.[53]

---

51. Berry, *The Great Work*, 118.
52. Mitroff and Denton, "Study of Spirituality," para. 10.
53. Martin, *The Opposable Mind*, 76–77.

Though Martin does not say it, I suggest that integrative thinking demands attention to the spiritual. The Spirit-led leader calls on prayer. Stevens adds, "Pray continuously to be in constant communication with the Guide."[54] The findings of my survey indicate that among people of professed faith or spirituality there is a sense that their spirituality grounds them and strengthens them, providing them with meaningfulness, vocational fulfillment and joy. This may be a sound response to complexity. A respondent stated, "I pray for the wisdom to make the most of every day."[55] Another states, "I frequently use meditation, reflection, and prayer as a means to resolve issues in my mind."[56] Another writes, "I spend time praying for discernment."[57] Could we introduce a period for contemplation into the workplace routine?[58]

Adaptive Capacity

Responding to disruptive market forces requires deeply embedded adaptive capacity. This can only become the norm if we prepare the adaptive skills of our teams well in advance of disruptive events.[59] Bennis states:

> Every development you get in the digital world that we are living in can be our enemy or can be our best friend, and leaders have got to understand that it has got to be our best friend . . . One of the things that is most important in effective leaders is their

---

54. Stevens, *Doing God's Business*, 206.
55. Verbatim respondent 9.
56. Verbatim respondent 14.
57. Verbatim respondent 18. At a key time in development of a company—a service business—for which I held a leadership role, we chose to introduce an unconditional service guarantee. Simply, we stated that 'If for any reason you are not satisfied, we will refund our fee.' We worried that many would take advantage of us: using our services and then simply ask for their money back. Not one client did.
58. Andrea Swinton writes, "Pre-COVID, some innovative employers have introduced into the workplace opportunities for contemplation, without the label of faith. Quiet Rooms and Yoga are examples. The pivot within the HR terminology of 'health programs' to 'wellness programs' allows for the inclusion of mental health into the workplace. I suspect that employers are sensing that people want time for contemplation but they avoid faith; rather they talk about wellness and mindfulness."
59. The relatively new digital environment in which we operate has become accelerated in a world struggling with new physical distancing measures required by the Covid 19 Pandemic.

adaptive capacity—and the digital environment can enhance adaptive capacity.⁶⁰

Analyzing and responding to complex situations requires *consultation, and then action*. These are inspired and learned practices. This is what we witness in the Book of Acts. Bennis suggests that adaptive capacity is perhaps the key competence of leadership. John Kotter suggests that this is critical for organizations on the threshold of rapid change. Kotter affirms:

> Cultures can facilitate change adaptation if they value performing well for organizational constituencies, if they really support competent leadership and management, if they encourage teamwork at the top, and if they demand a minimum of layers, bureaucracies and interdependencies.⁶¹

The thread that weaves this adaptive culture together is leadership that is fully invested in the people in the organization—each one, individually! When each person holds a depth of caring for each other, trust becomes instinctive, communication is pervasive, and the ethos of the organization is unquestioned. Workplace engagement soars. An example is the seeking out and support of *intrapreneurship*.⁶² Adaptive leaders seek out and nurture intrapreneurs, providing resources and reward mechanisms suited to the task/opportunity identified.

Adaptive leaders have the ability to understand, internalize and respond to the emotions and sensitivities of others.⁶³ The leader's foun-

---

60. Bennis, "Leadership in a Digital World," 635.

61. Kotter, *Leading Change*, 179.

62. Known as the act of behaving like an entrepreneur while inside a company, intrapreneurship can nurture critical elements of change and new approaches. Harriet Ekperigin writes, "In my current role about a year ago, my peers and I were encouraged to be intrapreneurs, We welcomed this autonomy whole heartedly until one of the VP's began referring to us as the 'one throat to choke'. This did not go down well and in fact soured our initial excitement.

63. Several leadership programs incorporate the use of horses. These training programs build self-awareness skills through human-horse interactions. Tom Widdicombe writes: Communication is a remarkably powerful thing: if the horse knows that you know, then you're on your way. Look at it from the other point of view: if the horse knows that you don't know, then he [sic] has every right to worry. He [sic] is basically 'on his own,' and that is the one place the horse does not want to be. If you can show the horse that you are with him [sic, taking care of him [sic] and you are not going to let him [sic] down, then he [sic] will put his [sic] trust in you." (Widdicombe, *Be*, 17). Horses live in the moment. They are concerned about safety and leadership. We may not choose to participate in programs involving horses, but we must deepen our sensitivity toward others.

dational job is *to build community*; to ensure safety. Our colleagues have safety-related questions, particularly about the security of their job and about their prospects. They ask, 'What's expected of me?' and 'How am I doing?' These are, at their most basic level, safety-related questions. Also, they frequently want to help, if only we invite them. We must *celebrate good works*. Strong team cohesion is in effect a workplace safety issue. Therefore, attention to cohesion is a leadership issue. Simon Taggar and Mitchel J. Neubert assert that "just one poorly performing member can impact the team directly or indirectly by influencing the motivation of peers to perform."[64]

Mentorship

Building adaptive capacity, and the feedback loop that supports it, requires a heightened self-awareness. A respondent stated, "I pray for the wisdom to make the most of every day."[65] Here is a person seeking opportunities for growth. We constantly witness situations at work where a misinterpretation or misunderstanding escalates into intransigence, even hatred. Jesus teaches us to reflect on our own record (cf. Matthew 7:5), to de-escalate the situation where we can seek change, not revenge. Grenz writes, "God is love—the divine essence is the love that binds together the Trinity."[66] We must not forget that have access to this love, and that it is ours to share.

It is crucial, if we are to seek the presence of the Holy Spirit in our work, that we consider the call to love our enemies. We should not respond to aggression with aggression but, rather, forgiveness. We should, simply and through reflection, put the situation squarely in God's hands. When we do this, paradoxically, we become genuine, we become someone in whom others can put their trust. We become authentic. At the same time, we find new inner peace. An attitude of *forgiveness*—accepting and building on errors, then, is a foundation of adaptive capacity.

Mentorship is the selfless act of passing along knowledge, which itself is a gift from God, together with skill in the service of others. For people of faith, this act, following invitation, is essential to all that we do. Mentorship begins with responding to a call to engage. Susan Phillips

---

64. Taggar and Neubert, "A Cognitive (Attributions)-Model," 167.
65. Verbatim respondent 9.
66. Grenz, *Theology for the Community of God*, 69.

observes that, "All Christians are called to the ministry of listening."[67] We cannot listen simply to the words we hear, but the emotions within them. Radical listening frees us from our own agenda, and deepens our ability to respond. We must *maintain high levels of communication.*

As stated earlier, there have been significant, and in some cases dramatic, reductions in institutionalized mentorship in the workplace. This includes a reduction in formal apprenticeship programs together with on-the-job training and development. In their place we are witnessing a demand for 'just-in-time' expertise, similar to the demand for 'just-in-time' material and parts. As stated, a significant reason for this loss in mentorship has been the widespread reduction in middle-management ranks. Sydney Finkelstein states:

> The sad truth is that middle management is on its way to becoming virtually extinct. While there will always be some people supervising the work of other people, changes in technology, business culture and demographics are all conspiring to upend what has long been standard practice in companies. We should no longer expect traditional job ladders for managers to move up the ranks, or even retaining the notion that middle managers are the glue that connects workers and ensures goal alignment up and down the hierarchy.[68]

With the dissolution of middle management comes a dramatic erosion in close guidance. At the centre of mentorship is both skill development and encouragement. Pollard says, "It is not just what we are doing, but what we are *becoming* in the process that gives us our distinct value and is uniquely human."[69] This calls for a constant search for new methods and structures that promote mentorship, understanding that mentorship sometimes requires intervention. We must *nurture* workers, finding new ways to achieve this nurturing—this must be viewed as missional.

Transformative Leadership

A vigorous approach to identifying new methods and tools is foundational to transformation. Hope is at the heart of transformation. To repeat what has been said earlier, we must have the *words of our mission*

---

67. Phillips, "Spiritual Direction," 163.
68. Finkelstein, "The End," para.1.
69. Pollard, *The Soul of the Firm*, [emphasis original] 26.

and values in front of us every morning. Indeed, it does not take a lengthy conversation with someone to know if they uphold this practice. Bill Cosgrave writes:

> [A]s one develops a hopeful outlook and disposition over time one is thereby strengthening the virtue of hope as a vital dimension of one's moral character . . . Hope provides us with dynamism for action . . . Hope looks to the future, not as the end or a threat to what is, but as an open field of possibilities of human fulfilment and achievement.[70]

Building leadership implies bringing transformative, hopeful, change. We bring about a complete conversion from one state of practice to another. The word 'transform' has several interpretations: change, sometimes dramatic change, in form, function, appearance, and value. Indeed one interpretation of the word transformation suggests that the degree of change is close to *miraculous*. Peter Northouse writes, "Transformational Leadership is a process that changes, and transforms people. It is concerned with emotions, values, ethics, standards and long-term goals."[71] Thus work must allow for *alignment with values*.

Bringing about transformative change is not going to happen in a workshop—although this may be the beginning of the recognition of a need for change—but in deep, sometimes challenging dialogue. The findings of my survey indicate that it is possible that an epistemological social foundation is emerging to which we must respond. This suggests that in preparing for transformative change, a thorough understanding of value-sets must be explored and understood. For example, cognizance of the breadth of spiritual perspectives may be an outcome of this exercise. Thiessen writes, "There are different types of religious nones, from atheists to agnostics, to unchurched believers."[72] Indeed, essentially all of these perspectives, and more, were expressed by various respondents.

Developed in a way that is *nurturing*, transformative change may awaken the emotions, values and deeply held morality of a person in such a way that they are moved to a new plane of consciousness and ability in their work. To be a transformational leader is to become completely engrossed in the lives of one's staff; in their motivations and emotions; in their purpose at work. Thus, leaders are called to provide an environment

---

70. Cosgrave, "Hope, Human and Christian," 490.
71. Northouse, *Leadership Theory and Practice*, 185.
72. Thiessen, *Meaning of Sunday*, 95.

that is intentional. This requires earning a deep level of permission and trust. There is an iterative dimension to this. These iterations cannot be condensed or skipped. This requires discipline. Importantly we need to know when to leave people to themselves; to be absent—to let them process and work through lessons on their own. Transformative change simply cannot occur while we are standing there, with someone; in the moment. It can take months. Transformative change requires us to create a movement or flow in a new direction. This is where we move into a discussion that introduces new concepts, and offers alignment with personal goals and values. Then we must simply leave people alone. Noddings writes, "The receptive mode seems to be an essential component of intellectual work. We do not pass into it under stress . . . Indeed, we must settle ourselves, clear our minds, and reduce the racket around us."[73]

Whenever we re-engage, we should begin by seeking permission to move the dialogue ahead.[74] It will be clear when the transformation has occurred. Teams and leaders will be working at levels that they have not experienced before. Much of the change will have occurred when the leader is not around. Noddings asserts, "The one-caring, in caring, is *present* in her acts of caring. Even in physical absence, acts at a distance bear the signs of presence: engrossment in the other, regard, desire for the other's well-being."[75] A respondent stated, "I try to communicate my faith through action and had the opportunity to foster an environment that treated people kindly, fairly and honestly. I also spoke up when people wanted to bend the truth."[76] Advocating for workers implies that we cannot ignore dissonance. We must identify the source of dissonance, and respond to it. This is key. Once understood, failure to respond may lead to disaster.

Responding to Dissonance

Dissonance is generally accompanied by the expression of a lack of control or ability to improve the situation. There are infrequent opportunities

---

73. Noddings, *Caring*, 34.

74. As a colleague once opined, we learn to sail in the winter and we learn to ski in the summer.

75. Noddings, *Caring*, 19 [emphasis original]. There have, thankfully, been many individuals with whom I have interacted in my career whose advice still finds application for me decades later. I can recall each word offered.

76. Verbatim respondent 3.

to discuss workplace challenges in a constructive way with co-workers, supervisors or counsellors. With the virtual disappearance of middle management, resulting in an erosion of mentorship,[77] this leads to many instances of feeling adrift. A respondent stated:

> There is also always the gender question in terms of pay. There is little transparency around pay. But I am creating something—it is tangible and meaningful, something I can hopefully be proud of. Some co-workers are driven only by money, 'lifestyle,' or power.[78]

There is dissonance here, and we must seize on every opportunity to ameliorate it.

Work expectations are received well when they *align with expressed values*, Timely and regular detailed communication is critical, especially in times of change.

A non-leader respondent stated, "I pray for the wisdom to make the most of every day."[79] Prayer and meditation are expressed by respondents, both leaders and non-leaders, as means to cope with challenges, yet most organizations eschew the opportunity to offer a place or a means to do this in the workplace. It is leadership that is called upon to engage with such phenomena, and to create workplace environments that respond to them and in doing so *build community*. It is leadership, when Spirit-called and equipped, which can find resolutions to challenges. Through addressing such challenges leaders and workers will perceive a deeper sense of meaningfulness, a sense of energy, and a sense of well-being. Enterprises will experience a significant increase in productivity and reputation as workers feel uplifted and valued as individuals. Families and entire communities will flourish. This is equality. Volf asserts:

> The two most potent images of human flourishing in the Western cultural traditions come from the Bible, from the opening chapters of its first book and from the final chapters of its last. For those who embrace them, these images aren't merely dream-clouds, floating around in the sky of religious fancy. They are part of a grand narrative arc starting with the world's creation and ending with new heavens and the new earth of which

---

77. It may be that 'flattened' organizations become structural environments for more autonomous teams which develop new approaches to peer-mentorship and situation-specific contracted, real-time training and coaching. This would be a potentially rich area for further research.

78. Verbatim respondent 29.

79. Verbatim respondent 9.

Spiritual Leadership in a Secular World

the Hebrew Bible and the Christian Scriptures tell; and both, the grand arc and the visions of flourishing, are rooted in the convictions about the reality of the One who dwells in light.[80]

Throughout the biblical narrative we find individuals, called up at critical moments, often reluctantly at first, to step into leadership (cf. Jonah 1:3). We *must allow faith to guide us.* A respondent stated, "I enjoy a sense of fulfillment and vocation."[81] Leadership is a sacred calling. *Leadership is not a path to self-aggrandizement, power, or status.*[82]Spirit-led leaders influence, they do not seek power.[83] Allowing one's faith to guide us through difficult decisions is valuable.[84] A respondent stated, "I strive to be more like Jesus in the way I work and interact with my colleagues."[85]

The Safest Place in the Organization

We can make our office the safest place in the organization. The expression, 'being called on the carpet' is a common idiom. Getting summoned to the boss' office[86] seems seldom to be equated with something good happening. More generally we anticipate a reprimand. Imagine the empowerment that flows from a workforce where literally everyone feels they can walk into their superior's office, offer an idea, or make a point about something and feel not only truly embraced, but that they will

---

80. Volf, *Flourishing*, x–xi.

81. Verbatim respondent 25.

82. I have offered, in a speech, the question, "Are you building a monument to yourself, or a park bench for others to rest?"

83. Harriet Ekperigin writes, "I recall a time when a colleague of mine was interested in an internal director position. Based on his personality and work ethics, I did not think he would make a good people leader. When I asked him in conversation about his interest in the role he responded 'well when you have enough money the only thing left is power' Needless to say he was not a spirit-led leader and I was glad he did not even get an interview for the job."

84. I have learned the value of causing a break in dialogue, of following Jesus model of separating oneself from others for prayer and contemplation.

85. Verbatim respondent 8.

86. Andrea Swinton writes, "When I became a people leader, I was aware if asked someone to come into my office that people could immediately tense up. I made a point of prefacing invitations to join me in my office with 'don't worry, it is not bad' sometimes loud enough so others did not panic too. There are a wide variety of reasons to have a private conversation with staff. As leaders, we know this, however, staff tend to equate it to trouble."

likely see the outcome of their contribution as it becomes a reality. We can prove that our office is the safest place in the organization by showing our own vulnerability. This liberating for others and for us. Vulnerability, the admission, in effect, that we can be, and perhaps have been, wounded, is at the root of authenticity and authenticity is the foundation for leadership.[87] The findings of my survey indicate that the person and model of Jesus is valued by many. Are we safe to be with, even when we are admonishing someone? Are we fit to be a leader? Will we serve those that seek to serve the organization, and to grow in the process? *We are the custodians of the organization's ethics and values.* Right and wrong are truly powerful concepts and are borne aloft in the culture that we permit, uphold, and celebrate! An entrepreneur respondent stated, "It can be scary and overwhelming at times. All my efforts and funds go into the business. My workers and family are my peers."[88] Treating coworkers as peers is empowering. Safety and empowerment are the antithesis of mistreatment.[89] Marie Hutchinson et al. assert:

> Workplace bullying, mobbing, incivility, and emotional abuse are increasingly recognized as features of the modern workplace . . . Exposure can result in severe psychological trauma, lowered self-esteem, depression, anxiety, and posttraumatic stress disorder . . . Traditional models of power and conflict have theorized that conflict creates a situation where the personal power of one actor over another is sought and increased through bullying behaviours.[90]

Bullying, intimidating behaviour is present in the workplace. We have all witnessed it. Boddy adds, "Workplace incivility, expressed in such measures as rudeness, is associated with workplace performance."[91] Presenting the leader's office—your office—as the safest place in the organization creates, in effect, a sanctuary where critical conversations can take place. A respondent stated, "I believe that good engenders good."[92] Making our

---

87. From experience, I know that there is risk to this, but it is still the right thing to do.

88. Verbatim respondent 8.

89. A person relayed a story to me of a day when following a presentation, she received accolades from coworkers. As she left the room with her immediate supervisor, he said to her, "aren't you little miss perfect!"

90. Hutchinson et al., "Bullying as Circuits of Power," 25–26.

91. Boddy, "Corporate Psychopaths," 108.

92. Verbatim respondent 24.

environment a safe place engenders *hospitality*; it builds *community*—it may even produce a course-changing innovation.

Some prefer opaqueness over transparency. Some find it easy to put the proverbial thumb on the scale, to get a little more than they deserve. So where do we draw the line? It is the moment we sense that we are on the slippery slope toward a quest for power over an obligation to serve. If work is eschatological, then leadership is about legacy. When we see every act as an element of our legacy, each act takes on a new status. We can think of legacy as sending the product of our labour on to the future. A respondent stated, "My work satisfies my economic needs, and that does lead to a sense of calling as we are able to contribute money to causes important to us."[93] Gary Hamel writes:

> Imagine a retailer where frontline employees decide what to stock; where the pressure to perform comes from peers rather than from bosses; where teams, not managers, have veto power over new hires; and where virtually every employee feels like he or she is running a small business. Try to envision a company where everyone knows what everyone else gets paid, and where senior execs limit their pay to 19 times the average wage. Picture, if you can, a company that doesn't think of itself as a company, but as a community of people working to make a difference in the world, where the mission matters as much as the bottom line. Conjure up all this, and you'll have a portrait of Whole Foods market.[94]

This is an impressive vignette which has, at its core, the recognition of good work and the engagement of talent. These are acts of hospitality in the sense that people feel included and welcome, perceiving themselves as full participants.

Recognizing Good Work

Fundamental to leadership is the *recognition and celebration of good work*. Pawar states, "[L]eadership that adopts personal spiritual values and practices in its own conduct can contribute to workplace spiritual facilitation."[95] Recognition of good work assures a person that they are

---

93. Verbatim respondent 17.
94. Hamel, *The Future of Management*, 69.
95. Pawar, "Workplace Spiritual Facilitation," 384.

valued and needed. A respondent stated, "Everyone wants to feel 'needed' at their workplace."[96] Recognition of good work is a fundamental act of caring. Dell reminds us that the Book of Proverbs asserts the slothful/diligent comparison. She writes, "Careful, steady work is better than chasing rainbows, 'A slothful man [sic] will not catch his [sic] prey, but the diligent man [sic] will get precious wealth' (Prov 12:27)."[97] Leadership has the means to embed the *crafting of tasks within a vocational framework*, thus raising work up to spiritual meaningfulness.[98] Noddings writes, "The cared-for is free to be more fully himself [sic] in the caring relationship."[99] When people become aware that they are cared for, freedom replaces a sense of being stuck. The person blossoms with confidence and renewed vigour. Jay Lombard offers, "God knits us human beings together in love. It is a memory that goes back to the creation of the universe. And it is in love that we live forever."[100] Leadership shines when it brings these thoughts—truths, one might argue—to our daily work, in a world where our work may be at risk of being stripped of its greater value to our sense of vocation, and of its divine purpose. Lombard asserts that our existence is made complete by our deep awareness and knowledge of our divine purpose. He writes:

> True freedom is a key to a seemingly locked door. We are all handed the key and invited to open the door. But it's our choice whether or not to progress. Once through the doorway, we find on the other side a wide-open expanse of possibility. We embrace true freedom; we are free to live the lives we were meant to live. We can live lives of real purpose.[101]

This empowers us to make decisions that are *moral in nature*, without contingencies. It is supposed to be this way. From the earliest of the

---

96. Verbatim respondent 9.

97. Dell, *Seeking a Life*, 35.

98. Some decades ago, I was given a role that was designed as remedial in nature. I spent a few days with a person struggling a little in terms of achieving assigned goals. At the end of a day together, I asked the person, 'What do you like to do?' The person replied, 'Well I like this, and I like that.' I said, 'Why don't you take the next couple of weeks off—I won't tell anyone—see if you can find work that includes this and that. At the end of the two weeks the person resigned. I got a call to tell me that the person had found a job that included this and that!

99. Noddings, *Caring*, 73.

100. Lombard, *The Mind of God*, 179.

101. Lombard, *The Mind of God*, 113.

ancient Hebrew texts, the people of Israel were expected to conduct their daily lives in an attitude of obedience to the Law. Leviticus tells us this, as does Deuteronomy. All aspects of life were considered to be integral to a covenantal relationship with God (cf. Deut 6:4–9). Tremper Longman and Raymond Dillard write, "In some respects, Deuteronomy portrays what an ideal Israel would be. It presents an Israel with 'one God, one people, one land, one sanctuary, and one law.'"[102] A person's attitude toward their labour in those days was central to a virtuous life. Implicitly, I sense from many of their narratives the respondents to my research questionnaire echo this.

Inflection Points

My research suggests that the workplace is at a significant threshold as social, technological, economic, and market forces converge to result in significant organizational restructuring. The world's response to Covid 19 is a glaring example. This requires that we are students of organizational theory and are conscious of the human impact of organizational structure in our particular environments. The demands on leaders and workers alike are often overwhelming. Forced frictional unemployment is dramatic and is often debilitating as those laid off frequently experience an employment hiatus of six to twelve months and often take new work at compensation levels well below their prior experience.[103] The 'gig' economy appears to be more debilitating than empowering. Workplaces experience high levels of absenteeism. In addition, substance abuse seems to be increasing.[104]

The way that we treat one person will shape the expectation of others. A respondent stated, "Many events have placed a sense of doubt in my job security; e.g. others not being supported; not being assigned to a position that I felt qualified to do; being assigned a role that suited the

---

102. Longman and Dillard, *An Introduction to the Old Testament*, 114.

103. Frictional unemployment is the unemployment in an economy due to people in process moving from one job to another.

104. Many Canadian provincial governments have sponsored special training for the recognition and amelioration of substance abuse in the workplace. For example, *Health Newfoundland* states that problematic substances include: Cannabis, Alcohol, sleeping medications, sedatives, tranquilizers, solvents, gasoline, numerous opiates and stimulants. Problem gambling is also referenced. See: https://www.health.gov.nl.ca/health/publications/addiction_substance_abuse_workplace_toolkit.pdf.

company, but which impeded my development."[105] In a previous work, I have stated that our colleagues at work "have two simple questions to which they deserve answers: 'What are the standards against which I will be measured?' and 'Where do I stand?'"[106] These questions are central to the leadership approach that is presented here. People want to understand what is expected of them, and how their results will be measured and rewarded. This is *advocacy*—supporting and encouraging our employees.[107] Knowing the answers to these questions lies at the very beginning of flourishing. What can we do in terms of influencing organizational structure and leadership that will be catalytic in promoting vitality and flourishing? If we consider that a true sense of vocation is linked to flourishing, what can we do to enhance/equip employees' identification of their vocation and their progress toward feeling that they are achieving their goals and desires as related to vocation? How might we identify an optimal range of human functioning in the environments within our organizations and then how might we quantify, and measure progress in reaching that optimal range? Beyond fair pay, job security and equitable treatment, what can we build into our leadership activities matrix to promote dignity, generativity, growth and resilience? These are critical questions. Providing employees with a clear vision and a sense of security in their work seems fundamental to these goals. Constant *reflection* is required, founded in thoughtful dialogue—especially with those who challenge us.

A respondent stated:

> My chosen industry was not at all 'secure.' I believe that it was my calling. I was given human resources responsibilities that afforded me the opportunity to learn and grow. It also meant firing people—although it was always difficult, it was done as kindly as possible.[108]

Another respondent states:

> My work does provide a deep sense of meaningfulness. I find it very satisfying to know I have had a positive impact. I have

---

105. Verbatim respondent 22.
106. Bates, *Sales Force Management*, 93.
107. When an immediate supervisor learned that I was studying for a new industry designation—a designation that he held—he told me to stop wasting my time, because it had nothing to do with the job I was doing.
108. Verbatim respondent 3.

also worked in the not-for-profit sector. [That said] I will be working out of financial necessity until I am at least seventy. My work is a calling.[109]

Is it possible to create environments that provide for a deep sense of meaningfulness? Is it possible that *agape* and economically satisfying work should be tied together? Veith writes:

> Good works, for the most part, are done in vocation. Sin, too, takes place in vocation, in the myriad ways we violate our callings. Approaching moral issues from the perspective of vocation can illuminate *why* certain actions are right or wrong. The vocational angle can also help us understand what our duties are in our various jobs and social roles and, just as important, what the limits are in what we are called to do. It also illuminates what we are *not* called to do.[110]

Ethical, loving treatment of subordinates and co-workers will lead to an ethos upon which human flourishing is sustained. This ethos assures that we retain *humility*; that we are *present* in the lives of employees.[111] Frostensen adds emphasis, adding that humility, "is conducive to behaviours or attitudes among followers that are in one way or the other beneficial to the company or to leadership."[112] There is reciprocity in humility.

Connecting the Present to the Future

In organizations, inflection points occur when a sharp bending away from a positive trajectory for the enterprise arises. Overcoming inflection involves creating a contiguous linkage from present to future. In a time when we can reach for Twitter, regardless of our frame of mind and

---

109. Verbatim respondent 13.

110. Veith, *God at Work*, 133 [emphasis original].

111. When interviewing potential new leadership hires, I frequently invited them for breakfast. First I wanted to find out if they could be on time, second, I wanted to see if they chose the most expensive item on the menu, finally I wanted to see if they were respectful, or dismissive, of the wait person. Andrea Swinton adds, "This reminded me of the time I flew to the New York area for an interview for a role with an international organization. A car service picked me up at LaGuardia Airport. I recall chatting with the driver and not giving it much thought. On another car service ride to the US head office from the airport, a driver told me that he was always asked by the CEO for his feedback on the interviewees. I was floored; it didn't occur to me at all."

112. Frostensen, "Humility in Business," 94.

alertness, this decision to pause can be crucial. We are remembered most for how we behave in times of challenge—as a very old proverb states, 'anyone can sail the ship when the sea is calm.' In a Conference Board of Canada article, I wrote:

> Do you really understand the financials? Have you scrutinized the balance sheet? If your organization needs cash, what is its borrowing and capital-raising capacity? What are the tough decisions to be made? In what order are they to be made, and who will execute on them? How can you determine if some of the choices being considered could cripple the organization's ability to recover and grow? If personnel changes are to be made, how will you ensure they are carried out without damaging the values of the organization—both for those that will be leaving and for those that will be staying? How can the organization reposition itself for a more stable and successful future? Are you ensuring that your management team has the tools it needs to get the job done? What are the expectations that need to be established for all stakeholders? Is there risk of disconnect between what is being stated and how those in management are actually behaving?[113]

This commentary is focused ultimately on arriving at the correct organization structure for the tasks ahead. We must *consult, and then act*.

The Impact of Organizational Structure

How does organizational structure affect meaningfulness and a sense of belonging? Hatch and Cunliffe discuss varying structures. Functional organizations, which are known well, "are so called because they group activities according to a logic of similarity in work functions (the nature of the work people perform)."[114] Departmental structures maximize economies of scale, and focus control at the top of the organization. Hatch and Cunliffe point out that this structure also leads "to greater loyalty [among employees] to their function rather than the organization as a whole, leading to the problem of organizational silos."[115] Hatch and Cunliffe go on to describe M-form organizations, which "group people, positions, and units in one of three ways: by similarities in products or production

---

113. Bates, "The Corporation with Integrity," 2.
114. Hatch and Cunliffe, *Organization Theory*, 273.
115. Hatch and Cunliffe, *Organization Theory*, 273.

processes, customer type, or geographic region of activity."[116] Hatch and Cunliffe write, "When they are treated as profit centres, multi-division designs allow for a type of accountability that is not possible in functional designs."[117] Further organization designs include matrix organizations, designed to "combine the efficiency of the functional design with the flexibility and responsiveness of the M-form."[118] Hatch and Cunliffe go on to describe hybrid organization designs. They write:

> A research and development division may use a matrix, while other divisions are organized functionally. Hybrids may occur either because designers deliberately mix forms in an attempt to blend the advantages of two or more different types, or because the organization is changing and is only part way to realizing its new structure.[119]

There are a number of organizational structures in use. These include strategic alliances and joint ventures. For example, the mining industry is an environment where exploration companies form joint venture partnerships with extraction and production companies.[120] Yet another structure involves networks and virtual organizations. Many communications and marketing services businesses, as well as consulting businesses operate this way. We must be *students of organizational structure*; choosing the most effective ways to *build community*, together with a structure that upholds our ethos.

A growing number of people work alone, remotely. Erica Lenti writes, "Loneliness is emerging as a public health crisis. When workers feel lonely, it can affect their productivity."[121] Loneliness can leave one spiritually bereft. Leadership that is *nurturing* is required. Leadership for remote workers requires new reflection. This is an element of leadership practice seldom required in recent decades.

---

116. Hatch and Cunliffe, *Organization Theory*, 274.
117. Hatch and Cunliffe, *Organization Theory*, 275.
118. Hatch and Cunliffe, *Organization Theory*, 275.
119. Hatch and Cunliffe, *Organization Theory*, 275.
120. Such partnerships can be particularly challenging. Large, structured extraction and production companies are frequently in strategic partnerships with small, entrepreneurial exploration companies. Cultures and operating structures can be completely different.
121. Lenti, "All the Lonely People," 18.

Hatch points out, "Non-hierarchical relationships comprised of human points of contact, called nodes, form a network structure."[122] Frequently virtual companies are networks whose connections take place primarily or entirely via electronic media, as opposed to face-to-face interactions.[123] Autry writes:

> Here's the conundrum: as more and more of our businesses become driven by knowledge, information and service, thus absolutely dependent on people for success, [many will] think of themselves as free agents of their own careers ... What happens to loyalty in this scenario?[124]

Fractured, networked, and remote organization structures require a new *intentionality of caring*.[125] Autry writes:

> Loyalty in the community of work has both personal and professional aspects: There must be a balance between a loyalty to one's peers and team members, one's colleagues, one's manager, and one's employees, and the loyalty extended to the community itself, including the organization and its vision.[126]

Hatch writes, "[T]he beliefs of organizational members determine not only how a leader will be regarded, but who will be regarded as a leader."[127] Leaders are embedded. Leaders are not above. Stanley McChrystal writes, "As an enabler of the system, leaders are nodes in a network, rather than being the top of the apex of [the organization or department]."[128] Leaders must identify power dynamics and respond in ways that uphold the organization's ethos.

---

122. Hatch and Cunliffe, *Organization Theory*, 275.

123. Hatch and Cunliffe, *Organization Theory*, 281.

124. Autry, *The Servant Leader*, 161.

125. Andrea Swinton writes, "With the remote working conditions [wrought by] COVID, I find myself asking people, 'how are you?' and likewise others asking me how am I? We are actually listening to each other instead of the throw-away ice-breaker that it might have been before COVID. I do worry about the long-range impact of remote working, loneliness, less mentoring and disengagement. It could be easier for management to trim payrolls because employees will become two-dimensional people on a Zoom screen."

126. Autry, *The Servant Leader*, 161.

127. Hatch and Cunliffe, *Organization Theory*, 293.

128. McChrystal, *Leaders*, 399.

Situational Leadership

Leaders are in the community that is the organization. It is leadership more than structure that is key to human flourishing. A clear response to circumstances is one way to build community. In a stark narrative regarding very different situational responses. Nicholas Christakis chronicles very different outcomes for survivors of two shipwrecks in 1864. He writes:

> Two ships, the *Invercauld* and the *Grafton*, were wrecked on opposite sides of Auckland Island, two hundred and ninety miles south of New Zealand... Although they struggled for their lives on the same island at the same time, the crews of the *Invercauld* and the *Grafton* were not aware of each other. In the case of the *Invercauld*, nineteen of twenty-five crew members made it ashore, and only three survived. In the case of the *Grafton*, all five people on board made it ashore and all five made it off the island nearly two years later.[129]

The comparative experiences presented by Christakis reveal a dramatic and wrenching set of events. What is apparent is that the critical difference in the outcomes of these two situations, was leadership—*leadership that focussed on community*, and on *flourishing*. These lessons are real for us today. Trebesch states:

> When we flourish, we experience emotional, psychological, and social well-being. We are full of life—peaceful, cheerful, satisfied and productive. We accept ourselves as we are, knowing our strengths and weaknesses. We engage challenges, enjoy learning and embrace an overall sense of purpose. We expect our days to be useful and hopeful. Flourishing people have strong relationships and connectedness to community, contributing as well as receiving.[130]

Being a solely task-oriented leader, even when acting in a kind manner, will likely bring short-term results, but may squander the long term.

To be explicit that our leadership approach is grounded in faith may be problematic—there is a cost to discipleship that we must understand. Linda Brook writes:

> Though there may be some, I have personally not heard any leaders address the real cost of going public as Christians at

---

129. Christakis, *Blueprint*, 40–42.
130. Trebesch, *Made to Flourish*, 12.

work. In fact, I have not heard it so much as hinted at that there is or *might* be a cost, when there most assuredly is, and most often, it is a high one . . . This is the whole truth. There is a cross and a cost to following Jesus no matter what field one may be in or how much favour one may have. While salvation is free, *following* Jesus is not.[131]

Some, however, are noticing the value of faith-led leadership. Patricia Best writes:

> You can with impunity on Bay Street give self-serving advice to your clients, or you can be a foul-mouthed, back-stabbing, son of a bitch to your colleagues in the office. But you cannot, in the normal course of events, talk about loving your fellow human being, and you cannot talk about the tragedy of layoffs or the responsibility of the CEO to the mail-room clerk. And you certainly cannot wonder aloud about the role of spirituality in the hard-edged canyons of the financial diocese.[132]

Perhaps, it's time we did.

A respondent stated, "Everyone wants to feel needed."[133] Responding to this call in a deep, authentic, way is the grounding of leadership. We should never stop working on relationships. Being brilliant on our own gets the enterprise nowhere, unless we are a sole proprietor.

Deep self-awareness in times of conflict is critical. Dennis Sandole et al. write:

> Theorists often make a distinction between personal identity, or self-identity, and collective or social identity. Personal identity focuses on an individual's sense of him- or herself as an autonomous, unique person . . . Individuals have a sense of self, an identity or public image they want others to see. In incorporates particular traits, attributes and skills along with self-descriptions and self-evaluations that together constitute a personal identity . . . When the emergent circumstances of a conflict call into question one's sense of self, the conflict itself shifts.[134]

When our identity is fully aligned with our understanding of our goals, our identity is aligned with the vision that is cast.

---

131. Brook, *Frontline Christians*, 190 [emphasis original].
132. Best, "Awakenings," 69.
133. Verbatim respondent 8.
134. Sandole et al, *Handbook of Conflict Analysis and Resolution*, 20–21.

Situational leadership implies that situations of injustice must be responded to and remedied immediately.[135] Blakely et al. assert that, "[A]s perceptions of justice increase, so does the level of Organizational Citizenship Behaviours . . . a fair working environment is important for promoting the performance of Organizational Citizenship Behaviours."[136] The Apostle Paul wrote, "Let all things be done for *building up*."[137]

Vision

Among the critical attributes of leadership is *vision* (cf. Prov 29:18). Vision requires perspective and sometimes elevation. Jesus shows us, many times, to go to higher places. When we allow ourselves to break away from the fray; to go, figuratively, to a higher place, we can contemplate the end-state of what we are in the middle of now. We can look down on our work, not as a work in progress, but as a completed whole. We can 'peer' downstream from a decision we are about to take and imagine the effect of our prospective decision from that place in the distance, and through that figurative lens we can see if it has turned out the way we had hoped it would. We can see prospective paths to a solution that are not necessarily immediately visible from ground level. In a role where the work is never really done, perspective is a key leadership trait. People know when there is no vision. Following vision, *leaders should consult, and then act*. They must identify, and present the path forward. A respondent stated, "I feel secure for now. [That said] as I walked into the fog and did all I could—God met me and journeyed with me."[138] Leaders experience liminal moments—indeed, withdrawing to a 'higher place' can be a liminal experience. We must *allow faith to guide* us.

Conscious separation of oneself from the moment-to-moment demands of our work is not a luxury, but an absolute necessity. In fact we owe it to our organizations and stakeholders to do it. This may be one of the most critical changes in behaviour when moving into leadership: letting go of those activities which are no longer our job, and focussing on the bigger picture. The disciples offered a clear example when they

---

135. I have found this particularly crucial in an environment governed by a negotiated labour contract.

136. Blakely et al., "The Moderating Effects of Equity Sensitivity," 268.

137. 1 Cor. 14:26 [emphasis added].

138. Verbatim respondent 7.

immediately let go of their existing jobs to follow Jesus' call: in effect an eschatological call to a new destiny.

Jesus found solitude, but also community. The Christian life is lived in quiet solitude *and* in community. Leadership may be learned in solitude, but it is practised and honed in serving community. *Nurturing* is foundational. Indeed there can be no proportionality to our offer of help to others. This is serious business. Mentoring cannot be done from a safe distance. Pollard amplifies the need for this dialogue at work. He writes:

In all of this uncertainty and change there is a constant—people:

- People who are looking for a mission and purpose in their work.
- People who are seeking to understand the why, not simply the how to of their job.
- People who have a growing appetite for more participation and ownership in results.
- People who are increasingly looking to the work environment for security and, in some cases, relief from the confusion in their personal lives.
- People who are creative, productive, and want to contribute.
- People who have been created in God's image with dignity and worth.[139]

Engagement with others is the connecting thread of virtually every comment made by the respondents to my survey. A respondent stated, "I think my peers and co-workers want that deep sense of meaningfulness but I'm not sure that everyone knows how to get that."[140] Noddings writes, "[I]f we commit ourselves to receptivity, natural caring occurs more frequently, and conflicts may thereby be reduced."[141] Receptivity, openness and willingness to accept new ideas, on the part of the leader, engenders receptivity in all. This is a Spirit-led ethos. Leaders are custodians of this ethos. This is central to the notion of shepherding (cf. John 10:27ff).

When our colleagues, employees, stakeholders and customers know exactly what we stand for, the value of our organization's ethos in the market-place rises. Our *price-to-ethos ratio* improves! Our workplace will

---

139. Pollard, *The Soul of the Firm*, 128–29.
140. Verbatim respondent 2.
141. Noddings, *Caring*, 104.

be sought out by those wishing to find work where vocation might be fulfilled. It will be a place where people flourish.

The paradigm 'knowing, being and doing'[142] is valuable to the role of leadership. It is *being* that may be most critical to employee engagement. This is easily seen in the ethos of a company when the founder's name hangs above the door, the leader's *presence* imbues every decision in the organization, for better or worse.[143]

A respondent stated, "There were times when the sense of being tested really could be borne through a sense of faith."[144] Readiness to *confront situations that are potentially destructive* of the need for hope is key. This calls for a well-articulated and often repeated statement of vision for the organization. Strong vision, infused with our mission and values, reignites hope.

Carver and Oliver state that, "The CEO shall not fail to plan so as to safeguard the company from unacceptable financial conditions."[145] The centrality of financial stewardship is the role of leadership; an area of responsibility that must exemplify the organization's ethical values. Ethos establishes purpose. Purpose dictates our approach to stewardship. Ethos lays out 'the narrow road' that we travel.

Purpose

In a sense, we can see Spirit-led leadership as a form of outrage; a welling up of indignation regarding unacceptable situations. The Spirit-led leader determines the urgent need for things to be done differently. R. Latta writes, "[A] purpose is a possible course of action, conceived and adopted for execution, but not yet executed . . . Activity and purpose are each teleological: every activity and every purpose is a tendency to an end."[146] Purpose, then, connotes aiming for something that is better than the current situation. Purpose implies constant improvement. A

---

142. The McMaster Divinity College paradigm is 'Knowing, Being and Doing.'

143. A company that I became familiar with had a founder whose first name was Charles. I would frequently hear employees voice the question, 'what would Chuck do?'

144. Verbatim respondent 14.

145. Carver and Oliver, *Corporate Boards That Create Value*, 169.

146. Latta, "Purpose," 17–20.

respondent stated, "I actually need to feel a deep sense of purpose."[147] Gary Burnison writes:

> Large or small, Fortune 500 or community group, every great organization is established for a reason that goes beyond profit. Leadership begins with that purpose—the 'why' of the organization. Certainly your people are working for their own self-interest; that's why you pay them . . . People long for meaning in their lives, and so must the organization. Understanding the *why* behind what we're doing lets us connect our individual actions to a larger, deeper, purpose.[148]

While Burnison does not speak of purpose in spiritual terms, I present service to, and alignment with God's Kingdom as that larger, deeper purpose. We might contemplate God's Kingdom as a holy nation without physical borders: a place that has been purified: cleansed through Christ. In a way, we can think of purification as simplification. Thus leadership is presented as a divine calling. Leadership is divinely inspired. *This is a calling not to the deserving—or the demanding. It is a calling to the ready*, as it was for Isaiah (cf. Isa 6:8). Sometimes the reward for leadership is hard to perceive. Moses was called to lead his nation to the Promised Land. He personally did not enter in. "The Lord said to him, this is the land of which I swore to Abraham, to Isaac, and to Jacob, saying, 'I will give it to your descendants;' I have let you see it with your eyes, but you shall not cross over there (cf. Deut 34:4)." Leadership is about legacy rather than immediate reward. Leadership is not a path to position, but rather it is a path to an obligation of service to others.[149]

A respondent stated, "I try to communicate my faith through action and had the opportunity to foster an environment that treated people kindly, fairly and honestly. I also spoke up when people wanted to bend the truth. God gave me strength.[150] This testimony is contrary to so many accounts of what makes for strong leadership. For example, Lane Greene writes:

---

147. Verbatim respondent 2.

148. Burnison, *Lead*, 29 [emphasis original].

149. A second year undergraduate student once told that me he was heading for a career in the military, and could not wait to receive a role as a commissioned officer. I asked him why. He told me that he could not wait to have people under him.

150. Verbatim respondent 3.

> We live in a culture that promotes democratic values of being fair to one and all . . . The problem for us is that we are trained and prepared for peace, and we are not at all prepared for what confronts in the real world—war. The world has become increasingly competitive and nasty. In politics, business, even the arts, we face opponents who will do almost anything to gain an edge.[151]

There is a dimension of leadership that is beginning to be articulated in schools of business. It is about weaving our deepest spiritual values as human beings formed in the image of God into the all-engaging work of leadership. Leadership must involve creating an ethos worthy of those who seek purpose and meaningfulness in work. We literally owe our best to our people.[152] It is about responding to the call to leadership for those who seek a productive life. As Dell describes, "the desire to do something fulfilling with one's life."[153] Parkin discusses the difference between being a leader and leadership. She states:

> A leader is a post-holder and may be elected, chosen, or appointed to lead something—an army, an organization, a project team. The post-holder is viewed as the source of leadership. The holder [i.e. manager] may or may not be good at leadership. Leadership may be exercised by anyone, from anywhere in an organization or group. Even when an appointed leader exists, others may exercise leadership.[154]

To add the Christian perspective to this, Stevens writes, "Business itself is an opportunity for the business person to function in a redemptive manner."[155] We are redeemed, or 'bought back' by God through our attitude of service, humility, and creative effort.

Training programs have little value if they do not conform to an ethos of flourishing. Indeed, if a training initiative is not linked to this ethos, it is money down the drain. Bartleby states, "American companies spent U.S. $91bn on training [in 2017] almost a third as much again as they did in 2016."[156] We may be overlooking a critical issue. There is a

---

151. Greene, *The 33 Strategies*, xv.

152. An academic colleague states that of all the activities of a professor, they need to bring their 'A Game' to the classroom.

153. Dell, *Seeking a Life*, 34.

154. Parkin, *The Positive Deviant*, 94.

155. Stevens, *Doing God's Business*, 26.

156. Bartleby, "Time to Get in Training," 49.

universal and deep thirst for meaningfulness and purpose, as expressed through our work. However, as James Burns writes, "We have long known that persons are complex bundles of motivations."[157] Generally, although not always, among the respondents, this thirst for meaningfulness and purpose clearly is linked to the respondents' spiritual orientation. It is also linked to a desire for an ethical, caring, and constructive environment.

We learn something new fully when it comports with our motivations and orientation. It is fundamental that leaders know the life stories and aspirations of those they work with. Training must adhere to the achievement of aspirations if it is to be effective. True satisfaction is expressed when people feel they are doing the work they feel called to, and when they understand that the work they are doing is their calling. This is true among those respondents who express faith and those who do not. This requires the creation and preservation of a workplace that includes regular, trusting, and engaging conversations around work and progress that is focussed deeply on the personhood of the worker. Persons are packages of emotions, needs, fears, aspirations and dreams. All of these elements wind up in front of us, waiting for guidance.

Work environments and structures, the nature of work, the ways in which work is woven into our daily lives and values, are changing, sometimes dramatically. Vocation, economic necessities, family, all require compromise. These compromises should be understood well and embedded in our leadership imperatives. A respondent stated, "I used to wear rose-coloured glasses and then get crushed when people weren't as justice minded or compassionate as I was. We are all broken."[158] *Discernment* is called for.[159] Discernment and calling are paired together. Elizabeth Liebert writes:

> Discernment, the Christian spiritual practice of seeking and responding to God's call in the midst of all the forces, options, and decisions that mark our lives, may very well be the most

---

157. Burns, *Leadership*, 457.

158. Verbatim respondent 2.

159. At one point, I had a leadership role where the majority of the team were women. I used to call team meetings at the end of the workday, sometimes slipping into after-hours. Several of the women explained to me that this caused great tension, because they had children in day-care, and going overtime in daycare caused a greatly increased expense. This was a critical lesson.

important practice for dealing with the complexity of our contemporary lives.[160]

Barton speaks of discernment as "the capacity to recognize and respond to the presence and the activity of God—both in the ordinary moments and the larger decisions of our lives."[161]

Symmetry of Information

Assurance of symmetry of information is a critical leadership trait and is tied directly to the demand for justice. Simply put, don't hide the ball. Those of us who know cannot and must not take advantage of those who do not know. In the investment industry this known is as a lack of symmetry, wherein those who have less financial knowledge than experts are at risk of being taken advantage of. Experts must ask themselves, 'if the other party reasonably knows everything that I know, would they still make the deal?'

Generosity is paired with symmetry. Jesus offers, "From everyone to whom much has been given, much will be required (Luke 12: 48)." This is a call to fiduciary stewardship. To expand on this, we should take a legacy view on all the gifts that we have received. In other words our gifts are used to create legacy. These gifts are not consumables that we can simply use up for ourselves, but rather are given to us to enrich the world around us. Russell Shorto writes:

> It was largely the broader workplace where the faith dialogue occurred . . . [T]he Word spread 20 centuries ago. And as it did, it transmitted itself less in houses of worship than in the tents of carpet sellers, in the wine shops and bakeries and maybe most of all at the tables found in every market town where stacks of coins signaled the indispensable presence of the moneylender. The market was the central place of human interaction. It was where change happened, where ideas lighted from one mind to the next. It is up to us to decide whether our activities at work lead others toward faith, or away from it. One way or the other this will be our legacy.[162]

---

160. Liebert, *The Soul of Discernment*, 19.
161. Barton, *Pursuing God's Will Together*, 10.
162. Shorto, "Faith at Work," para. 4.

Like it or not, it is the workplace where we develop the morals by which we act in essentially all our spheres of existence. Acting our faith will encourage others to ask what drives us: opening a space for a Spirit-led conversation.

Corrective Leadership

Leaders occasionally must confront corruption. Grant Wahlstrom and Anita Chowdury explain:

> [T]he forensic audit team at Midnight Sun Inc. (MSI), sat with Justin Planter, a regional sales manager at the solar power company, as he rolled his eyes. MSI's procurement department forwarded Planter's travel and expense (T&E) reports to Cathy Francis, the human resource manager, after and employee noted that spending was not consistent with the company's T&E policy . . . During the interview, Planter admitted to purchasing a personal cell phone using his company credit card. In addition, he frequently used the credit card for alleged business meetings in establishments that bordered on adult entertainment.[163]

Sadly, such situations are not uncommon. Indeed, if we have not experienced such behaviour in our own work environments, we have certainly read about them. They must be addressed swiftly. *Leaders must confront destructive situations.* As with confronting corruption, leadership involves confronting workplace aggression. A respondent stated, "Two males in the same job before me [were] paid more."[164] How has this phenomenon become acceptable? Gender income inequality is workplace aggression. Another respondent stated, "[I feel] that I have been taken advantage of."[165] This, too, is workplace aggression. In 1986, three short decades ago, Hall wrote:

> Obviously, determining comparable worth [of a woman in the workplace] is a *formidable task*, because myriad factors have to be

---

163. Wahlstrom and Chowdury, "The Double Dipper," 23. Harriet Ekperigin writes, "This reminds me of the eHealth Ontario 'muffin scandal', where a senior independent consultant charged back expenses for a muffin as 'business expense'. This certainly did not speak well of her decision making and it later came to be in the front pages of Ontario newspapers. in government roles especially, we must do everything possible to be fiscally responsible to tax payers."

164. Verbatim respondent 1.

165. Verbatim respondent 22.

considered . . . The opposition to comparable worth will remain strong, however, for economic, political and social reasons.[166]

It's time. Leadership response is urgent. Trust evaporates when it is clear that correction is required, yet not addressed.

Leaders must act! As a leader with, or without, direct profit and loss accountability, one's task is to act strategically and tactically to increase profitability while enhancing customer experience.[167] In a market economy where our business win/loss ratio is a moment-to-moment measurement, an ethos that extends equally to customer experience as well as profitability is critical.

Leading from Beside

The simplest and most effective correction occurs on the job and in the moment. This is curbside leadership—the essence of the 'master-apprentice' relationship described earlier. Leadership is about focussing on those who might work beside us, whether they are the head of finance or they work in the mail room. A leader's task is to bring others to greater knowledge and ability—sometimes beyond our own knowledge and ability.

There is an optimal level of performance to be aspired to in every business endeavour. This is where the enterprise achieves perfect equilibrium between client satisfaction, employee meaningfulness, and an appropriate profit margin. Many service providers are skewed in one direction or another; giving up client satisfaction for the sake of profitability, or profitability for the sake of the client experience. Often, employee purpose and meaningfulness may be forgotten altogether. Leadership should keep all these priorities in careful balance. This is a product of leading from beside, gained through dialogue—hearing all voices. When we lead from alongside, through conversation we become aware of the inequities that are inhibiting true flourishing. This calls for us to move decisively to remove inequities in the workplace. As observed, the gender salary gap is a stark example. Deborah Gin and Chris Meinzer write:

---

166. Hall, *Dimensions of Work*, 219 [emphasis added].

167. This is also where trusted counsel is invaluable. The CFO of the parent company of the firm where I held a leadership role, when I outlined prospective new initiatives to him, would ask, "Paul, what's your test for reasonableness?" It became an automatic practice.

> In a recent survey of female constituents at *Association of Theological Schools* (ATS), we included a question of whether participants thought they were paid less than men at the same rank/level in their school. Of the 520 women currently serving in ATS schools, 40 percent said yes, 30 percent said no, and another 30 percent said they didn't know.[168]

While it appears that there has been improvement in recent years, gender inequity is still present, and it is blatantly discriminatory. Gender-based compensation inequity is just one example of discrimination. In an interview, Karen Christensen adds depth to this issue. She states:

> In any organization—whether it is public, private, or not-for-profit—internal processes create power dynamics, and those dynamics foster cultures where gender-based discrimination, racial discrimination, and discrimination towards other vulnerable populations proliferate. Organizational practices—many of which have become taken-for-granted—perpetuate inequality by privileging some groups over others in hiring, promotion, reward and other decisions.[169]

Trust grows out of deep engagement with colleagues.[170] Our task is to affirm and to encourage at the same time that we correct. When we find organizational circumstances that require correction, it is up to us to act—quickly and decisively. The findings of my survey indicate that acting our faith—being guided by our faith, may be the most important way to bring faith into our workplaces.

Punctuality: The Simplest Example

The most fundamental form of correction is personal example. A respondent stated, "I am here in this lifetime to be of service to others."[171] Jesus

---

168. Gin and Meinzer, "What about the Salary Gap," 12.

169. Christensen, "Tackling Inequality," 123.

170. When I occupied the Dean's office in a business school, a second-year commerce student knocked on my door. Haltingly, she told me that she had cheated on an exam. I asked her what she was going to do about it. She knew that she had to confess. We talked for a while, and she knew that there would be a penalty. Her transgression cost her a lost term. For a while I wondered if this might be the last time I encountered her. It was not. She returned, completed her studies, and graduated with distinction. Somewhere deep in her hope and self-respect welled up.

171. Verbatim respondent 28.

said, "We must work the works of him who sent me while it is day; night is coming when no one can work (John 9:4)." Here is perhaps the simplest leadership service lesson of all: *time management*. Leaders are frequently missing the point about respecting simple punctuality, and this is causing the unnecessary wasting of resources. It is giving a very unfortunate message to peers and subordinates in the enterprise. When someone shows up late occasionally, there are often good reasons, and we should acknowledge that. However, when someone shows up late persistently, they are making a choice to be late. When that person is the senior member of the group, or worse, the entire enterprise, the message they are giving is that they are quite comfortable with squandering the organization's resources. They are also confirming their view that their own agendas rank ahead of those who are frustrated and waiting for them to show up! Either way it is a very short-sighted discipline and a bad message. Is there a more simple way to set the tone for collegiality and the importance of the stewardship of resources than by being on time? More than this, add up the aggregate time lost by people waiting on a habitually late leader. Multiply that through their compensation rates, and then multiply that through the number of events where this is allowed to happen. The net loss goes straight to the bottom line. Above all this is about respect. There is an expression, "they do not care what you know until they know that you care." We have to show up—on time.[172]

Vulnerability

Leadership involves resolving the convoluted, the complex, the tangled and the torturous conundrums of the workplace. A respondent stated, "I am wrestling with how [we] should approach gender identity and sexuality issues—this is not a safe discussion." David McLean presents this:

> Empirically, I believe the relational aspects of leaders and their followers are key . . . Specifically, relational agility, or the ability to establish and nurture deep inter-connectedness, respect and trust with others in the organization is foundational to organizational resiliency . . . I am defining organizational resiliency as

---

172. This issue of being on time may seem relatively unimportant, until we recognize that if cannot get this right, why bother with anything else?

the capacity of the organization to successfully navigate change while delivering positive results.[173]

Establishing deep connectedness is particularly challenging when spans of control are broad and organizational sections and departments are very large. Hamel offers:

> In many companies, the major staff groups, such as HR, finance, and planning, employ hundreds, if not thousands, of people. Yet how many of these folks feel personally responsible for helping their company build a bona fide 'management advantage? In my experience, most are focussed on compliance and efficiency issues.[174]

Regular, detailed and useful sharing of information creates a community. Regular communication requires integrity and vulnerability. It is in accepting our vulnerability—acknowledging that anything we might achieve is the indwelling of the Holy Spirit—that the road to authenticity begins. Robert Clinton writes:

> At the heart of any assessment of biblical qualifications for leadership lies the concept of integrity—that uncompromising adherence to a code of moral, artistic, or other values that reveals itself in sincerity, honesty, and candour, and avoids deception or artificiality. The God-given capacity to lead has two parts: giftedness and character. Integrity is the heart of character.[175]

Given the power that they hold over such critical elements as the allocation of scarce resources, workforce composition, compensation and benefits, leaders must have, and act with, integrity. A stark example of this is the decision to discriminate, or as discussed earlier, the failure to correct discriminatory practices. This becomes apparent in decisions to hire majority workers over minority workers, male over female. Describing integrity as a primary virtue, Walter Fluker writes:

> Integrity informs the leader's actions and practices . . . It is the practice of speaking and living straight from the heart without neglecting the rational processes of the mind . . . At a deeper level, the leader must examine the motivational content of his or her behaviours as they relate to integrity. While integrity has

---

173. McLean, "Relational Agility," 4.
174. Hamel, *The Future of Management*, 246–47.
175. Clinton, *The Making of a Leader*, 50.

to do with wholeness, harmony, and integration at the personal level, it is also the product of critical self-examination.[176]

Intense, and frequent introspection—self-examination is core to growing in leadership. An example is the issue of reflection on the power imbalance that exists in the workplace. This requires virtually constant self-examination and reflection on the way authority is exercised and the resulting impact on morale and self-esteem in the workplace. Such reflection enables change. James Autry confirms, "If you change yourself, you've already changed the workplace environment."[177] In the long run we triumph over hubris. However, as Tomas Chamorro-Premuzic writes, "men [sic] are rarely rewarded for behaving more humbly, and we have far too much tolerance for male leaders who behave like narcissists."[178] In their discussion of the story of Job, Bartholomew and O'Dowd assert, "Wisdom grows only with humility before the Lord."[179] This is a challenging assertion in a workplace culture that, literally, promotes confidence. Chamorro-Premuzic discusses the pitfall of "confidence disguised as competence."[180] Chamorro-Premuzic writes regarding his subject, Ryan:

> Ryan's self-regard is apparent not only during job interviews, but also in internal team assignments, client presentations and networking events. Ryan speaks more, and louder, and he is much more likely to interrupt other people . . . He's less likely to qualify his statements with caveats and more likely to speak in bold strokes—something his boss sees as 'having vision.'[181]

By contrast, there is a critical and seemingly, sometimes, unattainable strength that is required of leaders—the strength of decision-making intertwined with deep empathy. Richard Chewning et al. write "Practicing corporate shalom by ensuring that relationships, profits, products and ethics correspond with God's intention for humanity."[182] Kindness does not mean softness; indeed servant leadership is a challenging calling. Northouse writes, "Servant Leadership is an approach focussing on leadership from the point of view of the leader and his or her behaviours.

176. Fluker, *Ethical Leadership*, 66–67 [emphasis original].
177. Autry, *Servant Leadership*, 50.
178. Chamorro-Premuzic, *Why Do So Many*, 50.
179. Bartholomew and O'Dowd, *Old Testament*, 185.
180. Chamorro-Premuzic, *Why Do So Many*, 17.
181. Chamorro-Premuzic, *Why Do So Many*, 17–18.
182. Chewning et al., *Business*, 193.

Servant leadership emphasizes that leaders be attentive to the concerns of their followers, empathize with them and nurture them."[183] Servant leadership may ensure that leaders are more open to negative feedback. Chamorro-Premuzic writes, "One reason overconfident leaders are more prone to reckless decisions is that they are immune to negative feedback."[184] This ties back to communication. We can resolve this by constant, and meaningful dialogue in 'town hall' type events, or simple one-on-one conversations. Such conversations encourage cooperation. Clive Beed and Clara Beed write that following the cooperative relations between each member of the Trinity, "Jesus' advocacy is toward collaboration, mutual assistance and support, enhancing trust, partnership, alliance and teamwork."[185]

Actions will be Imitated

For better or worse, leaders will be emulated. The findings of my research indicate that acting our faith and being guided by our faith, may be the most important way to bring faith into our workplaces. It is remarkably powerful simply to be the kind of colleague that one desires everyone else in the organization to be. They will watch you intently. They will listen to your words, your tone, and your responses to questions. They will watch your body language, even without realizing it. This enables you to carry your organization's lexicon to every person in the organization, and this will translate into the way folks treat one another and how they respond to customers as well. Such conversations also enable you to recognize and respond more immediately to instances of ineffectiveness, or gaps in knowledge and approach. This gives rise to the opportunity to be a curbside coach—giving meaningful guidance right in the thick of day-to-day activity.

Recognizing the person is a trait of strong leadership. A Deputy Head Master of a School in the UK, together with a colleague, would stand outside the school entrance in the morning and greet everyone as they entered. Often a conversation would ensue. A simple act that creates an ethos of connection. People grow not only in capability, but in a deep sense of purpose in their work; finding trust in others. The findings of my

---

183. Northouse, *Leadership Theory and Practice*, 219.
184. Chamorro-Premuzic, *Why Do So Many*, 35.
185. Beed and Beed, "Jesus on Cooperation," 32.

survey indicate that the person and model of Jesus is valued by many of the respondents to my research questionnaire. This vignette also emphasizes the need for presence.

Acting our Faith Grounds Others

The findings of my survey indicate that among people of professed faith or spirituality there is a sense, as evidenced by several respondents, that their spirituality grounds them and strengthens them; providing them with meaningfulness, vocational fulfillment and joy. Some simply left for new environments over changing their existing environment. We can retain valued employees by paying greater attention to our values, and finding a forum in which to discuss them. By example, a respondent stated, "I feel trusted."[186] Can anything be more straightforward?

Short term performance can be forced through purely transactional means. Long-term performance is tied, inextricably, to ethics and culture. The values that leaders model are the values that are embraced. If values are not aligned, it is time to think about moving on. People listen to what we say in the boardroom or the classroom, and then they watch how we behave in the hallways and at the curbside. If our behaviour is inconsistent with our statements, others are confused, or they write the relationship off completely. In particular, they are watching us intently at inflection points. This becomes intense in times of error and of challenge. Do we obfuscate when challenged with an issue or do we address the issue plainly and openly? If there is compensation to be made for an error, do we deal with it forthrightly or do we try to negotiate the least we can get away with? The bottom line is that opacity might work for a while, but generally not for long. The findings of my survey indicate that among people who expressed meaningfulness, vocational fulfillment and joy, there was also expression of a degree of fatigue and powerlessness. The root of this is inconsistency of leadership. Also evident was the resignation that finding greater purpose required economic compromise. This moment of resignation represents a significant inflection point, becoming debilitating to the point where one simply goes through the motions of work.

---

186. Verbatim respondent 9.

Work is Sacramental

Leaders need counsel. As suggested, what can sometimes be the fog of current circumstances can be cut through only if we can stand in the future and describe that future in a level of detail that is as specific as our organization's current circumstances. Sometimes the clarity we need can only be achieved by bringing trusted and impartial advisors into the dialogue.

While this is a critical discipline when contemplating strategic decisions, it also has important value in everyday business. Dealing decisively and transparently with missteps can be costly, but never as costly as the impending financial or reputational hit that lurks when the first error is not dealt with head-on. Don Tapscott and David Ticoll write, "Leaders see transparency as a threat or an opportunity."[187] To this I add that work is sacramental. We must treat work with reverence. The Psalmist writes, "He makes grass grow for the cattle, and plants for man to cultivate—bringing forth food from the earth: wine that gladdens the heart of man, oil to make his face shine, and bread that sustains his heart (Ps 104:14–15)." In a fundamental sense these gifts are sacraments from God—they bring together his gifts of natural resources to us, and his gifts of `skills within us that we might use to put such gifts to our use. Thus, we arrive at work as sacrament.

The Latin *sacramentum* was used to describe a thing, sometimes money, pledged as a down-payment or a non-refundable bond. In this sense, some turn to the book of Acts for evidence of the sacred nature of this down-payment. We read, "Keep watch over yourselves and over all the flock, of which the Holy Spirit has made you overseers, to shepherd the church of God that he obtained with the blood of his own Son (Acts 20:28)." With this passage in mind, we should think of our life's work as sacrament—as our down-payment—a first instalment—on our participation in God's kingdom. We may be happy in the knowledge that the Holy Spirit will equip us—authorize us—to carry out our work.

As Spirit-filled people, we are carrying out our purpose in our efforts to assure shelter, sustenance and self-actualization. Such work is sacramental and will endure through the ages and beyond, into the new kingdom—this is *legacy*. The word legacy has, as its root, the Latin *legatus*, the same root as the words legate and delegate. In effect, through our legacy we are sending the product of our labour on to the future: a future that is beyond our earthly lives. As good leaders we delegate to and equip

---

187. Tapscott and Ticoll, *The Naked Corporation*, 3.

those with whom we work alongside. *They ultimately become stronger than us, and that is our reward.* We pass the torch into strong hands.

Prayer invokes Legacy

Prayer is a critical practice for sustaining self-awareness. In private prayer, as Williams writes, "[We] might say that we are being encouraged to flee from 'projection'—from other people's projections onto us, ours onto them, our own inflated expectations of ourselves."[188] Prayer cannot help but consciously place our mission into God's hands.

In addition to having our mission in front of us every day, so must our perspective on legacy be in front of us. Leading from faith is eschatological. We must adapt constantly, in cooperation with others; as the Spirit calls us. The workplace has changed since yesterday. As leaders, we must be *all* in. Leadership is *never* part-time. McChrystal writes, "Leadership is far more difficult than we realize. This calls for us to be clear-eyed to the burden we have inherited. Leadership is not glamorous or straightforward. It is painful and perplexing, even at its best."[189] Leadership without counsel (cf. Prov 15:22) will ultimately fail. Jesus says:

> You are the light of the world. A city on a hill cannot be hidden. Neither do people light a lamp and put it under a bowl. Instead, they put it on its stand, and it gives light to everyone in the house. In the same way, let your light shine before others, that they may see your good deeds and praise your Father in heaven (cf. Mt. 5:14–16).

What a literally awesome gift leadership is. When we are given this gift, we are *seen* by God and identified for a specific task. We become an 'I.' Gibbs speaks of:

> [An] ethics of responsibility, arising out of the need not merely to speak and act responsively, but more out of the need to think: to give an account to others of why we should respond for other people . . . Responsiveness is the fulfillment of a responsibility, but my bearing of the responsibility is independent of whether I act ethically or not.[190]

---

188. Williams, *Silence and Honey Cakes*, 63.
189. McChrystal, *Leaders*, 399.
190. Gibbs, *Why Ethics*, 3.

This is the leadership task that we are called to. We are bound to an ethical exigency. We cannot simply respond to situations. We must respond ethically. Thus Gibbs states, "Responsibility in this ethics is asymmetric: I am responsible for others in a way that they are not responsible for me."[191] *Sometimes there is a price to pay, but there is reward in paying the price.*

We should pray that our calling to leadership is sure. A respondent stated, "I pray most nights that I am making the right/best decisions."[192] This *is* the response to the call of leadership. Leadership is *always* about the future. We look back, but we act forward. It is about righting things that are not working. This is why leadership is hard.

Leadership requires endurance and forbearance. Leaders are steady and diligent. It bears repeating that leadership is transformational, not transactional. Richard Cassidy reminds us of Paul's unfolding progress towards his testimony before the Roman Empire's highest official. He writes:

> Is it true that Luke fails to show Paul engaging in any particularly significant endeavour at the ending of Acts? It is important to observe that the encounters which Paul has previously had with various provincial officials effectively prepare the way for such a 'summit' encounter with Caesar. Luke has portrayed Paul receiving divine visions guiding him to judgement and testimony before the emperor (cf. Acts 23:11 and 27:24). The perspective afforded by the allegiance-witness theory is crucial. What emerges when Acts and its conclusion are viewed from this perspective is: (1) that Luke's ending shows Paul's faithful testimony before Caesar to be complete *in principle,* and (2) that Luke's ending indicates that Paul's 'ordinary' ministry of behalf of Jesus continues for the immediate future.[193]

Thus we learn that leadership, divinely-inspired, unfolds at a speed that God chooses. We do not, necessarily, get the entire blueprint in one instant. We must walk the path laid before us, hopefully bolstered as we require it. It is a marathon, not a sprint.

Finally, rest is required. Barton writes:

> In solitude we learn to wait on God for our own life so that when leadership brings us to the place where the *only option* for us is to wait on God, we believe it all the way down to the bottom of our being. Because we have met God in the waiting place (rather

---

191. Gibbs, *Why Ethics*, 3.
192. Verbatim respondent 18.
193. Cassidy, *Society and Politics*, 168.

than running away or giving in to panic or deceiving ourselves into thinking things are better than they are), we are able to stand firm and believe God in a way that makes it possible for others to follow suit.[194]

We should build into our routine sufficient time for rest, prayer, contemplation, and renewal.

Conclusion

This chapter has asserted that leadership must focus on the ethos of the organization as strenuously as structure is given to the material imperatives that guide organizational composition. This results in a leadership *gestalt* that combines human flourishing with output-oriented requirements. Neither is left behind. In fact both are enhanced.

To achieve this, multiple practices of leadership are recast and embedded in spiritual discernment, thus assuring that all leadership practices are moral in nature.

Deep focus is given to the individual person in a given situation. Leadership is considered to be co-related to human flourishing. Specific leadership activities are offered as imperative when those activities are conceived as equal in importance to flourishing in terms of organizational results.

Love is presented as the foundation to leadership, leading to moral choices that are automatically in concert with the *agape* imperative. Spirit-led leadership is comprehensive; it cannot be compartmentalized. This leads to adaptive capacity that facilitates situational response without erosion or loss of a divine-human endeavour that is constantly adapting and transforming as legacy to God's unfolding kingdom.

---

194. Barton, *Strengthening the Soul of Your Leadership*, 98.

5

Leadership as a Divine Calling

> *It was he who gave some to be apostles, some to be prophets, some to be evangelists, and some to be pastors and teachers, to prepare God's people for works of service, so that the body of Christ may be built up until we all reach unity in the faith and in the knowledge of the Son of God and become mature, attaining to the whole measure of the fullness of Christ.*
>
> (EPH 4:11 NIV)

SOMEWHERE IN OUR CAREER there is a jolt; a shake-up, a disturbance. There is a proverbial knock at the door. We find ourselves questioning not only our methods, but our entire approach.[1] Such an experience may be described as a personal inflection point—a bending away to a new trajectory. In particular for many, thoughts turn to a reflection on work and leadership as manifestations of faith. Veith offers us this, "The doctrine of vocation offers a theological way of thinking about work."[2] The vocation of leadership has at its core an ethic of recognition, which I shall develop more fully in this chapter. This ethic of recognition may be contemplated through the image of leadership as a form of shepherding,

---

1. I was well into the second half of my career before coming to faith let alone considering my work as a divine calling.
2. Veith, *God at Work*, 157.

Leadership as a Divine Calling

in the fullest biblical sense of the term (cf. John 10: 27–28). It is leadership for others to follow.

Of the respondents, five discuss some level of discussion with a minister or counsellor. One discusses attending a teaching series. Another discusses annual visits from church elders. Two describe conversations with 'advisors.' One describes praying with a supervisor. The balance of the respondents are essentially silent on the matter.[3]

While there were few respondents who spoke of meaningful conversations with a minister or spiritual advisor, many testified to the role that their faith played in their daily working lives and their reflection on the purpose of their work. One respondent spoke of adherence to the teachings of what this respondent described as Eastern Religions. Several specifically referred to their spirituality as separate from a religious affiliation.

A study by Anushri Rawat and Shiva Nadavulakare state that:

> [Their] study results demonstrate that having a strong work calling is beneficial for both individuals and organizations. Results show that individuals who have a strong work calling are more committed to their organizations, have less emotional exhaustion and exhibit higher levels of contextual performance. Thus, in order to reap positive outcomes from their work individuals should engage in work that enables them to pursue their calling. Also, organizations will have increased work outcomes by hiring individuals who have a strong work calling. Further, organizations will benefit greatly by creating conditions that enable individuals to pursue their calling. Findings indicate that individuals with a high calling thrive in organizations that have more participative decision-making practices and which offer high work discretion.[4]

While Rawat and Nadavulakare offer different sources of one's calling, there is suggestion that one's calling is the result of a "transcendent summons originating beyond one's self."[5] It appears critical that a discussion of calling is valuable. That is the subject of this chapter.

Many of the respondents assert that they are people of Christian faith. Several of these, however, do not see value in the teachings of the

---

3. Workplace ministry will be the subject of another work.
4. Rawat and Nadavulakare, "Examining the Outcomes of Having a Calling," 499.
5. Rawat and Nadavulakare, "Examining the Outcomes of Having a Calling," 499.

church; in fact some cite discord in their Church. A respondent stated, "I am wrestling with how the church should approach gender identity and sexuality issues—this is not a safe discussion."[6] Nor is it clear that they are regular church attendees. To be clear, I personally affiliate with the Anglican Church, where I serve as an ordained Deacon. I do not, however, suggest that joining a church is critical to what I have to offer here. Also, while I value so very deeply the friends and associates who have enriched my life who are adherents of faiths which are other than mine, I can only speak of my own faith and experiences as a Christian. Richard Niebuhr writes:

> A Christian is ordinarily defined as 'one who believes in Jesus Christ,' or as 'a follower of Jesus Christ.' He [sic] might be more adequately described as one who counts himself [sic] as belonging to that community of men [sic] for whom Jesus Christ; his life, words, deeds, and destiny, is of supreme importance as the key to an understanding of themselves and their world—the main source of the knowledge of God and man [sic]. Good and evil, the constant companion of the conscience, and the expected deliverer from evil.[7]

Niebuhr's words may still have heft for those that carry a strong grounding in faith, seeing work as divine calling. One respondent stated:

> I experience very deep joy and meaningfulness in my work. In my mid-thirties I followed God's leading toward a career using more of my gifts and a desire to help/serve. My views, which stem from a deep-rooted belief in Christian life, are not popular amongst peers. I feel quite powerless at times. I have chosen to work in a non-Christian environment where I can model Christ.[8]

This respondent would appear to model the definition of a Christian as provided by Niebuhr, and this respondent certainly reflects the challenge, even struggle experienced in being in community with others who may not share the same views. Broadly, however, as I have said it is clear that a church affiliation is seldom identified among the respondents as a place that anchors them in coping with their workplace travails. A respondent stated:

---

6. Verbatim respondent 1.
7. Niebuhr, *Christ and Culture*, 11.
8. Verbatim respondent 6.

> I believe that there is something higher, but not through the lens of religious faith. In terms of my spiritual beliefs, I believe that we are all connected and that the energy we bring to our interactions effects the quality of connection, and other things like loyalty, trust, etc. I also believe that on the whole, people are good.[9]

Another writes:

> I do not subscribe to an organized religion; however I do hold to my own spiritual beliefs. I believe that my work's meaning is driven by my desire to contribute to others' growth and development. I am also deriving meaningfulness from volunteering.[10]

Such responses imply an orientation to *believe* in a divine power, but not necessarily to *belong* to a denominational church or other faith community. Morisy adds, "The loss of familiarity with religious symbols . . . means that an important level of awareness, critical in providing coherence and giving depth to one's faith, remains inaccessible."[11] The gospel message may be accepted when it is perceived to affirm personhood and provides an affirmation that the person and model of Jesus presents a path to deeper meaningfulness. Gibbs and Coffey suggest that many "will engage in open and honest dialogue with people they know well and consider credible witnesses."[12] This underscores the thought that perhaps the best way to present the message of the Gospel is to fully recognize the person.

The Search for Meaning

Sometimes verbalized, often not, there is a search for meaning in our work, as in our life broadly. A respondent stated, "Most people either believe in nothing, or believe in something so rigid and prescriptive that there is no point in discussing it."[13] This suggests a perception that coworkers may be entrenched in a particular dogmatic view and that any attempt at dialogue would be pointless, even contentious. Marty offers that, "[T]he human self is a rather fragile thing. Social scientists and theologians

---

9. Verbatim respondent 4.
10. Verbatim respondent 5.
11. Morisy. *Beyond the Good Samaritan*, 45.
12. Gibbs and Coffey, *Church Next*, 194.
13. Verbatim respondent 24.

of different stripes have long pointed out the deep insecurities, the persistent struggles with meaning and significance, and the persistent search for lasting relations that so steadily define nearly every human life."[14] Several respondents expressed insecurity. For example, one respondent stated, "In terms of fully satisfying a sense of calling, that is more difficult. I'm still trying to figure it all out." Lake Lambert writes, "The search for meaning . . . can include opportunities to volunteer through work and a focus on a company's social responsibility. Researchers note that Millennials more than any other generation have experience with community service."[15] This is deeply encouraging.

The workplace can frequently be more chaotic than calm. Pattison writes, "While there may be some general, formal principles of management, these may be unevenly applied in practice and the actual work of managers may be rather chaotic and *ad hoc*. Real Managers may not do the things they say managers should do."[16] We get caught up in the demands of the immediate. We all begin every task by responding, consciously or unconsciously, to our perception of our environment. This bears repeating, our situation shapes our reaction. A situational response frames our engagement with the task at hand. Edward Farley writes:

> All human beings exist and act in situations and engage in interpretations of situations. This interpretative dimension of human existence does not cease with faith and with life in the community of faith. On the contrary, faith and the world of faith shape the perspective, the 'taken-for-granted stock of knowledge,' the weighting of what is important, all of which affect the interpretation of situations. In other words interpreting situations from the viewpoint and in the context of faith does create a special hermeneutic task, differentiable from other hermeneutic or interpretive dimensions of theology.[17]

The respondents' collective perspectives largely describe an in-harmony, or tension: what I have described as dissonance. The causes of such tensions become so entrenched in the routines and mores of the environment that we compartmentalize them until we can no longer, and then there is fracture.

14. Marty, "Shaping Communities," 308–9.
15. Lambert, "The Future of Workplace Spirituality," 158.
16. Pattison, *The Faith of Managers*, 13.
17. Farley, "Interpreting Situations," 119.

There are truly wrenching dynamics at play as society and organizations transition from the modern to the postmodern. In one organization, many generations of workers[18] are navigating changing structures and ethics in the same environment, but each one of us filters these changes through different frameworks based on experiences and upbringing. Care must be taken while navigating the changes from those circumstances which were more in tune with traditions from earlier times. Pattison argues that:

> Within and beneath the everyday practice of management lie hidden religio-ethical assumptions that mostly go unnoticed by the casual observer. Just because they are unnoticed does not mean that they are not important or influential—indeed, some of the foundations of management may rest upon them.[19]

As said, our frames of reference can be vastly different. When leaders are brought together to discuss their work, their challenges, and their spirituality, resilience is built. Zylla states, "Resilience is measured by the ability, given similar resources of a person or organization, to bounce back, recover, and even thrive after a significant trauma or event."[20] Thus, thoughtful conversations around pivotal events, especially inflection points, not only restore and strengthen the organization, but leaders within the organization are also restored and strengthened. These events confirm and uphold leaders' efforts as they navigate their way towards a greater sense of fulfillment and purpose of their work. Eventually, these dialogues of reflection may lead to further discussion of spirituality.

John Van Sloten writes:

> One of the best parts of my job is meeting with small groups of workers from any given field to learn about their jobs as they better discern God's active presence at work. This collective effort is not only an effective way for *them* to discover God's on-the-job presence; it is also a means through which everyone in our community can do the same . . . When they realize they can know God through their unique passions and abilities, their experience of work is transformed. Their jobs become more

---

18. Silents (Born between 1925 and 1946), Baby Boomers (Born between 1946 and 1964), Generation Xers (Born between 1965 and 1980), and Generation Ys or Millennials (born after 1980).

19. Pattison, *The Faith of Managers*, 1.

20. Zylla, "Cultivating a Resilient Congregation," 103.

God-aware, and this epiphany has led to a profound sense of delight and gratitude.[21]

Sponsorship of study groups will facilitate discussions of such challenges as cross-generational work practices and the integration of multiculturalism in the workplace. Philip A. Woods and Glenys J. Woods discuss "cultural networking—that is understanding symbols, meanings and customs."[22] While Woods and Woods discuss this concept in the context of educational environments, here is a relatively straightforward activity to bring to the workplace, through discussion groups and/or the placement of cultural artefacts. Lambert writes, "A desire for 'balance' is frequently invoked when referring to the Millennials at work and this echoes a Boomer theme as well as the workplace spirituality movement's quest for holism."[23] It may take many, many interactions to reach a deep conversation. The Spirit-led leader will patiently look for moments where discernment will spring forth. The point of view that I have arrived at is that to act my faith, and then simply to wait for someone to ask me what drives me. Even then, I ask permission to discuss my faith.

Discernment

Everyone is too busy achieving and surviving. They are too busy getting somewhere, and too busy trying to figure out what to do next while doing their best for their families. Federico Suarez writes, "We are all so busy 'finding ourselves' that the divine request to deny ourselves becomes practically unintelligible."[24] Busy-ness is a common underlying theme among the respondents. There is a risk in this. Parker Palmer writes, "As we become more obsessed with succeeding, or at least surviving, in the world, we lose touch with our souls and disappear into our roles."[25] In the midst of all this, however, is hope. The findings of my research indicate that hope is stronger than lived experiences in many cases. It is hope that we put our trust in. Suarez offers a dialogue focused on Matthew's account of the Sermon on the Mount:

---

21. Van Sloten, *Every Job a Parable*, 74 [emphasis original].
22. Woods and Woods, "Deepening Reflective Practice." 234.
23. Lambert, "The Future of Workplace Spirituality," 156.
24. Suarez, *The Narrow Gate*, 22.
25. Palmer, *A Hidden Wholeness*, 15.

> Paradoxical as it may seem, it is not the wide road, the affirmation of the ego; that enables us to find ourselves and attain the fullness of our personality. It is the narrow road, the denial of self (which is the affirmation of God) that leads us to this end. For it is only along this narrow road and through the narrow gate—through Jesus Christ—that one can arrive at the death of the old man [sic] or the false self, and to the birth of the new man [sic], or the authentic self.[26]

This passage emphasizes the paracletic nature of Spirit-led leadership. A divine call to leadership demands us to find ways to come alongside colleagues struggling with workplace demands, disappointments, disagreements and challenges. Lloyd-Jones adds, "We are meant to be participators in this; it is a call to action. You notice the words, 'Enter ye;' they are an invitation and an exhortation at one and the same time."[27] Somewhere inside, this call is heard. There is an innate sense that there is more. A respondent stated, "He is still revealing."[28] This is not intellectual. It is spiritual.[29] As Palmer states, "The soul wants to tell us the truth about ourselves."[30] Listening is required. Our soul is the focus of the Holy Spirit—God's agent of our interior growth.

A respondent stated, "My views, which stem from a deep-rooted belief in Christian life, are not popular amongst peers. I feel quite powerless at times. I have chosen to work in a non-Christian environment where I can model Christ."[31] This respondent echoes a critical premise of this study—that work, and the leadership of work, are of eschatological importance. I accept the Wesleyan perspective offered by Kenneth Collins, that "there is no man [sic] unless he [sic] has quenched the Spirit, who is wholly devoid of the grace of God."[32] Thus, *there is, in all persons, at least a faint glimmer of the divine light which when made brighter brings rebirth, and restoration.* This is achievable.

---

26. Suarez, *The Narrow Gate*, 24.
27. Lloyd-Jones, *Studies in the Sermon on the Mount*, 487.
28. Verbatim respondent 2.
29. On occasion, I will spend time with someone who wants to talk. I will ask them, 'do you want faith to be part of this conversation?' Invariably, the answer is yes. Though they may not say it explicitly, their soul wants to speak.
30. Palmer, *A Hidden Wholeness*, 15.
31. Verbatim respondent 6.
32. Collins, *The Theology of John Wesley*, 74.

Spiritual Rebirth

God is always the first mover, the initiative-taker, both in the rebirth of the soul, and in its restoration. Soul rebirth and restoration is effected by Jesus Christ through the working of the Holy Spirit. Christ will move through us, and beyond us.

To imagine our leadership role as including the call to care for souls may be too daunting to contemplate. We should remember, however, that we shall be equipped divinely for the task. When we are ready, active listening is at the heart of soul-care. Palmer writes:

> The soul is like a wild animal—tough, resilient, savvy, self-sufficient and yet exceedingly shy. If we want to see a wild animal, the last thing we should do is to go crashing through the woods, shouting for the creature to come out. But if we are willing to walk quietly into the woods and sit silently for an hour or two at the base of a tree, the creature we are waiting for may well emerge, and out of the corner of an eye we will catch a glimpse of the precious wildness we seek.[33]

Active listening, perhaps the very first step in responding to the call of Spirit-led leadership involves a deeply engaged presence. Deborah Antai-Otong writes, "Active listening involves all of the senses, not just hearing. It requires tremendous energy, discipline, and concentration, and requires recognizing and screening out internal and external influences and barriers that interfere with communication.[34] As suggested earlier, presence, or being, must precede doing. Presence involves paying attention. Ananias' first task was to 'be' with Paul (cf. Acts 9:10). Our task is to be present with others before dialogue can begin. Ananias was to represent God, and to invigorate the situation by his presence. Doohan writes:

> Recent spiritual renewal focuses on a rediscovery of the essential source values of faith and an opening to the autonomous values of the world. These discoveries have led to a simplification of spiritual life and a fundamentally positive attitude to the world. This has also led to new ways of thinking and living Christianity that imply a new value for human and earthly realities, an

---

33. Palmer, *A Hidden Wholeness*, 58.

34. Antai-Otong, "Active Listening at Work," 24. Harriet Ekperigin writes, "Earlier in my first career while working as a nurse therapist in mental health, I would often come home exhausted after a heavy day with clients. I was convinced that active listening was sometimes more draining than a hard day's manual labour."

awareness of personal responsibility for others, and a new community consciousness in believers.[35]

This consciousness centres on presence—a presence that excludes all but the focus of our prayer. Osmer writes:

> In recent decades discussion of the spirituality of presence has been widespread and has moved in a number of directions. Here it describes a spiritual orientation of attending to others in their particularity and otherness within the presence of God. The key term here is 'attending,' relating to others with openness, attentiveness and prayerfulness. Such attending opens up the possibility of an I-Thou relationship in which others are known and encountered in all their uniqueness and otherness, a quality of relationship that ultimately depends on the communion-creating presence of the Holy Spirit.[36]

Sometimes, perhaps even most of the time, our simple, quiet and attentive, presence is enough to make a profound impact on others. At its most fundamental, Spirit-led leadership is simply *presence*. Think about this for a moment: when so many feel invisible, simply being present in their lives changes everything. *Presence* invites a person's soul to speak.

Kate McLelland offers that the soul is "in its broadest sense, the essence of a person, the thing that defines them, the thing that makes them who they are."[37] We should seek ways to join colleagues; to come alongside them, in conversation about our mutual work *before* we approach the spiritual dimension of our lives and aspirations. This is a soul-full engagement. Barton states, "I am talking about the part of you that is most real—the very essence of you that God knew before he brought you forth in physical form, the part of you that will exist after your body goes into the ground."[38] The soul is shaped, formed, and nurtured by the Holy Spirit to perform those intellectual and physical tasks that we are being called to do, and that we are being equipped, spiritually, to carry out. Thomas Oden writes, "Soul, according to its classical Christian conception, is the unitive centre of the person . . . Soul is that by which we most deeply feel, know, and will, and by which the body is animated. The soul

---

35. Doohan, *Spiritual Leadership*, 108.
36. Osmer, *Practical Theology*, 34.
37. McLelland, *Call the Chaplain*, 15.
38. Barton, *Strengthening the Soul of Your Leadership*, 13.

lives out of God, and its life transcends this mortal sphere."[39] Though we may never articulate it specifically, the caring of souls is at the very centre of the task of leadership: ensuring that souls are healthy and capable of doing what Ronald Rolheiser describes as "keeping us energized, vibrant, living with zest and full of hope . . . keeping us fixed together."[40] When our soul is given freedom of expression, the intellect is ignited.

Transformation and Shalom

This book has emphasized the view of leadership as the work of transformation—of constantly growing from what *is* to what *can be*. Biblical accounts of leadership are almost entirely about the call to bring about transformation. Osmer states, "Transforming leadership . . . is leading an organization through a process in which its identity, mission, culture, and operating procedures are fundamentally altered."[41] Conversations regarding transformation are central to the calling of leadership. Such conversations can be a prelude to a way of thinking that previously could not be contemplated. By example, Northouse points out that from the mid-1960s there was a turn away "from the view of women as inferior to men (e.g. some had posited that women lacked skills and traits necessary for managerial success) to the view that extols the superiority of women in leadership positions."[42] Yet, here we are—as discussed, in large part we have not resolved the fundamental issue of gender-based compensation inequity. To take this one step further, Northouse suggests that women's styles tend to be more transformational than men's.[43] So, clearly, women's leadership skills are at least equal to their male counterparts. Chewning et al. write that organizations practise "corporate shalom by ensuring that relationships, profits, products, and ethics correspond with God's intention for humility." [44] In effect, experiencing dissonance is suffering inequality in the workplace. Shalom is the elimination of suffering. Shalom means the elimination of inequality. Williams states, "In case we've forgotten, it's worth reminding ourselves that the Bible seems fairly clear

---

39. Oden, *Pastoral Theology*, 187.
40. Rolheiser, *The Holy Longing*, 14.
41. Osmer, *Practical Theology*, 177.
42. Northouse, *Leadership Theory and Practice*, 349.
43. Northouse, *Leadership Theory and Practice*, 351.
44. Chewning et al. *Business*, 194.

that we are given to one another as believers so that we may know and experience more of God than we would on our own."[45] There can be no 'camps' that may be formed or implied—no assertion that there is a zero-sum game at hand where one group will triumph over another. We really need to let this sink in. Sarah Moses states:

> Rowan Williams' theological understanding of the non-competitiveness of Christian community and ecclesial unity as given provides a necessary framework for an analysis of the ethics of recognition. With regard to moral discernment, Williams identifies moments when new questions and potential new practices force communities to determine whether an ethical judgment is 'continuous' with the historic tradition. It is such situations that the exercise of recognition functions as the practice that allows a community to embody communion and to facilitate ethical discernment in the context of disagreement.[46]

This is a critical conversation. Williams is reminding us of the practices of the first Christian community (cf. Acts 4:32–37). Each member of the community was both seen as a contributor, and recognized for their right to participate and for their respective gifts. In an essay on moral decision-making, Williams wrote, "We watch to see if our partners take the same kind of time, sense that they are under the same sort of judgment or scrutiny, and approach the issue with the same attempt to be dispossessed by the truth with which they are engaging."[47] Williams learned, as we all do, that not all processes achieve the desired outcome.[48] *Sometimes it is because insufficient time has been taken.* This is a leadership lesson. Moses writes, "Cultures are products of historical processes in interpretation and meaning which are always in flux and changing."[49]

---

45. Archbishop's Presidential Address. [n.d.]. I add to this that my experience of God has grown substantially through conversations with colleagues whose faith is different than mine.

46. Moses, "The Ethics of Recognition," 151.

47. Williams, "On Making Moral Decisions," 304.

48. I, too, have witnessed such breakdowns. Sometimes it is because one party holds views so strongly that they are blind to the opportunity for recognition. I have witnessed the ugliest of situations as chair of university tenure and promotion committees, where academic rivalry and jealousy descends into an attempt to prevent a colleague from receiving deserved recognition.

49. Moses, "The Ethics of Recognition," 154. Patience is a virtue, as my father told me often.

Reflection and Hopeful Regeneration

A respondent stated:

> There were times when the sense of being tested really could be borne through a sense of faith. Although not an attender at any religious ceremony, I frequently use meditation, reflection, and prayer as a means to resolve issues in my mind. I do have a strong sense of spiritual guidance.[50]

This respondent is reflecting on a deeply personal experience. Bass and Dykstra write, "Practical theologians have long insisted that theological reflection finds its most generative starting point in concrete, nearby situations."[51] A respondent stated, "I find it hard to have honest, open conversations without fear of reprisal."[52] Such perspectives seem to call out for a leadership response. While only one respondent literally used the word 'suffering' many described situations that were troubling. Zylla describes "the essence of the compassionate response: *to move into the suffering of others with active help.*"[53] We may ask if this is too much to ask of leaders, being helpful is clearly in the job description. Leaders bear massive burdens. Prayer will equip us to bring hope, resilience, and forgiveness to others. Nouwen writes:

> When we live with hope, we do not get tangled up with concerns for how our wishes will be fulfilled . . . In the prayer of hope, there are no guarantees asked, no conditions posed and no proofs demanded . . . Hope is based on the premise that the other gives what is good. Hope includes an openness by which you wait for the promise to come through, even though you never know when, where, or how this might happen.[54]

The findings of my survey indicate that hope is stronger than actual lived experiences. *Hope is a yearning for transformation.* Hope implies trust and reliance. A respondent stated, "I feel called to this time and place for a reason."[55] This is a hope-full statement. Another respondent stated,

---

50. Verbatim respondent 14.
51. Bass and Dykstra, *For Life Abundant*, 355.
52. Verbatim respondent 1.
53. Zylla, *The Roots of Sorrow*, [emphasis original] 100.
54. Nouwen, *With Open Hands*, 73.
55. Verbatim respondent 2.

"I am able to leverage my gifts."[56] Hope is what shores up the entrepreneur in the early days and months of a start-up business.[57] Hope is what empowers an employee to bring an idea to the Chief Executive Officer.[58] Hope underpins vocation. Hope leads to prayer.[59] As Nouwen affirms, "Prayer leads you to new paths."[60]

Hope leads to a willingness to improvise when the perfect tools may not be available. It is hope that underpins resilience. Hope leads to trust, and trust leads to the empowerment of others. Hope leads to a forgiving attitude toward failure. Failure leads to innovation.

Hope leads to perseverance. The letter to the Hebrews states:

> So do not throw away your confidence; it will be richly rewarded. You need to persevere so that when you have done the will of God, you will receive what he has promised. For in just a very little while, He who is coming will come and will not delay. But my righteous one will live by faith. And if he shrinks back, I will not be pleased with him. But we are not of those who shrink back and are destroyed, but of those who believe and are saved (Heb 10: 35–39).

When the workplace is imbued with hope. Workers will take that hope home with them. Zylla states, "*A resilient community of faith has an 'ethos' of hopefulness and a narrative that evokes a hopeful view of the world.*"[61] This statement epitomizes the organization that is vibrant, innovative, and joyful.[62]

Spirit-Led Boards

I want to turn for a moment to governance. While this work is focussed primarily on those in functional leadership roles, and finding ways to provide ministry to them, there is another tier of leadership that requires discussion. This tier is the group charged with the legal oversight of the enterprise: the Board of Directors. John Carver and Caroline Oliver write

---

56. Verbatim respondent 15.
57. I know this.
58. I have witnessed this.
59. I do this.
60. Nouwen, *With Open Hands*, 122.
61. Zylla, "Cultivating a Resilient Congregation," 108 [emphasis original].
62. I have participated such situations.

emphatically, "[E]xecutives are under control of the board."⁶³ Carver and Oliver go on to state that, "Governance operates at a level that transcends current issues and specific company traditions and elevates people to a higher conceptual plane, one from which accountability can be seen more clearly."⁶⁴ Michael Willis and Michael Fass emphasize, "One of the key discussions at the board will be about trust because trust is an essential ingredient for success and will need to be created and nurtured."⁶⁵ David Gyertson suggests, "When mission and/or identity crises occur, it is not unusual to find the root causes in the relationship between the governing board and the CEO."⁶⁶ Pattison adds, "Ethical and values issues become more apparent and more contested when radical change takes place. Custom, tradition and 'common sense' can no longer serve as a complete guide to behaviour."⁶⁷ There is a very real need for deeper and structured dialogue at the board table regarding ethos and culture. Boards must articulate approaches to the circumstances described by the grounded theories presented in this work during retreats that are focussed on organizational mission and core values. Such exercises reinforce the ethos that the owners of the enterprise regard as essential. Roger Martin, Alison Kemper and Rod Lohin discuss *virtuous capital* as "those assets and capital expenditures [that] relate to positive contributions to society or reduced risk to the environment."⁶⁸ This is a clear demonstration of the organization's ethos.

Deep Caring and Spiritual Yearning

The critical, central, quality of Spirit-led leadership is caring. Palmer writes, "Deep caring about each other's fate does seem to be on the decline."⁶⁹ However, the natural tendency to care is still there, even if suppressed by circumstances. A respondent stated, "It is meaningful to work alongside people to help them explore their lives and life

---

63. Carver and Oliver, *Corporate Boards That Create Value*, xi.
64. Carver and Oliver, *Corporate Boards That Create Value*, xxi.
65. Willis and Fass, *Faith in Governance*, 50.
66. Gyertson, "Christian Leadership," 34.
67. Pattison, *The Faith of Managers*, 103.
68. Martin et al., "Virtuous Capital," 76.
69. Palmer, *A Hidden Wholeness*, 37.

circumstances."[70] When the circumstance is provided, this tendency to care will be re-energized.

Nouwen writes:

> The spiritual life is first of all, a patient waiting, that is, a waiting in suffering (*patior*—suffer), during which the many experiences of unfulfilment remind us of God's absence. But it is also waiting in expectation which allows us to recognize the first signs of the coming God in the centre of our pains. The mystery of God's presence, therefore, can be touched only by a deep awareness of his absence. It is at the centre of our longing for the absent God that we discover his footprints.[71]

Respondents articulate their spiritual yearning, as a means of coming to terms with the purpose of their work, in numerous ways. A respondent stated, "I'm still trying to figure it all out."[72] Intuitively, one can imagine vast numbers of people saying something like this. This is an invitation to ask someone to tell us their story. Listening to stories is Spirit-led—it lays a foundation for transformative change (cf. Mark 5). Nowhere, perhaps, is this more critical than in the workplace. Thomas Attig writes that "you must learn the details of each life story . . . you must learn the details."[73]

A respondent stated, "I feel that most of my colleagues share the same passion, although there are definitely some who don't."[74] Another writes, "I'm not sure if my co-workers share the same views."[75] Another writes, "I'm not convinced my colleagues share my sense of vocation."[76] Another writes, "I don't feel a high degree of meaningfulness."[77] Incompleteness gnaws at people, particularly leaders. Bass provides a simple but moving example of incompleteness. She writes, "Most days, I do not live on a mountain top, rather, I poke along in the weeds, my eyes turned

---

70. Verbatim respondent 12.
71. Nouwen, *Reaching Out*, 128.
72. Verbatim respondent 1.
73. Attig, *How We Grieve*, 18–19.
74. Verbatim respondent 8.
75. Verbatim respondent 30.
76. Verbatim respondent 10.
77. Verbatim respondent 32.

down toward my own path rather than out toward God and neighbour. Even then, of course, I retain a certain kind of knowledge of God."[78]

Workaholism

A challenge that is perhaps pervasive today is workaholism, particularly among those in leadership roles. Thomas W.H. Ng et al write:

> The changing nature of careers in recent years further accentuates the need to increase our understanding of Workaholism . . . [W]ith the advance of technology (e.g., internet and telecommunication), more and more employees are able to work outside the traditional office and outside traditional work hours, these changes can induce more workaholism especially in managerial employees, who now have both greater incentives and greater opportunities to invest more heavily in work . . . On one hand, workaholics are addicts who cannot control themselves; on the other hand, they are particularly diligent and dedicated workers.[79]

This deserves exploration, especially in the wake of Covid 19. Scott Hahn writes, "We have become stuck in creation's sixth day, unable to get perspective on life, unable to get a decent rest . . . If we do not make time to stop and think we lose our ability to sense God's being and his presence."[80] For people practicing their faith this means attending to the rhythm of work and Sabbath rest. We also need encouragement. Nouwen writes, "We need someone who encourages us when we are tempted to give it all up."[81] This phenomenon may be a primary reason for increased mental leaves of absence. Stefan Wyszynski offers a simple counselling discussion regarding praying at each stage in our work. He states:

> [There] is a kind of supernatural organization of work: a division of work into a number of little activities, each of which we give back to God in a separate act of love. It is possible to set all of the activities of the day into this framework. However, it is sufficient to get through some determined task well once during

---

78. Bass, "Practical Wisdom," 69.
79. Ng et al., "Antecedents, and Consequences, of Workaholism," 111–12.
80. Hahn *Ordinary Work*, 51.
81. Nouwen, *Reaching Out*, 137.

the course of the day in order to acquire wonderful fruits in the sanctification of the temporal.[82]

Empowered by Surrender

While there may be a need for intervention by experts, we must open a space for God to take over. This is our surrender. James Loder writes that in the moment of surrender we are, "known, seen and authorized [by God]."[83] Loder describes Paul's experience on the Road to Damascus, which we may view as a leadership preparation event. He writes, "Not only is Saul, seen, known and understood, he is authorized; first by this direct meeting and later by confirming events . . . He is called into the making of history."[84] Paul's experience is an extreme example of a transformative circumstance that we may experience ourselves: trauma followed by understanding. Pattison writes:

> Managers have to determine whether there is a need for change, and whether they have any choice about this. In doing so, they must identify the core mission or *raison d'etre* of their organization to discriminate between competing priorities and courses of action . . . Often, these issues have substantial ethical and practical implications. They should be taken seriously before change management is embarked upon.[85]

This is vital. Introducing change before there is an intellectual, even visceral, recognition that change is required will be futile. A period of contemplation is required.

For many the struggle to find purpose can be significant, if not monumental. Flourishing must involve spiritual intimacy. Before we can reach intimacy with God, and indeed greater intimacy with another person, we should first find stillness in solitude, which becomes a path to prayer. However, the silence that is prelude to solitude that may be the most significant threshold to cross. For those who have not yet accepted faith; indeed, even for those who have accepted faith—to ask them to be still—to enter solitude, can be a daunting request. Moreover, many

---

82. Wyszynski, *All You Who Labor*, 82.
83. Loder, *The Transforming Moment*, 22.
84. Loder, *The Transforming Moment*, 22.
85. Pattison, *Faith of the Managers*, 121–22.

will actively resist such an imperative. *We avoid silence, out of fear of the darkness of our existence, and out of fear of a struggle with the errors of our past.* Nouwen writes, "Whether it is good or bad I do not know, but there is no doubt that solitude leads me often to think about my past."[86] If this is Nouwen's experience, then we can imagine how profoundly difficult it might be for us to devote time to silence, without distractions, without the glittering lights of computer screens, mobile devices, televisions, and so on, in order to enter into solitude. To say the least it can be painful to confront past errors and perceived missed opportunities. We may even feel that it is too late—we have too much baggage—to contemplate a relationship with the divine. As Woody Guthrie wrote, "You've got to walk that lonesome valley."[87]

Liminality

We do have to go to the lonesome valley by ourselves. This is a liminal space. We find ourselves standing at a threshold, not knowing whether to step forward or to step back. It is a lonely place—it has to be. Paul Tournier adds:

> How many men and women around about us there are, with whom we rub shoulders daily, living in secret loneliness? The doctor, a sort of confessor, knows it better than anyone else. Often at the close of an interview I have heard the client tell me, without realizing it, I have been looking for someone for many years, someone to whom I could say just what I've told you now, someone I could trust without reservation and without any fear of being condemned.[88]

Loneliness certainly can be a place where we are stuck; unable to move. As stated, loneliness can indeed be a *liminal* place—a threshold ultimately to pass through, perhaps with guidance. Gianpiero Petriglieri et al. write:

> We set out to investigate how management education may foster the transformational learning that supports leaders' ongoing development. On the basis of [our] qualitative analysis we propose that this occurs through a process of *personalization* by which

---

86. Nouwen, *The Genesee Diary*, 93.
87. Song lyrics by Woody Guthrie.
88. Tournier, *Escape from Loneliness*, 14.

individuals examine their experiences and revisit their life stories as part and parcel of management learning.[89]

Silence is the first foothold on this threshold. The next step is into solitude.

The Spirit-led leader will be alert to people moving through reflection and contemplation. Martin Buber makes clear the divine exhortation that each human being is fully seen and identified. Buber writes, "The It is the chrysalis, the You the butterfly."[90] We metamorphose into whole human beings when we are seen as whole beings—when we are loved. This is at the heart of what Rowan Williams presents as an ethic of recognition. Loneliness, then, is a state of being an It; being solitary, unnoticed, isolated. Intimacy is non-existent in loneliness. To be seen—to be fully known—is to dispel loneliness. When someone sees us, acknowledges us, notices us, speaks to us, and tells us that we are a whole and unique being, we are no longer alone. When we know that we are no longer alone, a movement toward intimacy begins. This can be instantaneous.[91]

Solitude is not loneliness. It is across the threshold from loneliness and the fears of silence. Solitude is being *alone* without being *lonely*. It is the other side of the threshold. It is an act of withdrawal for reflection, meditation and, for a person of faith, a source of spiritual growth. This is a moment of surrender to God, who knows us completely. Evelyn Whitehead and James Whitehead write:

> My former state and its values and motives are no longer satisfying; they no longer make sense. Disorientation and confusion can result. Such a passage is, for one who would believe, a potentially sacred time, a *kairos*. Experienced initially as disorienting and even debilitating, this time is also one of special opportunity—an extraordinary chance to encounter God and to reorient oneself in more loving and generous directions.[92]

When we contemplate this transforming moment occurring while a person is also attempting to navigate all the myriad responsibilities of work-related tasks, we can understand why this may well be a time that intense consternation and uncertainty could occur. Whitehead

---

89. Petriglieri et al. "Up Close and Personal," 436 [emphasis original].

90. Buber, *I and Thou*, 69.

91 Artefacts can be important elements of intimacy. In my home office there are quite a number of small items given to me by former students—each bringing a warmth to my environment, and each bringing reminders of moments of connection.

92. Whitehead and Whitehead, *Christian Life Patterns*, 140.

and Whitehead write, "This *kairos* at mid-life, like every other such potentially frightening moment, is often avoided. Busying oneself in work or fleeing into distractions are but two such attempts."[93] We need a mechanism; a journal perhaps.[94]

As stated earlier, many respondents who identify as leaders refer to prayer and meditation. For example, "I frequently used meditation, reflection, and prayer as a means to resolve issues in my mind."[95] Prayer also begins in solitude. Through prayer, intimacy begins. A respondent stated, "There is definitely a sense of calling. This has led me to much time in prayer.[96] As intimacy begins first with God, we are prepared for intimacy with one another. The more willing we are to spend time in reflection, the more ready we are for complete and constructive participation in community. Nouwen asserts that prayer is the most essential element of the faithful life. However, he writes, "Praying is no easy matter. It demands a relationship in which you allow someone other than yourself to enter into the very centre of your person, to see there what you would rather leave in darkness, and to touch what you would rather leave untouched."[97] `Prayer may be perceived, in effect, as a portal—between the eternal and the temporal; between the now and the not yet. These thoughts shed light on a great challenge for the person who relies on their perceived ability to go it alone, feeling no need for reliance on the Divine. Research suggests that this may be a growing syndrome in the increasingly pervasive worldview that excludes the existence of God.[98] For people who are working hard to maintain control of their lives in sometimes chaotic environments, it is entirely reasonable that standing at a liminal threshold brings great anxiety, particular when those around

---

93. Whitehead and Whitehead, *Christian Life Patterns*, 140. Abuse of narcotics is an example.

94. Some support groups include the notion of creating 'accountability partners' who are there to support and encourage other members during difficult moments.

95. Verbatim respondent 14.

96. Verbatim respondent 23.

97. Nouwen, *With Open Hands*, 19.

98. I have often used the metaphor of standing on a coastal beach, watching the tide flood and ebb, and standing on the sand as if in a liminal place. We cannot remain on the beach as the tide approaches, and we cannot stand forever at the threshold of a decision to accept God.

us are simply ignoring the issue altogether. A respondent stated, "I barely hear the word 'God,' let alone a discussion about who Jesus is."[99]

Work in the Realm of God

How can we bring work into the realm of God? Paul Stevens points to several conversations that we might attempt to ignite in a Spirit-led leadership practice. He suggests:

- A theological framework for marketplace activity.
- An understanding of corporate culture and the task in cultivating it.
- An explanation of how faith relates to vocation, work, and ministry in the workplace and gives it lasting and satisfying meaning.
- A perspective on how spirituality is not merely a way of cranking up motivation in weary workers but the very source of creativity and entrepreneurship.
- A motivational perspective on dealing with awkward ethical dilemmas.
- A plan for living contemplatively in the thick of a demanding career.[100]

While not explicitly stated in the questionnaire verbatim responses, it is clear that these elements of leadership practice should be integrated into a living and dynamic action plan, constantly reviewed and refined. In particular, the act of providing regular feedback and frequent affirmation of progress is critical. Amabile and Kramer write:

> Through exhaustive analysis of diaries kept by knowledge workers, we discovered the *progress principle*. Of all the things that can boost emotions, motivation and perceptions during a workday, *the single most important is making progress in meaningful work*. And the more frequently people experience that sense of progress, the more likely they are to be producing creatively in the long run.[101]

---

99. Verbatim respondent 6.
100. Stevens, *Doing God's Business*, 13.
101. Amabile and Kramer, "The Power of Small Wins," [emphasis added] 2.

Opening a conversation about progress on a task may yield a very valuable conversation. While we are explicitly charged with achieving goals related to profit and output, leading a conversation that ties such goals to the personal aspirations related to human flourishing is an opportunity. Somewhere in our conversation with someone, there will be a clear transforming event, initiated by God. The effect will be recognizable. Human flourishing enhances organizational performance. Anton Boisen underscores the view that transformation often occurs at moments of deep inflection. These are moments when we experience risk of loss, moments of tragedy, or simply moments when we finally come face to face with the fundamental question, 'who is God to me?' Even more deeply, we may ask 'who am I to God?' Boisen writes, "My thesis is that religious experience is rooted in the social nature of man [sic] and arises spontaneously under the pressure of crisis situations . . . As one stands face to face with the ultimate realities of life and death, religion and theology tend to come to life."[102] Moments in our work endeavour ignite poignant experiences. These are moments of deep introspection—of looking inside ourselves. Patton writes, "For Boisen, crisis could be a tragedy or an opportunity, the making or breaking of a person, the discovery of possibility and direction in life . . . Boisen understood crisis as involving the disorganization of a person's world . . . something has happened which has upset the foundations upon which ordinary reason is based."[103] These are hefty words. Transforming moments can be equally powerful in the ways that our views of life are influenced.

Being transformed into a person that is in communion with the Holy Trinity makes possible a deeper intimacy with others. It is the removal of the fear of such intimacy. Intimacy with another may make significant crises far more manageable. Nouwen writes, "Contemplative Prayer often brings us to an intimate encounter with the love of God, revealed in Jesus. In such an experience we come to know even more deeply that God is not against us, but for us; not far from us, but with us; not outside of us, but deeply within us."[104]

At Evangel Hall Mission in Toronto, Ontario, Canada, this is witnessed every day. Just one example is the story of Bill, as presented in their 2016 Annual Report:

---

102. Boisen, *Religion in Crisis and Custom*, 3.
103. Patton, "Physicians of the Soul," 165.
104. Nouwen, *Spiritual Formation*, 12.

> When Bill first stepped through the doors of Evangel Hall Mission, he had reached the end of his rope. He was out of work, living under a truck, and struggled with a crippling drug addiction. Discovering EHM through word of mouth, Bill came here looking for help when there was nowhere left to go. He started volunteering a few days a week, which was vital in helping him find a purpose again It also eased his mind of the hardships that plagued him. 'EHM made me feel like a somebody' he says. 'They lifted me out of the gutter and gave me a place to be.'[105]

This testimony of a transforming moment underscores Nouwen's words, "We need someone who encourages us when we are tempted to give it all up, to forget it all."[106] By encouraging others, we are encouraged.

Morality and caring are inextricable. Nel Noddings underscores this when she asserts that, "Moral behaviour arises out of our natural impulse to care."[107] We must encourage one another.

We ask significant questions: 'Am I worthy of love?' 'Are others capable of loving me?' These deeply personal, fundamental, and perhaps fearful questions may be emblematic of the threshold moment between silence and solitude. They represent central elements of the fear of intimacy. John the Apostle offers clarity:

> And so we know and rely on the love God has for us. God is love. Whoever lives in love lives in God, and God in him. In this way, love is made complete among us so that we will have confidence on the Day of Judgment, because in this world we are like him. There is no fear in love. But perfect love drives out fear, because fear has to do with punishment. The one who fears is not made perfect in love. We love because he first loved us (1 John 4: 16–19).

An attitude of forgiveness may be the deepest and most profound of opportunities that we are given. Forgiveness brings us to a sacred place. Forgiveness is at the heart of Jesus' ministry. Berel Lang writes, "We know that people may not feel forgiving or be able to act forgivingly even when they are aware that the circumstances warrant forgiveness."[108] This is, in effect, another liminal threshold which may be difficult to pass through.

---

105. Evangel Hall Annual Report 2016 No page number.
106. Nouwen, *Reaching Out*, 137.
107. Noddings, *Caring*, 51
108. Lang, "Forgiveness," 109.

Holy Ground

When we seek and are accepted into a caring relationship, we are effectively entering holy ground; blessed ground. Nouwen writes about a deeply meaningful conversation with a student that illuminates this. He writes, "It is the Christ in you, who recognizes the Christ in me."[109] Nouwen is suggesting here that evidence of care being received is the reciprocating notion of care being returned. To be clear, however, we seldom need to actually say this. We just have to act in such a way that that it is obvious. Patton speaks of a relationship beyond words. He writes of a "wholeness that exceeds what can be known, done, and said."[110] This wholeness of relationship may be the result of divine intervention in the caring moment. Jack Balswick et al. provide a Trinitarian foundation for this. They write, "to live as beings made in the image of God is to live as reciprocating selves, as unique individuals living in relationship with one another."[111] The indwelling of God is the underpinning of our reciprocating selves.

It is the indwelling of God that brings deeper leadership competence. It may take years to become aware of this. Capps discusses the competent self. Capps writes of, "[H]ow important it is [to be] recognized as competent . . . [This] also reveals that a person in the fourth decade of life is expected to be competent with regard to various interpersonal relationships—familial and work related—and that competence, in every one of these relationships, is very difficult to achieve."[112] These observations underscore the reality that this decade of life is a season of great risk—yet this may be a critical season for leaders. Anthony Storr introduces us to "the paradoxical notion that building stronger relations frequently requires time in solitude to restore relational damage that may have occurred in the past and provide for restoration to a sense of deeper self-worth."[113]

---

109. Nouwen, *Reaching Out*, 45.
110. Nouwen, *Lifesigns*, 55.
111. Balswick et al., *The Reciprocating Self*, 31.
112. Capps, *The Decades of Life*, 79.
113. Storr, *Solitude: A Return to the Self*, 149.

Leadership as a Divine Calling

Choice and Challenge

When we stand in the liminal space that is a threshold, we *must* make a choice. We can move on or move back, live in fear, or live in anticipation. As previously stated, solitude could be viewed as a moment of both fleeing and staying. Williams writes, "We might say that we are being encouraged to flee from 'projection'—from other people's projections onto us, ours onto them, our own inflated expectations of ourselves."[114] When we stay and contemplate in solitude, however, Williams continues, "we have to find somewhere dark enough for memory and imagination to join hands."[115] This is a profoundly intense statement. It is a statement of sorting out regrets and moving on to aspiration. Nouwen continues, "Our primary task in solitude, therefore, is not to pay undue attention to the many faces which assail us, but to keep the eyes of our mind and heart on him who is our divine saviour."[116]

Even for Nouwen, however, this is challenging at times. He confesses, "So what about my life of prayer? Do I like to pray? Do I spend time praying? Frankly the answer is no to all three questions. After sixty-three years of life and thirty-eight years of priesthood, my prayer seems as dead as a rock."[117] But Nouwen does not give up. He affirms that, "Prayer gives us the courage to stretch out our arms and be led."[118] For the self-assured aspiring leader this can be a difficult surrender—we must hand over control! Once the decision is made however, a convictional experience may come swiftly.

Getting on to the right path, especially as we reach mid-life, may have a great deal to do with forming a crystallized picture of one's legacy. *Moving to legacy means the giving up of purely personal interests in the acceptance of a transcendent demand.* In effect we account for those things we wish to leave behind. This may be the pinnacle of leadership. This is finding purpose—it is accepting our divine vocation. Rolheiser makes the statement, "Spirituality is about what we do with the fire inside us."[119] In other words it is accepting Christ as the source of our future. This is the movement from illusion to prayer. Nouwen writes, "Prayer is being

---

114. Williams, *Silence and Honey Cakes*, 63.
115. Williams, *Silence and Honey Cakes*, 96.
116. Nouwen, *The Way of the Heart*, 20.
117. Nouwen, *Sabbatical Journey*, 5.
118. Nouwen, *Making All Things New*, 42.
119. Rolheiser, *The Holy Longing*, 11.

unbusy with God instead of being busy with other things. Prayer is primarily to do nothing useful or productive in the presence of God."[120] This is a sea-change demand.

Intimacy

Workplace dissonance brings fear. To be intimate with another is to have overcome fear. This presents our presence in a prismatic way. This is to say that we reflect the light of God back to God, and we refract that light onto those around us. Once we recognize the possibilities in others, we cannot help but see the whole person, regardless of their circumstances. We can then offer to become the shepherd—the leader—guiding the person toward a convictional experience. It is when we step aside and let Christ take over. Referring to Phil 2:5–11, Loder writes:

> Christ, by his own initiative, enters into all 'worlds' (incarnation) by the proclamation of his world, he exposes the deepest possible conflict (sin) and then takes it into himself (crucifixion). He enters into the condemned and buried past of world history (descent into hell). Then he emerges as a radically new being, or new being breaks in on the earth through him (resurrection). The inherent continuity of God's action in Jesus Christ is exultantly affirmed (glorification), and it corresponds with public life in history (Pentecost) . . . Thus connecting human transformation to Christian history.[121]

Loder employs this passage to underscore that, "Convictional experiences are to be seen as initiated by Christ."[122] Loder continues by asserting that, "Transforming experiences initiated by Christ are characterized by a resulting sacrificial love in the one transformed." Loder makes a further comment that should be of great comfort to those struggling with the past, when he affirms that, "Convictional experiences are to be seen preeminently as a breakthrough from the future."[123] Rev 3:20 offers, "Listen! I am standing at the door, knocking; if you hear my voice and open the door, I will come in and eat with you, and you with me." This is none

---

120. Nouwen, *Spiritual Journey*, 19.
121. Loder, *The Transforming Moment*, 148.
122. Loder, *The Transforming Moment*, 148.
123. Loder, *The Transforming Moment*, 185.

other than God: requesting our hospitality. If we are deafened by our past, we cannot not hear God's knock at the door.

Change leadership requires stepping back. Nouwen asserts that we have to know when to leave a person alone—to let them listen for the knock at the door. He states:

> Paradoxically, we must then move away and leave solitude behind: The mystery of God's presence, therefore, can be touched only by a deep awareness of his absence. It is at the centre of our longing for the absent God that we discover his footprints, and realize that our desire to love God is born out of the love with which he has touched us . . . We discover how much he has filled our lives already.[124]

The task, then, is one of invitation. When invited, our conversations should open a space for the future. Nouwen writes that, "By slowly converting our loneliness into a deep solitude, we create that precious space where we can discover the voice telling us about our inner necessity—that is, our vocation."[125] Michael Knowles writes, "Christians bear witness to a saving grace that precedes any human response. Faith does not bear witness, first and foremost, to a particular act of reception, but to the divine primacy of divine action on behalf of humanity that makes reception possible."[126] Just as Jesus presented himself to Cleopas and his companion on the road to Emmaus, we should be fellow travellers with one another on this leadership journey. In this role, we invite others to join us in contemplation.

Conclusion

Do people experience a complete sense of spiritual flourishing in their work? Thirty-two individuals kindly agreed to share their experiences. These respondents represent a broad diversity of profession, age, role and geography. A majority of the respondents expressed faith or spirituality, together with tacit affirmation that work is vital to personhood. However a significant number went on to articulate varying levels of disharmony, or dissonance, in their workplace experience.

---

124. Nouwen, *Reaching Out*, 128.
125. Nouwen, *Reaching Out*, 40.
126. Knowles, *Of Seeds and the People of God*, 141.

The workplace has changed significantly in the last half-century as society transitioned from modern to postmodern. On the one hand, organizational systems are calculated and designed to achieve the hard goals of the enterprise. On the other hand, postmodern organizations are places for a wide range of behaviour, from humour to oppression and fierce competition.

If people experience dissonance at work, leadership is directly involved in the creation of such circumstances. This focus draws from my grounded theory emerging from qualitative study, which describes the workplace circumstances of the respondents. Arguably, virtually all of these circumstances flow effectively from specific leadership decisions. Therefore they also can be addressed by leadership decisions.

This book offers leaders a pathway to the creation of workplaces that nurture human flourishing *and* which achieve maximum possible output. The payoff is a community of workers and leaders who experience true flourishing. The enterprises that they are part of may experience significantly greater results.

All of the foregoing has come together to inspire an outline of innovative, Spirit-led leadership. Leadership that is modelled after the biblical concept of followership responding to Jesus' call to servant-hood and humility. Some of the observations result in challenging admonitions. Self-awareness is a foundation for those willing to reflect and respond. The rewards, however, are significant. The product of Spirit-led leadership is the creation of legacy in the broadest sense. Indeed, the outcomes, one might argue, are of eschatological dimensions.

The work of leadership is not easy. The workplace is going to change further. What will be a constant, however, is the relationship between satisfying work, in all its dimensions, and general well-being, both for individuals and entire communities.

Dreams of a 'middle class' life are being challenged. Many are debt-laden, to the point of being on the brink of financial insolvency. Many are holding down several jobs while harbouring fears of lay-offs. Commute-times are lengthening. Many are just tired.

In the midst of all this, people are doing their best to reflect on their spiritual nature, and a very significant number are, literally, praying for the ways in which their spiritual centre might be more fully expressed in the way they work. They care for their co-worker and they hope for an environment of equality, trust and integrity.

Spirit-led leadership is an 'all-in' profession requiring full commitment. It is a calling. The Bible recounts the stories of people who receive this sacred call. We hear of their initial and sometimes ongoing struggles to cope with their call. We also learn that, for the most part, no particular grand reward is given for their effort. Ultimately, however, their efforts change not only the lives of individuals, but entire communities.

As I finish this work, I also finish a day in the thick of the COVID 19 Pandemic. Like most of you, today I participated in a 'Zoom' call, a 'Microsoft TEAMS' call, and a 'WebEx' call. On the final call someone lamented that in this work-at-home environment we don't know if employees are at work or out shopping. Can someone not be working *and* shopping? Morisey writes:

> We have begun to recognize that, while our society has proved very effective in promoting industrial and scientific developments, we are far less competent in promoting humanizing processes; no longer are we able to take human flourishing for granted.[127]

It is about culture; it is about character; it is about ethos. We can learn to do this.

---

127. Morisey, *Beyond the Good Samaritan*, 123.

Reflections

By Tim Arnill, President and CEO of Verity International

As I was graduating from my Master's program and starting my business career, I used to debate with my best friend (who was studying for the Ministry) about the effectiveness of changing a system from the inside vs. the outside. My belief being that I would be able to have a far greater impact on individuals from within the business system than from without—you could create an environment where they could flourish by creating systems, structures, values that would support personal growth, development and connection thereby driving solid business results.

I often tell my career transition clients that business is more often than not played like a game. It is competitive, often both internally and externally and there are winners (at the market level) and losers (also at the market level). Work at the individual level by contrast, is not a game. It is often deeply personal and because we spend so much time at it, we strongly identify with it. To have alignment between the personal aspects of work and the broader ethos of the organization is the ultimate goal of a job search.

I have always sought to leave an organization 'better' than when I joined it. A core philosophy here is to control what you can control, influence what you can influence and the rest, don't worry about it. As a leader, you can 'control' how your team shows up and the value set that underlies their behaviour. I have had many lessons through my journey at Verity, one of the biggest being that if you hire somebody (or inherit them) who is not aligned with the values that are the foundation of the business, then make the decision fast to move them on before they impact the rest of the team and damage the credibility/integrity of the team and you as a leader. Sometimes it is the old dilemma that Leadership teams face when doing talent reviews; what do we do with the high performer who does not live the values?

Dissonance is pervasive in organizations. Interestingly, I think there is more of it in publicly traded organizations than privately held (other than VC). The master of the market often drives short term behaviours/strategies that do create dissonance in the organization. Whereas privately held, especially family owned establish far closer connections with their people and often feel like 'family'. It is also interesting when you encounter people of faith who end up being some of the most cutthroat business people around. I once worked for one who would play mind games with the team, undermining trust. The whole organization knew when you had a target on your forehead and were done . . . nothing was ever really communicated until the severance package was given out but the leader's behaviour towards the individual clearly changed and everybody else saw it.

By Harriet Ekperigin, Senior Business Lead in the Virtual Healthcare Sector

IN MY CAREER, I have always gone where my work makes me happy and for 7 years after leaving a management consultant role where I was unhappy, I worked as an independent consultant in the public sector moving between several contracts and several organizations. I saw all kinds of 'leaders', but only one that I can say consciously or sub-consciously acted in faith.

Most recently, a new CEO was announced at my current organization. He exudes spirit-led leadership to the point that I have asked my peers who knew him before if he is genuine . . . they responded that he has always been the same person, working for the people, learning from his staff and actively listening to improve their lives. Most days when I hear him speak, I still wonder if he really is this nice. It is easy to wonder if he clocks off and becomes a completely different person where his positive words and attitude are not translated behind closed doors. My negative experiences with unauthentic leaders have made me skeptical. Whenever I get these thoughts, I pray for him and for God to give me the grace to trust.

By Andrea Swinton, Board Director and former Executive in the Healthcare Sector

An experience of a former colleague kept coming to mind as I read this work. This individual, following completion of graduate studies in Theology, moved from the not-for-profit sector to a full-time role in the Church, only to find that the politics and conflict he was seeking to leave behind were equally at play in his new role. He left the role. I was struck with sadness that his strong commitment to the Church was negatively impacted by the bad work experience.

Bibliography

Ackerman, Denise M., and Riet Bons-Storm, eds. *Liberating Faith Practices: Feminist Practical Theologies in Context*. Leuven, Belgium: Peeters, 1998.

Agrell, Goran. *Work, Toil and Sustenance: An Examination of the View of Work in the New Testament, Taking into Consideration Views Found in Old Testament, Intertestamental, and Early Rabbinic Writings*. Lund, Sweden: Hakan Ohlsons, 1976.

Alderson, Wayne T., and Nancy Alderson McDonnell. *Theory R Management: How to Utilize the Value of the Person*. Nashville: Thomas Nelson, 1994.

Allison, James. *Behavioural Economics*. New York: Praeger, 1983.

Amabile, Teresa, and Steven J. Kramer. "The Power of Small Wins." *Harvard Business Review* (May 2011). https://hbr.org/2011/05/The-Power-of-Small-Wins.

Anglican Church of Canada. *The Book of Alternative Services*. Toronto: Anglican Book Centre, 1985.

Aristotle. *The Art of Rhetoric*. Translated by by J. H. Freese. Cambridge, MA: Harvard University Press, 1926.

Attig, Thomas. *How We Grieve: Relearning the World*. Oxford: Oxford University Press, 2011.

Autry, James A. *The Servant Leader*. New York: Three Rivers, 2001.

Baillie, John. *Our Knowledge of God*. London: Oxford University Press, 1952.

Ballard, Paul. "The Use of Scripture." In *Practical Theology*, edited by Bonnie J. Miller-McLemore, 163–75. Malden, MA: Wiley, 2014.

Ballard, Paul, and Steven R. Holmes. *The Bible in Pastoral Practice: Readings in the Place and Function of Scripture in the Church*. Grand Rapids: Eerdmans, 2006.

Balswick, Jack O., et al. *The Reciprocating Self: Human Development in Theological Perspective*. Downers Grove, IL: InterVarsity, 2005.

Barbalet, Jack. "The Experience of Trust: Its Content and Basis." In *Trust in Contemporary Society*, edited by Masamichi Sasaki, 12–18. Leiden, Netherlands: Brill, 2019.

Barth, Karl. *Church Dogmatics 1/2: The Doctrine of the Word of God*, edited by G.W. Bromiley and T. F. Torrance. New York: T. & T. Clark, 2009.

Bartholomew, Craig G., and Ryan P. O'Dowd. *Old Testament Wisdom Literature: A Theological Introduction*. Downers Grove, IL: IVP Academic, 2011.

Bartleby. "Time to Get in Training." *The Economist* (2018) 49.

Barton, Ruth Haley. *Strengthening the Soul of Your Leadership*. Downers Grove, IL: InterVarsity, 2008.

———. *Pursuing God's Will Together*. Downers Grove, IL: InterVarsity, 2012.

Bass, Dorothy C. "Practical Wisdom in Everyday Life." In *Christian Practical Wisdom: What It Is, Why It Matters*, edited by Dorothy C. Bass et al., 86–87. Grand Rapids: Eerdmans, 2016.

Bass, Dorothy C., and Craig Dykstra, eds. *For Life Abundant: Practical Theology, Theological Education, and Christian Ministry*. Grand Rapids: Eerdmans, 2008.

Bates, Paul K. "Paracletic Ministry: A Study in Pastoral Encounters with Male Mid-career Spiritual Searchers." *Practical Theology* (2017) 66–78.

———. *Sales Force Management in the Financial Services*. Toronto: Carswell, 1990.

———. "The Corporation with Integrity: A Well-Found Vessel in an Angry Sea." *Executive Action; Conference Board of Canada* (May 2009) 1–3.

———. "Work: An Eschatological Imperative." MTS thesis, McMaster Divinity College, 2014.

Bates, Paul K., and Al Emid. *What I Have Learned So Far and How It Can Help You*. Winnipeg: Knowledge Bureau, 2010.

Beach, Lee. *The Church in Exile: Living in Hope after Christendom*, Downers Grove, IL: InterVarsity, 2015.

Beckett, John D. *Loving Monday: Succeeding in Business without Selling Your Soul*. Downers Grove, IL: InterVarsity, 2006.

Beed, Clive and Cara Beed. "Jesus on Cooperation." *Transformation* (2015) 97–111.

Bell, Kimberley A. *Spirituality in the Workplace: Differences in Employee Well-Being and Job Satisfaction across Spiritual and Secular Learning Institutes*. Monee, IL: self-published, 2019.

Bennis, Warren. *On Becoming a Leader*. New York: Addison-Wesley, 1989.

———. "Leadership in a Digital World: Embracing Transparency and Adaptive Capacity." *MIS Quarterly* 37 (2013) 635–36.

Berry, Thomas. *The Great Work: Our Way into the Future*. New York: Three Rivers, 1999.

Best, Patricia. "Awakenings." *Toronto Life* (November 2000) 69–74.

Blakely Gerald L., et al. "The Moderating Effects of Equity Sensitivity on the Relationship between Organizational Justice and Organizational Citizenship Behaviors." *Journal of Business and Psychology* 20 (2005) 259–73.

Boddy, Clive R. "Corporate Psychopaths, Conflict, Employee Affective Wellbeing and Counterproductive Work Behaviour." *Journal of Business Ethics* (2014) 107–21.

Boisen, Anton. *Religion in Crisis and Custom: A Sociological and Psychological Study*. New York: Harper, 1953.

Bonhoeffer, Dietrich. *Ethics*. New York: Simon & Schuster, 1955.

Booth, Richard. "Toward an Understanding of Loneliness." *Social Work* 28 (1983) 116–19.

Brook, Linda Rios. *Frontline Christians in a Bottom-Line World*. Shippensburg, PA: Destiny, 2004.

Brown, Rosalind. *Being a Deacon Today: Exploring a Distinctive Ministry in the Church and in the World*. New York: Morehouse, 2005.

Brown, William S. "Technology, Workplace Privacy and Personhood. *Journal of Business Ethics* (1996) 1237–48.

Browning, Don S. *A Fundamental Practical Theology: Descriptive and Strategic Proposals*. Minneapolis: Fortress, 1996.

Bruno, Robert A. *Justified by Work: Identity and the Meaning of Faith in Chicago's Working-Class Churches*. Columbus, OH: Ohio State University Press, 2008.

Buber, Martin. *I and Thou*. New York: Simon & Schuster, 1996.
Burnison, Gary. *Lead*. Hoboken, NJ: Wiley, 2013.
Burns, James MacGregor. *Leadership*. New York: Harper Perennial, 1978.
Butler, James. "The 'Long and Winding Road' of Faith: Learning about the Christian Life from Two Methodist Congregations." *Practical Theology* (2020) 277–89.
Butler Bass, Diana. *Christianity after Religion: The End of Church and the Birth of a New Spiritual Awakening*. New York: Harper Collins, 2012.
Cameron, Helen, et al., eds. *Studying Local Churches: A Handbook*. London: SCM-Canterbury, 2005.
Capper, Colleen A. *Organization Theory for Equity and Diversity*. Abingdon, UK: Routledge, 2018.
Capps, Donald. *Agents of Hope: A Pastoral Psychology*. Eugene, OR: Wipf & Stock, 1995.
———. *The Decades of Life: A Guide to Human Development*. Louisville: Westminster John Knox, 2008.
Carr, Wesley. "Can We Speak of the Spirituality of Institutions?" In *The Hidden Spirit: Discovering the Spirituality of Institutions*, edited by James F. Cobble and Charles M. Elliott, 109–17. Matthews, NC: CMR, 1999.
Carter, Matthew. "4 Leadership Lessons from Nehemiah." *Novo*, February 2019. www.novorenewal.com.
Carver, John, with Caroline Oliver. *Corporate Boards That Create Value: Governing Company Performance From the Boardroom*. San Francisco; Jossey-Bass, 2002.
Cassidy, Richard J. *Society and Politics in the Acts of the Apostles*. Maryknoll: Orbis, 1988.
Chamorro-Premuzic, Tomas. *Why Do So Many Incompetent Men Become Leaders?* Boston: Harvard University Press, 2019.
Chewning, Richard C., et al. *Business through the Eyes of Faith*. New York: HarperOne, 1984.
Clinton, Robert J. *The Making of a Leader*. Colorado Springs: NavPress, 1988.
Collins, Kenneth J. *The Theology of John Wesley: Holy Love and the Shape of Grace*. Nashville: Abingdon, 2007.
Cosden, Darrell. *A Theology of Work: Work and the New Creation*. Eugene, OR: Wipf & Stock, 2005.
Covey, Stephen M. R. *The Speed of Trust*. New York: Free Press, 2018.
Christakis, Nicholas A. *Blueprint: The Evolutionary Origins of a Good Society*. Boston: Little, Brown Spark, 2019.
Christensen, Karen. "Tackling Inequality: The Role of Business." *Rotman Management* (2019) 123–26.
Dell, Katharine. *Seeking a Life that Matters: Wisdom for Today from the Book of Proverbs*. London: Dartman, Longman & Todd, 2002.
DePree, Max. *Leadership Is an Art*. New York: Crown, 2004.
Doohan, Leonard. *Spiritual Leadership: The Quest for Integrity*. New York: Paulist, 2007.
Drath, Wilfred. *The Deep Blue Sea: Rethinking the Source of Leadership*. San Francisco: Jossey-Bass, 2001.
Drori, Israel, et al. "Researching Transnational Entrepreneurship: An Approach Based on the Theory of Practice." In *Transnational and Immigrant Entrepreneurship in a Globalized World*, edited by Benson Honig et al., 3–30. Toronto: University of Toronto Press, 2010.
Drucker, Peter F. *Management*. Revised and updated by Joseph A. Maciariello. New York: Harper, 2008.

Dykstra, Craig, and Dorothy Bass. "A Theological Understanding of Christian Practices." In *Practicing Theology: Beliefs and Practices in Christian Life*, edited by Miroslav Volf and Dorothy Bass, 13–35. Grand Rapids: Eerdmans, 2002.

Ellul, Jacques. *Essential Spiritual Writings*. Maryknoll, NY: Orbis, 2016.

———. *The Technological Society*. New York: Vintage, 1964.

Evangel Hall Mission. *Annual Report*. Toronto: 2016.

Farley, Edward. "Interpreting Situations: An Inquiry into the Nature of Practical Theology." In *Pastoral and Practical Theology*, edited by James Woodward and Stephen Pattison, 118–27. Malden, MA: Blackwell, 2000.

Feng, Bing, et al. "Harnessing Behavioural Insights: A Playbook for Organizations." *Rotman Management* (2019) 7–12.

Finkelstein, Sydney. "The End of Middle Management." *BBC* (June 2015). http://www.bbc.com/capital/story/20150624-the-end-of-middle-management.

Finn, Daniel. "Human Work in Catholic Social Thought." *The American Journal of Economics and Sociology* (2012) 874–85.

Fluker, Walter Earl. *Ethical Leadership: The Quest for Character, Civility and Community*. Minneapolis: Fortress, 2009.

Folke, Carl, et al. "Resilience Thinking, Integrating Resilience, Adaptability and Transformability." *Ecology and Society* (2010).

Frankl, Viktor E. *Man's Search for Meaning*. Boston: Beacon, 2006.

Friedman, Milton. *Capitalism and Freedom*. Chicago: University of Chicago Press, 1962.

Frost, Peter J. *Toxic Emotions at Work*. Boston: Harvard University Press, 2003.

Frostensen, Magnus. "Humility in Business: A Contextual Approach." *Journal of Business Ethics* (2016) 91–102.

Ghebreslassie, Makda, et al. "Ontario Workplace Safety Board Reviewing Uber Eats Following Marketplace Investigation." *CBC News*, November 2018. https://www.cbc.ca/news/canada/marketplace-food-delivery-apps-labour-issues-1.4895801.

Gibbs, Eddie, and Ian Coffey. *Church Next: Quantum Changes in Christian Ministry*. Downers Grove: InterVarsity, 2000.

Gibbs, Robert. *Why Ethics: Signs of Responsibilities*. Princeton: Princeton University Press, 2000.

Gin, Deborah H., and Chris A. Meinzer. "What About the Salary Gap in Theological Education?" *In Trust* (2019) 12–14.

Golomb, Egon. "Model Theoretical Considerations on the Organisation of Urban Pastoral Work." *Social Compass* 10 (1963) 357–75.

Greene, Lane. "Losing Faith." *The Economist* (2018) 41.

Greene, Robert. *The 33 Strategies of War*. New York: Penguin, 2006.

Grenz, Stanley J. *Theology for the Community of God*. Nashville: Eerdmans, 2000.

Grey, Mary. "Survive or Thrive? A Theology of Flourishing for the Next Millennium." *An Irish Quarterly Review* 88 (1999) 396–407.

Grise-Owens, Erlene, and J. Jay Miller. "Responding to Global Shifts: Meta-practice as a Relevant Social Work Practice Paradigm." *Journal of Teaching in Social Work* 34 (2014) 46–59.

Gustafson, Andrew. "Making Sense of Postmodern Business Ethics." *Business Ethics Quarterly* (2000) 645–58.

Gwartney, James D., and Richard L. Stroup. *Economics: Private and Public Choice*. 7th ed. Orlando, FL: Dryden, 1976.

Gyertson, David J. "Christian Leadership and the Identity and Mission of an Organization." In *Christian Leadership Essentials: A Handbook for Managing Christian Organizations*, edited by David S. Dockery, 24–45. Nashville: B & H, 2011.

Hahn, Scott. *Ordinary Work, Extraordinary Grace: My Spiritual Journey in Opus Dei*. New York: Doubleday, 2006.

Haig-Brown, Celia, and John Hodson. "Indigenous Thought in Canadian Education." In *Alternative Education for the 21st Century: Philosophies, Approaches, Visions*, edited by Philip A. Woods and Glenys J. Woods, 167–88. New York: Palgrave MacMillan, 2009.

Hall, Lucas. "Remember the Words He has Taught You." *Online Letter*, July 29, 2020.

Hall, R. H. *Dimensions of Work*. Beverly Hills: Sage, 1986.

Hall, Thelma. *Too Deep for Words: Rediscovering Lectio Divina*. New York: Paulist, 1988.

Hamel, Gary, with Bill Breen. *The Future of Management*. Boston: Harvard Business School Press, 2007.

Hamman, Jaco J. "Revisiting Forgiveness as a Pastoral Theological Problem." *Pastoral Psychology* 61 (2012) 435–50.

Haque, Eve. "Multiculturalism, Language, and Immigrant Integration." In *The Multiculturalism Question: Debating Identity in 21st-Century Canada*. 203–23. Kingston, ON: McGill-Queen's University Press, 2014.

Harvey, Nicholas Peter. "Revelation and Contemplation." *New Blackfriars* (1991) 152–60.

Hatch, Mary Jo, and Ann L. Cunliffe. *Organization Theory: Modern, Symbolic and Postmodern Perspectives*. 3rd ed. Oxford: Oxford University Press, 2013.

Heifetz, Ronald A. *Leadership without Easy Answers*. Boston: Harvard University Press, 1998.

Hendel, Ronald. "Mind the Gap: Modern and Postmodern in Biblical Studies." *Journal of Biblical Literature* (2014) 422–43.

Higginson, Richard. "Integrity and the Art of Compromise." In *Faith in Leadership: How Leaders Live out Their Faith in Their Work and Why it Matters*, edited by Robert Banks and Kimberley Powell, 34–45. San Francisco: Jossey-Bass, 2000.

Hobbes, Thomas. *Leviathan*. 1651. Reprint, Ware, UK: Wordsworth, 2014.

Hoover, Kristine F., and Molly B. Pepper. "How Did They Say That? Ethics Statements and Normative Frameworks at Best Companies to Work For." *Journal of Business Ethics* (2015) 605–17.

Hurley, Robert F. "The Decision to Trust." *Harvard Business Review* (September 2006). https://hbr.org/2006/09/the-decision-to-trust.

Hutchinson, Marie, et al. "Bullying as Circuits of Power: An Australian Perspective." *Administrative Theory & Praxis* 32 (2010) 25–47.

Johnson, Paul G. *Grace for the Workplace: Monday Morning Incentive*. Victoria, BC: Ecce Nova, 2004.

Kellerman, Barbara. *Bad Leadership: What It Is, How It Happens, Why It Matters*. Cambridge, MA: Harvard, 2004.

Kenny, Anthony, and Geraldine Smyth. "Secularism and Secularisation." *Studies: An Irish Quarterly Review* (1997) 315–30.

Keren, Michael. "Moses as a Visionary Realist." *International Political Science Review* (1988) 71–84.

Knowles, Michael P. *Of Seeds and the People of God*. Eugene, OR: Cascade, 2015.

———. *We Preach Not Ourselves: Paul on Proclamation*. Grand Rapids: Brazos, 2008.

Kotter, John P. *Leading Change*. Boston: Harvard University Press, 1996.
Kuypers, John. *The First Rule of Inner Peace*. Burlington, ON: Present Living and Learning, 2014.
Lambert, Lake. "The Future of Workplace Spirituality." In *Spirituality, Inc.* 158. New York: NYU Press: 2009.
Lang, Berel. "Forgiveness." *American Philosophical Quarterly* 31 (1994) 105–17.
Langton, Nancy, et al. *Organizational Behaviour: Concepts, Controversies, Applications*. 5th ed. Toronto: 2010.
Latta, R. "Purpose." *Proceedings of the Aristotelian Society* 8 (1907–8) 17–32.
Lenti. Erica, "All the Lonely People." *Pivot* (November/December 2018) 17–18.
Lewis, C. S. *Mere Christianity*. New York: Harper One, 1980.
Liebert, Elizabeth. *The Way of Discernment: Spiritual Practices for Decision Making*. Louisville: Westminster John Knox, 2008.
———. *The Soul of Discernment: A Spiritual Practice for Communities and Institutions*. Louisville: Westminster John Knox, 2015.
Loder, James. *The Transforming Moment*. 2nd ed. Colorado Springs: Helmers and Howard, 1989.
Lopez, Isabel O. "Finding Wisdom and Purpose in Chaotic Times." In *Faith in Leadership: How Leaders Live out Their Faith in Their Work and Why it Matters*, edited by Robert Banks and Kimberley Powell, 79–92. San Francisco: Jossey-Bass, 2000.
Lloyd-Jones, Martin. *Studies in the Sermon in the Mount*. Grand Rapids: Eerdmans, 1976.
Lombard, Jay. *The Mind of God: Neuroscience, Faith, and a Search for the Soul*. New York: Harmony, 2017.
Longman, Tremper, III, and Raymond B. Dillard. *An Introduction to the Old Testament*. 2nd ed. Grand Rapids: Zondervan, 2006.
Luhrmarin, Tanya. "Understanding the Work of Faith." *The Cambridge Journal of Anthropology* (2016) 147–49.
Lyotard, Jean-Francois. *The Postmodern Condition: A Report on Knowledge*. Minneapolis: University of Minnesota Press, 1979.
Malphurs, Aubrey. *Developing a Vision for Ministry in the 21st Century*. Grand Rapids: Baker, 1992.
Martin, Roger. *The Opposable Mind: How Successful Leaders Win through Integrative Thinking*. Boston: Harvard University Press, 2007.
Martin, Roger, et al. "Virtuous Capital: How to Measure Business's Contribution to Society." *Rotman Management* (2021) 73–77.
Marty, Peter. "Shaping Communities: Pastoral Leadership and Congregational Formation." In *For Life Abundant: Theological Education and Practical Christian Ministry*, edited by Dorothy C. Bass and Craig Dykstra, 306–26. Grand Rapids: Eerdmans, 2008.
Maslow, Abraham H. *Maslow on Management*. New York: John Wiley & Sons, 1998.
McChrystal, Stanley. *Leaders: Myth and Reality*. New York: Penguin, 2018.
McKee, Annie. "Being Happy at Work Matters." *Harvard Business Review* (November 2014). https://hbr.org/2014/11/being-happy-at-work-matters.
McLean, David. "Relationship Agility and Its Impact on Leader Success: A Case Study." Antioch University, 2011.
———. "Understanding Relational Agility: Exploring Constructs of Relational Leadership Through Story." PhD diss., Antioch University, 2014.

McLelland, Kate. *Call the Chaplain: Spiritual and Pastoral Caregiving in Hospitals.* London: Canterbury, 2014.

McNeal, Reggie. *A Work of Heart: Understanding How God Shapes Spiritual Leaders.* San Francisco: Jossey-Bass, 2000.

Money.Com. "Money Concerns." http://money.com/money/5634807/sears-eddie-lampert-employee-concerns/.

Meeks, M. D. *God the Economist: The Doctrine of God and Political Economy.* Philadelphia: Fortress, 1989.

Meng, Yishuang. Spiritual Leadership at the Workplace: Perspectives and Theories." *Biomedical Reports* (2016) 408–12.

Mercer, "Leadership, Stress, and the Importance of Self-Care." https://www.mercer.com/our-thinking/career/voice-on-talent/leadership-stress-and-the-importance-of-self-care.html.

Mercer, Joyce Ann. "Economics, Class, and Classism." In *Practical Theology*, edited by Bonnie J. Miller-McLemore, 432–44. Hoboken, NJ: John Wiley & Sons, 2011.

Merritt, Jonathan. "It's Getting Harder to Talk about God." *New York Times*, October 2018. https://www.nytimes.com/2018/10/13/opinion/sunday/talk-god-spirituality-christian.html.

Miller, David W., and Faith Wambura Ngunjiri. "Leadership View on Corporate Chaplains: Business, Sociocultural and Spiritual Justifications." *Journal of Management, Spirituality and Religion* 12 (2015) 129–55.

Mintzberg, Henry. *Managing.* San Francisco: Berrett-Koehler, 2009.

Mitroff, Ian and Elizabeth Denton. "A Study of Spirituality in the Workplace." *MIT Sloan Management Review* (1999). https://sloanreview.mit.edu/article/a-study-of-spirituality-in-the-workplace/.

Morisey, Ann. *Beyond the Good Samaritan: Community Ministry and Mission.* London: Bloomsbury, 1997.

Morrison, Elizabeth Wolfe, and Sandra L. Robinson. "When Employees Feel Betrayed: A Model of How Psychological Contract Violation Develops." *The Academy of Management Review* (1997) 226–56.

Moses, Sarah. "The Ethics of Recognition: Rowan Williams' Approach to Moral Discernment in the Christian Community." *Journal of the Society of Christian Ethics* 35 (2015) 147–65.

Mowry, Bill J. "A Reflective Approach to Research: Applying the Research Paradigm of Post-positivism to the Evangelical Church." *Christian Education Journal* (2016) 51–67.

Muschalla, B., et al. "The Significance of Job-Anxiety in a Working Population." *Occupational Medicine* 63 (2013) 415–21.

Niebuhr, H. Richard. *Christ and Culture.* New York: Harper Collins, 1951.

Nichols, Tom. *The Death of Expertise: The Campaign against Established Knowledge and Why It Matters.* Oxford: Oxford University Press, 2017.

Noddings, Nel. *Caring: A Feminine Approach to Ethics and Moral Education.* 2nd ed. Berkeley: University of California Press, 2003.

Norris, Pippa, and Ronald Inglehart. *Sacred and Secular: Religion and Politics Worldwide.* 2nd ed. Cambridge: Cambridge University Press, 2011.

Northcott, Michael, "Pastoral Theology and Sociology." In *Pastoral and Practical Theology*, edited by James Woodward and Stephen Pattison, 151–63. Malden, MA: Blackwell, 2000.

Northouse, Peter G. *Leadership: Theory and Practice*. 6th ed. Los Angeles: Sage, 2013.
Nouwen, Henri J. *In the Name of Jesus*. New York: Crossroad, 1989.
———. *Letters to Marc about Jesus: Living a Spiritual Life in a Material World*. New York: Harper Collins, 1988.
———. *Lifesigns: Intimacy, Fecundity and Ecstasy in Christian Perspective*. New York: Doubleday, 1966.
———. *Making All Things New: An Invitation to the Spiritual Life*. New York: HarperOne, 1966.
———. *Reaching Out: The Three Movements of the Spiritual Life*. New York: HarperOne, 2010.
———. *Sabbatical Journey: The Diary of His Final Year*. New York: Crossroad, 1998.
———. *Spiritual Formation: Following the Movements of the Spirit*. New York: Doubleday, 1966.
———. *The Genesee Diary: Report from a Trappist Monastery*. New York: Doubleday, 1976.
———. *The Road to Daybreak: A Spiritual Journey*. New York: Doubleday, 1988.
———. *The Way of the Heart*. New York: Ballantine, 1981.
———. *The Wounded Healer: Ministry in Contemporary Society*. New York: Doubleday, 1972.
———. *With Open Hands*. Notre Dame, IN: Ave Maria, 2006.
Oden, Thomas C. *Pastoral Theology: Essentials of Ministry*. New York: Harper Collins, 1983.
O'Malley, Ed. "Leadership in Uncertain Times." *Comment* (2020) 67–70.
Ooghe, Herbert, et al. "Venture Capital in the U.S.A., Europe and Japan." *Management International Review* 29 (1989) 29–45.
Osmer, Richard R. *Practical Theology: An Introduction*. Grand Rapids: Eerdmans, 2008.
Owram, Kristine. "The Other Side of Hunter Harrison's CP Legacy: White-Collar Workers Driving Trains." *National Post* (2016) 2.
Palmer, Parker J. *A Hidden Wholeness: The Journey Toward an Undivided Life*. Hoboken, NJ: Jossey-Bass, 2004.
———. *The Active Life: A Spirituality of Work, Creativity and Caring*. San Francisco: Wiley, 1990.
———. *To Know as We Are Known: Education as a Spiritual Journey*. New York: Harper Collins, 1993.
Parkin, Sara. *The Positive Deviant: Sustainability Leadership in a Perverse World*. London: Earthscan, 2010.
Pascale, Richard T., and Jerry Sternin. "Your Company's Secret Change Agents." *Harvard Business Review* (2005). https://hbr.org/2005/05/your-companys-secret-change-agents.
Patterson, Kyle R. *Transformational Leadership*. Lexington, KY: Self-published, 2019.
Pattison, Stephen. *The Faith of the Managers: When Management Becomes Religion*. London: Bloomsbury, 1998.
Patton, John, *From Ministry to Theology: Pastoral Action and Reflection*. Nashville: Abingdon, 1990.
———. "Practical Theology Asks." Presentation to Faculty Colloquium, McMaster Divinity College, Hamilton, ON. June 3, 2018.
———. "Physicians of the Soul." In *Turning Points in Pastoral Care: The Legacy of Anton Boisen and Seward Hiltner*, edited by Leroy Aden and J. Harold Ellens, 159–72. Grand Rapids: Baker, 1990.

Pawar, Badrinarayan Shanker. "Leadership Spiritual Behaviors Toward Subordinates: An Empirical Examination of the Effects of a Leader's Individual Spirituality and Organizational Spirituality." *Journal of Business Ethics* 122 (2014) 439–52.

Pennington, Jonathan T. *The Sermon on the Mount and Human Flourishing: A Theological Commentary*. Grand Rapids: Baker Academic, 2017.

Petriglieri, Gianpiero, et al. "Up Close and Personal: Building Foundations for Leaders' Development Through the Personalization of Management Learning." *Academy of Management Learning* 10 (2011) 430–50.

Pfeffer, Jeffrey. *Dying for a Paycheck*. New York: Harper Collins, 2018.

Phillips, Susan S. "Spiritual Direction as a Navigational Aid in Sanctification." In *Life in the Spirit: Spiritual Formation in Theological Perspective*, edited by Jeffrey P. Greenman and George Kalantzis, 160–79. Downers Grove: InterVarsity, 2010.

Phipps, Simon. *God on Monday*. London: Hodder & Stoughton, 1966.

Pollard, C. William. *The Soul of the Firm*. New York: Harper Collins, 1996.

Public Guardian and Trustee for Ontario Annual Report (2016–17).

Quatro, Scott A. "New Age or Old Age: Classical Management Theory and Traditional Organized Religion as Underpinnings of the Contemporary Organizational Spirituality Movement." *Human Resources Development Review* 3 (2004) 228–49.

Ramsey, Paul. *Basic Christian Ethics*. Louisville: Westminster John Knox, 1993.

Ravitch, Sharon M., and Matthew Riggan. *Reason and Rigour: How Conceptual Frameworks Guide Research*. Los Angeles: Sage, 2012.

Rawat, Anushri, and Shiva Nadavulakere. "Examining the Outcomes of Having a Calling: Does Context Matter." *Journal of Business and Psychology* (2015) 499–512.

Renjen, Punit. "A Guide to Resilient Leadership." *Rotman Management* (2021) 43–47.

Rescher, Nicholas. "Personhood." In *Metaphysical Perspectives*, Notre Dame, IN: University of Notre Dame Press, 2017.

Rigoglioso, Marguerite. "Spirit at Work: The Search for Deeper Meaning in the Workplace." *Research and Ideas*, October 1999.

Rolheiser, Ronald. *The Holy Longing: The Search for a Christian Spirituality*. New York: Doubleday, 1999.

Rushing, Sara. "Comparative Humilities: Christian, Contemporary, and Confucian Conceptions of a Political Virtue." *Polity* (2013) 198–222.

Sandole, Dennis J. D., et al., eds. *Handbook of Conflict Analysis and Resolution*. London: Routledge, 2009.

Sankey, Ira. *Sankey's Story of the Gospel Hymns and of Sacred Songs and Solos*. Philadelphia: The Sunday School Times, 1906.

Schiotz, Frederik. "A Christian Concept of Vocation." *Christian Education* (1944) 39–47.

Scott, Kim. *Radical Candor: How to be a Kickass Boss*. New York: St. Martin's, 2017.

Selznick, Philip. *Leadership in Administration: A Sociological Interpretation*. Berkeley: University of California Press, 1957.

Shideler, Mary McDermott. "Introduction." In *Are Women Human?* by Dorothy L. Sayers, 1–17. Grand Rapids, MI: Eerdmans, 1971.

Shorto, Russell. "Faith at Work." *New York Times*, October 2004. https://nytimes.com/2004/10/31/magazine/faith-at-work.html.

Simon, Y. R. *Work, Society and Culture*. Edited by Vukan Kuic. New York: Fordham University Press, 1971.

Sinek, Simon. *Start With Why: How Great Leaders Inspire Everyone to Take Action*. New York: Penguin, 2011.

Smith, Hazel, and Roger T. Dean. *Practice-Led Research, Research-Led Practice in the Creative Arts*. Edinburgh: Edinburgh University Press, 2009.

Snow, Carlton, J. "Rebuilding Trust in a Fractured Workplace." In *Faith in Leadership: How Leaders Live out Their Faith in Their Work and Why It Matters*, edited by Robert Banks and Kimberley Powell, 34–45. San Francisco: Jossey-Bass, 2000.

Snyder, Anne. "Why Character? Why Now?" *Comment: Public Theology for the Common Good* 37 (2019) 44–49.

So, Damon W. K. *The forgotten Jesus and the trinity you never knew*. Eugene, OR: Wipf & Stock, 2010.

Souba, Wiley W. "The Being of Leadership." *Philos Ethics Humanit Med* 6 (2011). https://www.ncbi.nlm.nih.gov/pmc/articles/PMC3050817/,

Stanton, Graham D. "A Theology of Complexity for Christian Leadership in an Uncertain Future." *Practical Theology* 12 (2019) 147–56.

Statistics Canada. "Statistics Canada report a 14% increase in annual days lost to absenteeism between 2014 and 2018." https://www150.statcan.gc.ca/t1/tbl1/en/tv.action?pid=1410019001

———. "Work Absence of Full-Time Employees by Geography, Annual (2014)." https://www150.statcan.gc.ca/t1/tbl1/en/tv.action?pid=1410019001.

Sternberg, Robert J. "Foolishness." In *A Handbook of Wisdom: Psychological Perspectives*, edited by Robert J. Steinberg and Jennifer Jordan, 331–52. Cambridge: Cambridge University Press, 2005

Stevens, R. Paul. *Doing God's Business: Meaning and Motivation for the Marketplace*. Grand Rapids: Eerdmans, 2006.

Stevens, R. Paul, and Alvin Ung. *Taking Your Soul to Work: Overcoming the Nine Deadly Sins of the Workplace*. Grand Rapids: Eerdmans, 2010.

Stevenson, Betsy. "What are the Economics of Happiness?" *Yale Insights*, February 2018. https://insights.som.yale.edu/insights/what-are-the-economics-of-happiness.

Storr, Anthony. *Solitude: A Return to the Self*. New York: Simon & Schuster, 1988.

Stott, John. *Basic Christian Leadership*. Downers Grove, IL: InterVarsity Press, 2002.

Suarez, Federico. *The Narrow Gate*. London: Sceptre, 2004.

Swinton, John. "What is Practical Theology?" PowerPoint Notes from a presentation at McMaster Divinity College, Hamilton, ON, Spring 2017.

Swinton, John, and Harriet Mowat. *Practical Theology and Qualitative Research*. Croydon UK: SCM, 2006.

Taggar, Simon, and Mitchel J. Neubert. "A Cognitive (Attributions)-Emotion Model of Observer Reactions to Free-Riding Poor Performers." *Journal of Business and Psychology* (2008) 167–77.

Tapscott, Don, and David Ticoll. *The Naked Corporation: How the Age of Transparency Will Revolutionize Business*. Toronto: Penguin, 2003.

Terkel, Studs. *Working*. New York: Ballantine, 1985.

Thiessen, Joel. *The Meaning of Sunday: The Practice of Belief in a Secular Age*. Montreal: McGill-Queen's University Press, 2015.

Tobaccowala, Rishad. *Restoring the Soul of Business: Staying Human in the Age of Data*. New York: HarperCollins, 2020.

Tournier, Paul. *Escape from Loneliness*. Translated by John S. Gilmour. Philadelphia: Westminster, 1977.

Trebesch, Shelley G. *Made to Flourish: Beyond Quick Fixes to a Thriving Organization*. Downers Grove, IL: IVP Academic, 2015.

Twenge, Jean M. "Are Mental Health Issues on the Rise?" *Psychology Today*, October 2015. https://www.psychologytoday.com/ca/blog/our-changing-culture/201510/are-mental-health-issues-the-rise.

USA Today. "Workplace Mass Shootings" [n.d.], https://www.usatoday.com/story/money/2019/06/06/workplace-mass-shootings-rare-and-puzzling-heres-history-them/1373276001/.

VanderWeele, Tyler J. "On the Promotion of Human Flourishing." *Proceedings of the National Academy of Sciences of the United States of America* (2017) 8148–56.

Van Sloten, John. *Every Job a Parable: What Walmart Greeters, Nurses and Astronauts Tell Us About God*. Colorado Springs, CO: NavPress, 2017.

Veith, Gene Edward Jr. *God at Work: Your Christian Vocation in All of Life*. Wheaton, Ill.: Crossway, 2002.

Vogt, Rosemary. "Workplace Loneliness and Spirituality." *Faith Today* (September/October 2018) 24.

Volf, Miroslav. *Flourishing: Why We Need Religion in a Globalized World*. New Haven: Yale. 2015.

———. *Work in the Spirit: Toward a Theology of Work*. Eugene, OR: Wipf & Stock, 1991.

Wahlstrom, Grant, and Anisa Chowdhury. "The Double Dipper: An Employee Tip Uncovers a Multimillion-dollar Travel and Expense Scam." *Internal Auditor* (April 2020) 23–25.

Whitehead, Evelyn Eaton, and James D. Whitehead. *Christian Life Patterns: The Psychological Challenges and Religious Invitations of Adult Life*. New York: Crossroad, 2015.

Whyte, David. *Consolations: The Solace, Nourishment and Underlying Meaning of Everyday Words*. Langley, WA: Many Rivers Press, 2017.

Widdicombe, Tom. *Be With Your Horse*. Newton Abbot, UK: David and Charles, 2005.

Wilcox, Ann Allart. "Reflections on Doing, Being and Becoming." *Australian Occupational Therapy Journal* 46 (1999) 1–11.

Wilcox, Tracy. "Ethics as Strategic Thinking: Creating Legitimacy in the Workplace." *Business and Professional Ethics Journal* 18 (1999) 73–92.

Williams, Rowan, "Archbishop's Presidential Address to the General Synod." (2011) no pages.

———. "On Making Moral Decisions." *Anglican Theological Review* 295–308.

———. *Silence and Honey Cakes: The Wisdom of the Desert*. Oxford: Lion Hudson, 2003.

Willis, Michael, and Michael Fass. *Faith in Governance: Renewing the Role of the Director*. London: Industrial Christian Fellowship, 2004.

Winquist, Charles E. "Revisioning Ministry: Postmodern Reflections." In *Formation and Reflection: The Promise of Practical Theology*, edited by Lewis S. Mudge and James N. Poling, 27–35. Minneapolis: Fortress, 2009.

Woods, C. Jeff. *Designing Religious Research Studies*. Eugene, OR: Wipf & Stock, 2016.

Woods, Philip A. and Glenys J. Woods. "Deepening Reflective Practice." In *Alternative Education for the 21st Century: Philosophies, Approaches, Visions*, edited by Philip A. Woods and Glenys J. Woods, 167–88. New York: Palgrave MacMillan, 2009.

Worth, Jennifer. *Call the Midwife*. London: Phoenix, 2002.

———. *In the Midst of Life*. London: Phoenix, 2010.

Wren, Daniel A. *Evolution of Management Thought*. New York: Ronald, 1972.

Wyszynski, Stefan. *All You Who Labor: Work and the Sanctification of Daily Life.* Manchester, NH: Sophia Institute, 1995.

Yeoman, Ruth. "Conceptualizing Meaningful Work as a Fundamental Human Need." *Journal of Business Ethics* 125 (2014) 235–51.

Zagorin, Lea Jeanne. "Beyond Economic Impact, The Psychic Impact Received by the Chapel Hill Community from Carolina Athletics." MA thesis, University of North Carolina at Chapel Hill, 2017.

Zylla, Phil C. *The Roots of Sorrow: A Pastoral Theology of Suffering.* Waco: Baylor University Press, 2012.

———. "Cultivating the Resilient Congregation: Theoretical Reflections and Constructive Proposals." *MJTM* 15 (2013–2014) 100–118.

www.ingramcontent.com/pod-product-compliance
Lightning Source LLC
Chambersburg PA
CBHW062019220426
43662CB00010B/1395

"Bates is an inspirational leader and researcher . . . This book depicts his knowledge on leadership approaches coupled with profound expertise in theology on challenging matters . . . His use of mixed methods, grounded theory, lived experiences of the participants through surveys, his own experiences, and a wide range of literature builds a channel for readers to think and appreciate the theme of Spirit-led leadership which may seem difficult for non-believers—quite admirable. This book is going to increase our values and those of others to realize that work is a calling rather than drudgery. Overall, it is a great piece of writing that will influence a lot of people."

—ESTHER WAITHERA KIEBERGER
Author of *Scattering Survivors*

"*For Others to Follow* is a must-read for anyone wanting to lead. As contemporary society loses faith in leaders, this book calls us back to leadership that is based on more than just positional power . . . Bates presents us with a work that calls us to a higher standard of leadership. As John Maxwell reminds us, the future of our organizations, businesses, and governments will rise and fall on the strength of its leaders. I envision a world where we have restored faith in our leaders. This can happen when leaders are truly Spirit-led. The sooner we live out this ethos, the better we will be."

—ANDREW RUTLEDGE
Assistant pastor and doctoral candidate

"Bates leads us into the best of his worlds: deep and careful academic research, broad and transparent personal experience, and a deep and transforming faith. His ethos of Spirit-led leadership has been shared with workplace and academic colleagues, clients, and students in such a way that his own search for meaning through work has encouraged and shaped the longings of others. In this book, Bates provides guidance that will spiritually anchor us at work by helping us navigate dissonance between purpose and work. Paul achieves his goal of seeking to construct leadership as the means to encourage workers to rediscover deeper meaning and purpose."

—LAURIE BUSUTTIL
Associate professor at Redeemer University

"Paul's study is relevant for Christians, persons of other faiths, and those of no religious faith. It is a wonderful contribution to effective leadership."

—PAUL M. MOORE
Corporate lawyer

"This is a well-researched, well-written work. Bates engages with conversation partners from many disciplines, including biblical scholars, practical theologians, and practitioners and researchers in various fields of business and commerce, leadership theory, and ethics. His model of Spirit-led leadership is based on a well-grounded theory supported by qualitative research. His emphasis on ethos, personhood, justice, servanthood, and genuine care (or cruciformity, to use a more obviously theological term) is grounded in a deeply reflective understanding of Scripture . . . The depth of his thoughts and his love for the church come through clearly in his writing. We are in dire need of true Spirit-led leaders. I cannot think of a timelier work for the benefit of the church. I wholeheartedly recommend this book."

—FRANCIS PANG
Professor at McMaster Divinity College

"I was pleased to read *For Others to Follow* . . . Bates gives a well-annotated thesis for helping employees to flourish in the workplace using a faith-based, largely Christian approach . . . He emphasizes the need for empathy and forgiveness while acknowledging difficult decisions about difficult employees and the use of quiet, thoughtful meditation and prayer at times of stressful decision-making . . . While not claiming to offer a panacea, Bates has useful concepts about the role of faith in leadership. I would encourage the reader to examine the arguments and see how they may be applied today in Canada and globally."

—JOHN ANTHONY SEFTON MARRIOTT
Retired psychiatrist